Rick Steves'

POC[illegible]
VENICE

Rick Steves & Gene Openshaw

Contents

Introduction 3
Grand Canal Cruise 13
St. Mark's Square Tour 31
St. Mark's Basilica Tour 45
Doge's Palace Tour 67
Frari Church Tour 85
St. Mark's to Rialto Loop Walk 97
Rialto to Frari Church Walk 109
St. Mark's to San Zaccaria Walk 117
Sights 125
Sleeping 153
Eating 163
Practicalities 185
Index 209

Introduction

Venice is a world apart. Built on a hundred islands, its exotic-looking palaces are laced together by graceful bridges over sun-speckled canals. Romantics revel in the city's atmosphere of elegant decay. And first-time visitors are often stirred deeply, waking from their ordinary lives to a fantasy world unlike anything they've ever seen.

Those are strong reactions, considering that Venice today, frankly, can also be an overcrowded tourist trap. But Venice offers so much. By day, it's a city of art-filled museums, trendy shops, and narrow alleyways. At night, when the hordes of day-trippers have gone, another Venice appears. Glide in a gondola through quiet canals. Dance across a floodlit square. Don a Carnevale mask—or just a clean shirt—and become someone else for a night.

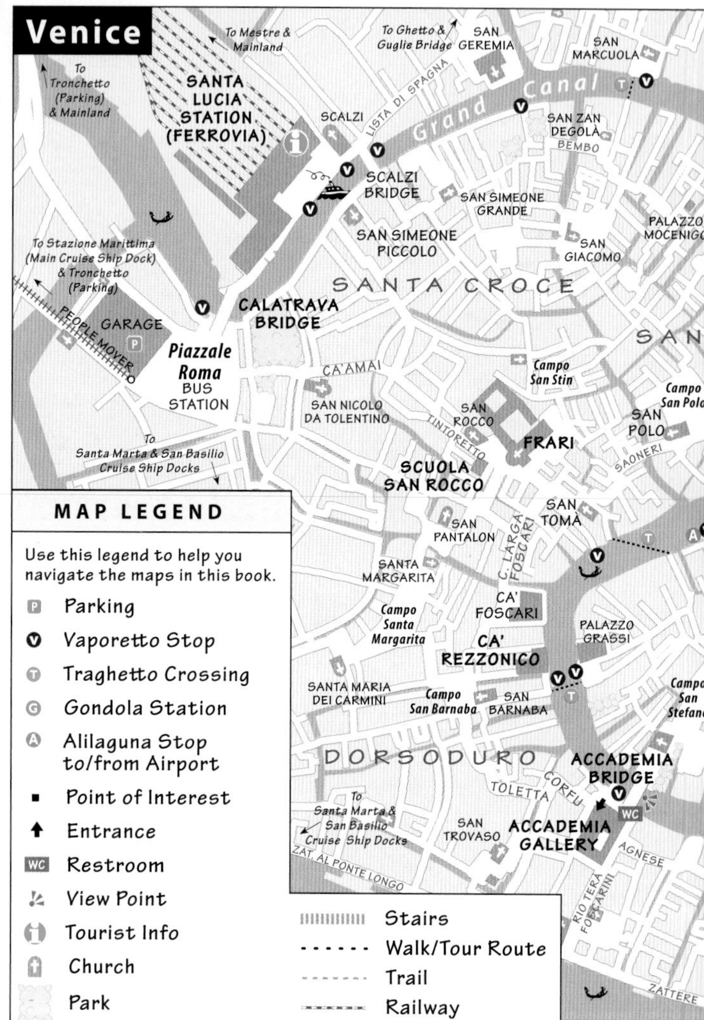
Venice
To Mestre & Mainland
To Ghetto & Guglie Bridge
SAN GEREMIA
SAN MARCUOLA
To Tronchetto (Parking) & Mainland
SANTA LUCIA STATION (FERROVIA)
LISTA DI SPAGNA
Grand Canal
SCALZI
SAN ZAN DEGOLÀ
BEMBO
SCALZI BRIDGE
SAN SIMEONE GRANDE
PALAZZO MOCENIGO
SAN SIMEONE PICCOLO
SAN GIACOMO
To Stazione Marittima (Main Cruise Ship Dock) & Tronchetto (Parking)
SANTA CROCE
CALATRAVA BRIDGE
PEOPLE MOVER
GARAGE
SAN
Piazzale Roma
BUS STATION
CA'AMAI
Campo San Stin
Campo San Polo
SAN NICOLO DA TOLENTINO
SAN ROCCO
TINTORETTO
SAN POLO
FRARI
SAONERI
To Santa Marta & San Basilio Cruise Ship Docks
SCUOLA SAN ROCCO
SAN TOMÀ
SAN PANTALON
C. LARGA FOSCARI
SANTA MARGARITA
CA' FOSCARI
Campo Santa Margarita
PALAZZO GRASSI
CA' REZZONICO
SANTA MARIA DEI CARMINI
Campo San Barnaba
SAN BARNABA
Campo San Stefano
DORSODURO
ACCADEMIA BRIDGE
TOLETTA
CORFU
To Santa Marta & San Basilio Cruise Ship Docks
SAN TROVASO
ACCADEMIA GALLERY
AGNESE
ZAT. AL PONTE LONGO
RIO TERA FOSCARINI
ZATTERE
MAP LEGEND
Use this legend to help you navigate the maps in this book.
Parking
Vaporetto Stop
Traghetto Crossing
Gondola Station
Alilaguna Stop to/from Airport
Point of Interest
Entrance
WC
Restroom
View Point
Tourist Info
Church
Park
Stairs
Walk/Tour Route
Trail
Railway

To Ghetto & Train Station
To San Michele, Murano, Burano & Torcello
SANTA MARIA MADALENA
STRADA
SAN FELICE
FONDAMENTE NOVE
Lagoon
SAN STAE
CA' D'ORO
CA' PESARO
NOVA
SANTI APOSTOLI
Campo Santi Apostoli
FOND. DEI MENDICANTI
HOSPITAL
SAN CANZIAN
FISH MARKET
SAN CASSIAN
Campo de le Becarie
PRODUCE MARKET
COLLEONI STATUE
SANTI GIOVANNI E PAOLO (SAN ZANIPOLO)
POLO
RUGA V. SAN GIO
RIALTO BRIDGE
Campo San Bartolomeo
SAN SILVESTRO
Campo San Aponal
RIVA DEL VIN
SAN LIO
SAL. SAN LIO
Campo Santa Maria Formosa
SAN LORENZO
2 APRILE
SANTA MARIA FAVA
MERCERIE
TEATRO GOLDONI
SAN SALVADOR
CASTELLO
SCUOLA DALMATA
Campo San Luca
SAN ZULIAN
FABBRI
Campo Manin
MANDOLA
SCALA CONTARINI DEL BOVOLO
ST. MARK'S
BRIDGE OF SIGHS
SAN ZACCARIA
Campo San Anzolo
LA FENICE OPERA HOUSE
CORRER MUSEUM
Piazza San Marco
CAMPANILE
LA PIETA
RIVA DEGLI SCHIAVONI
WC
SAN MARCO
DOGE'S PALACE
To Public Gardens & Santa Elena
22 MARZO
SAN MOISÈ
SAN MARCO & SAN THEODORE COLUMNS
Campo San Maurizio
Campo Santa Maria Zobenigo
Grand Canal
St. Mark's Basin
LA SALUTE
PUNTA DELLA DOGANA MUSEUM (CUSTOMS HOUSE)
To Lido
PEGGY GUGGENHEIM COLLECTION
SAN GIORGIO MAGGIORE
200 Meters
200 Yards
SAN GIORGIO
SPIRITO SANTO
ALLO

Key to This Book

Sights are rated:

▲▲▲	**Don't miss**
▲▲	**Try hard to see**
▲	**Worthwhile if you can make it**
No rating	**Worth knowing about**

Tourist information offices are abbreviated as **TI,** and bathrooms are WCs.

Like Europe, this book uses the **24-hour clock.** It's the same through 12:00 noon, then keep going: 13:00 (1:00 p.m.), 14:00 (2:00 p.m.), and so on.

For **opening times,** if a sight is listed as "May-Oct daily 9:00-16:00," it should be open from 9 a.m. until 4 p.m. from the first day of May until the last day of October (but expect exceptions).

For **updates** to this book, visit www.ricksteves.com/update. For a valuable list of reports and experiences—good and bad—from fellow travelers, check www.ricksteves.com/feedback.

About This Book

With this book, I've selected only the best of Venice—admittedly, a tough call. The core of the book is eight self-guided tours that zero in on Venice's greatest sights and neighborhoods.

My Grand Canal Cruise, snaking through the heart of the historic core, introduces you to this moist metropolis. Then hit St. Mark's Square, with its one-of-a-kind basilica and Doge's Palace. I've included several neighborhood walks that take you to both major sights (Rialto Bridge) and out-of-the-way places (Frari Church).

The rest of the book is a traveler's tool kit. You'll find plenty more about Venice's attractions, from shopping to nightlife to how to do a Venetian pub crawl. And there are helpful hints on saving money, avoiding crowds, getting around town, enjoying a great meal, and more.

Venice by Neighborhood

The island city of Venice (population 60,000) is shaped like a fish. Its major thoroughfares are canals. The Grand Canal winds through the middle of

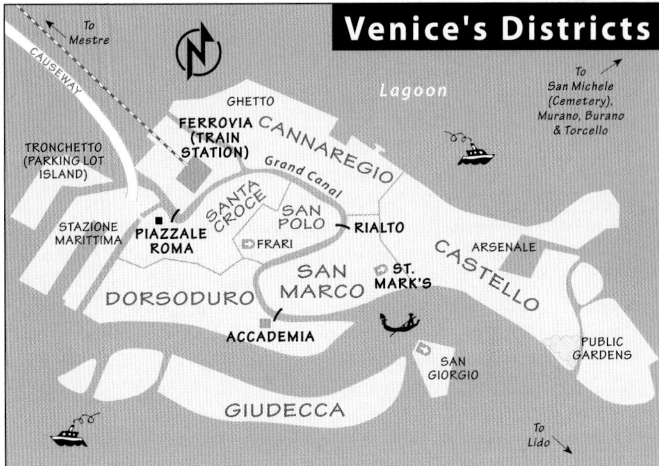

the fish, starting at the mouth where all the people and food enter, passing under the Rialto Bridge, and ending at St. Mark's Square (Piazza San Marco). Park your 21st-century perspective at the mouth and let Venice swallow you whole.

To find your way, navigate by landmarks. Many street corners have a sign pointing you to *(per)* the nearest major landmark. St. Mark's Square (San Marco) and Rialto Bridge are the center of the tourist action. Other major landmarks are Accademia Bridge (gateway to the charming Dorsoduro neighborhood), Ferrovia (train station), and Piazzale Roma (another transportation hub). I've organized this book—sights, hotels, and restaurants—around these major landmarks.

Officially, Venice is divided into six districts, called *sestieri* (see the map). Addresses generally list the district and house number (e.g. Cannaregio #221b), not the street. For more on the *sestiere* and addresses, ✪ see page 193. I find it easier to navigate by landmarks, not *sestiere*, addresses, or street names.

Venice is remarkably small. You can walk across it in an hour, and most sights are within 20 minutes of the Rialto Bridge or St. Mark's Square. Beyond the city's core lie several other interesting islands (Murano, Burano, Torcello, Lido) accessible only by boat.

Venice at a Glance

▲▲▲**St. Mark's Square** Venice's grand main square. **Hours:** Always open. See page 128.

▲▲▲**St. Mark's Basilica** Cathedral with mosaics, saint's bones, treasury, museum, and viewpoint of square. **Hours:** Mon-Sat 9:45-17:00, Sun 14:00-17:00 (until 16:00 Nov-March). See page 128.

▲▲▲**Doge's Palace** Art-splashed palace of former rulers, with prison accessible through Bridge of Sighs. **Hours:** Daily April-Oct 8:30-18:30, Nov-March 8:00-17:30. See page 128.

▲▲▲**Rialto Bridge** Distinctive bridge spanning the Grand Canal, with a market nearby. **Hours:** Souvenir stalls open daily, produce market closed Sun, fish market closed Sun-Mon. See page 141.

▲▲**Correr Museum** Venetian history and art. **Hours:** Daily April-Oct 10:00-19:00, Nov-March 10:00-17:00. See page 129.

▲▲**Accademia** Venice's top art museum. **Hours:** Mon 8:15-14:00, Tue-Sun 8:15-19:15. See page 135.

▲▲**Peggy Guggenheim Collection** Popular display of 20th-century art. **Hours:** Wed-Mon 10:00-18:00, closed Tue. See page 136.

▲▲**Frari Church** Franciscan church featuring Renaissance masters. **Hours:** Mon-Sat 9:00-18:00, Sun 13:00-18:00. See page 141.

▲▲**Scuola San Rocco** "Tintoretto's Sistine Chapel." **Hours:** Daily 9:30-17:30. See page 141.

▲**Campanile** Dramatic bell tower on St. Mark's Square with elevator

Planning Your Time

Plan your sightseeing carefully to avoid lines and work around closed days. (✪ See my sightseeing tips, page 198.) Venice is small enough that, even if you only had one day, you could see the biggies in a 12-hour sightseeing blitz. But let's assume you have at least three days.

Day 1: In the morning, take the slow vaporetto #1 down the Grand Canal from the train station/Piazzale Roma to San Marco. Stop off along the way to explore the Rialto market, grabbing an early lunch at the *cicchetti* bars nearby. Continue down the Grand Canal to St. Mark's Square. Spend the afternoon sightseeing the square, the basilica, the Doge's

to the top. **Hours:** Daily Easter-June and Oct 9:00-19:00, July-Sept 9:00-21:00; Nov-Easter 9:30-16:45. See page 131.
▲**Bridge of Sighs** Famous enclosed bridge, part of Doge's Palace, near St. Mark's Square. **Hours:** Always viewable. See page 129.
▲**San Giorgio Maggiore** Island across the lagoon featuring church with Palladio architecture, Tintoretto paintings, and fine views back on Venice. **Hours:** May-Sept Mon-Sat 9:30-12:30 & 14:30-18:00, Sun 8:30-11:00 & 14:30-18:00; Oct-April until 17:00. See page 132.
▲**La Salute Church** Striking church dedicated to the Virgin Mary. **Hours:** Daily 9:00-12:00 & 15:00-17:30. See page 138.
▲**Ca' Rezzonico** Posh Grand Canal palazzo with 18th-century Venetian art. **Hours:** April-Oct Wed-Mon 10:00-18:00, Nov-March Wed-Mon 10:00-17:00, closed Tue year-round. See page 139.
▲**Punta della Dogana** Museum of contemporary art. **Hours:** Wed-Mon 10:00-19:00, closed Tue. See page 140.
▲**Ca' Pesaro** International Gallery of Modern Art in a canalside palazzo. **Hours:** Tue-Sun 10:00-18:00, closed Mon. See page 143.
▲**Scuola Dalmata di San Giorgio** Exquisite Renaissance meeting house. **Hours:** Mon 14:45-18:00, Tue-Sat 9:15-13:00 & 14:45-18:00, Sun 9:15-13:00. See page 146.
Church of San Zaccaria Final resting place of St. Zechariah, plus a Bellini altarpiece and an eerie crypt. **Hours:** Mon-Sat 10:00-12:00 & 16:00-18:00, Sun 16:00-18:00. See page 120.

Palace, the Correr Museum, and the Campanile. Around 20:00, have dinner (make a reservation). Afterward, enjoy the dueling orchestras with a drink on St. Mark's Square.

Day 2: Spend the morning shopping and exploring (consider my Rialto to Frari Church Walk) as you make your way to the Frari Church. See the Frari and nearby Scuola San Rocco. Head over to the Accademia/Dorsoduro area and have lunch. Spend the afternoon seeing the Dorsoduro's main artsy sights: Ca' Rezzonico, Accademia, and the Peggy Guggenheim Collection. Or take a nap. Around 18:00, have a pub crawl

Daily Reminder

Sunday: While anyone is welcome to worship, most churches are closed to sightseers on Sunday morning. They reopen in the afternoon: St. Mark's Basilica (14:00-17:00, until 16:00 Nov-March), Frari Church (13:00-18:00), and the Church of San Zaccaria (16:00-18:00). The Naval Museum is closed all day, and the Rialto open-air market consists mainly of souvenir stalls (fish and produce sections closed). It's a bad day for a pub crawl, as most pubs are closed.

Monday: All sights are open except the Rialto fish market, Ca' Pesaro, Palazzo Mocenigo Costume Museum, Lace Museum (on the island of Burano), and Torcello Museum (on the island of Torcello). The Accademia and Ca' d'Oro close at 14:00.

Tuesday: All sights are open except the Peggy Guggenheim Collection, Ca' Rezzonico (Museum of 18th-Century Venice), and Punta della Dogana.

Wednesday/Thursday/Friday: All sights are open.

Saturday: All sights are open except the Jewish Museum.

Notes: The Accademia is open earlier (daily at 8:15) and closes later (19:15 Tue-Sun) than most sights in Venice. Some sights close earlier off-season (such as the Correr Museum, Campanile bell tower, St. Mark's Basilica, and the Church of San Giorgio Maggiore). Modest dress is recommended at churches and required at St. Mark's Basilica—no bare shoulders, shorts, or short skirts.

for dinner. Afterward, take a gondola ride (or, much cheaper, a moonlight vaporetto ride).

Day 3 and Beyond: Choose from among Venice's lesser sights: a trip to San Giorgio Maggiore, La Salute, modern art at the Punta della Dogana, or the area east of St. Mark's (Church of San Zaccaria, Scuola Dalmata di San Giorgio). Budget time for just exploring, using my walks as a jumping-off point. In the evening, have dinner and catch a Vivaldi concert. With more time in Venice, you could visit the lagoon islands (Murano, Burano, and more), but these require at least a half-day.

Quick Tips: Avoid the midday crowds around St. Mark's as best you can. Take advantage of my free Venice audio tours, covering the

Grand Canal Cruise, St. Mark's Square, St. Mark's Basilica, and the Frari Church—✪ see page 199 for details. A vaporetto pass and a Museum Pass may be worthwhile. Consider an afternoon nap to maximize energy for after dark. Stop often for gelato.

Finally, remember that Venice itself is its greatest sight. Make time to wander, shop, and simply be. When you cross a bridge, look both ways. You may be hit with a lovely view.

I hope you have a great trip! Traveling like a temporary local and taking advantage of the information here, you'll enjoy the absolute most out of every mile, minute, and euro. I'm happy that you'll be visiting places I know and love, and meeting some of my favorite Italian people.

Happy travels! *Buon viaggio!*

Grand Canal Cruise

Canal Grande

Take a joyride and introduce yourself to Venice by boat. Cruise the Canal Grande all the way from the train station (Ferrovia) to San Marco.

If it's your first trip down the Grand Canal, you might want to stow this book and just take it all in—Venice is a barrage on the senses that hardly needs narration. But these notes give the cruise a little meaning and help orient you to this great city.

I've organized this tour by boat stop. I'll point out what you can see from the current stop, and what to look forward to as you cruise to the next stop. Now, kick back and let Venice entertain you with its charms.

ORIENTATION

Length of This Tour: Allow 45 minutes.

Cost: €7 for a one-hour vaporetto ticket, or covered by a transit pass—the best choice if you want to hop on and off (✪ see page 195).

When to Go: Avoid the morning rush hour (8:00-10:00), when everyone is headed toward San Marco. In the uncrowded evening, sunset bathes the buildings in gold; after dark, chandeliers light up building interiors.

Getting There: This tour starts at the Ferrovia vaporetto stop (at Santa Lucia train station). It also works if you board upstream from Ferrovia at Piazzale Roma (bus station, parking lots).

Catching Your Boat: This tour is designed to be done on the slow boat #1 (which takes about 45 minutes). The express boat #2 travels the same route, but it skips some stops and takes 25 minutes, making it hard to sightsee. Also, some #2 boats terminate at Rialto; confirm that you're on a boat that goes all the way to San Marco.

Audio Tour: If you download my free audio tour (✪ see page 199), you won't even have to look at the book.

Stops to Consider: Consider hopping on and off along the way. Some interesting stops are: San Marcuola (Jewish Ghetto), Mercato Rialto (fish market and famous bridge), Ca' Rezzonico (Museum of 18th-Century Venice), Accademia (art museum and the nearby Peggy Guggenheim Collection), and Salute (huge art-filled church).

Sightseeing Tips: Try to snag a seat in the bow (though not all boats have them). You're more likely to find an empty seat if you catch the vaporetto at Piazzale Roma. Frankly, it's hard to sightsee while reading aboard a moving boat. Some readers do this cruise twice—once in either direction—to enjoy it all.

Starring: Palaces, markets, boats, bridges—Venice.

BACKGROUND

While you wait for your boat, here's some background on Venice's "Main Street."

At more than two miles long, nearly 150 feet wide, and nearly 15 feet deep, the Grand Canal is the city's largest canal, lined with its most impressive palaces. It's the remnant of a river that once spilled from the mainland into the Adriatic. The sediment it carried formed barrier islands that cut Venice off from the sea, forming a lagoon.

Venice was built on the marshy islands of the former delta, sitting on wood pilings driven nearly 15 feet into the clay (alder was the preferred wood). About 25 miles of canals drain the city, dumping like rivers (called *"rios"*) into the Grand Canal. Technically, Venice has only three canals: Grand, Giudecca, and Cannaregio. The 45 small waterways that dump into the Grand Canal are referred to as rivers (e.g., Rio Novo).

Venice is a city of palaces, dating from the days when the city was the world's richest. The most lavish palaces formed a grand architectural cancan along the Grand Canal. Once frescoed in reds and blues, with black-and-white borders and gold-leaf trim, they made Venice a city of dazzling color. This cruise is the only way to truly appreciate the palaces, approaching them at water level, where their main entrances were located. Today, strict laws prohibit any changes in these buildings, so while landowners gnash their teeth, we can enjoy Europe's best-preserved medieval city—slowly rotting. Many of the grand buildings are now vacant. Others harbor chandeliered elegance above mossy, empty, often flooded ground floors.

Grand Canal
To Jewish Ghetto
SAN GEREMIA
PALAZZO CORRER CONTARINI
San Marcuola
SAN MARCUOLA
CASINÒ
PAL. GRITTI
PAL. VENDRAMIN CALERGI
LISTA DI SPAGNA
PALAZZO FLANGINI
Riva di Biasio
Grand Canal
PAL. GIO-VANELLI
TURKISH "FONDACO" EXCHANGE
SANTA LUCIA TRAIN STATION (FERROVIA)
SCALZI
PALAZZO CALBO-CROTTA
PAL. MARCELLO
PAL. GRITTI
PALAZZO DONÀ BALBI
SAN ZAN DEGOLÀ
PALAZZO CA' TRON
SCALZI BRIDGE
Ferrovia
SANTA CROCE
TOUR BEGINS
SAN SIMEONE PICCOLO
CALATRAVA BRIDGE
GARAGE
PIAZZALE ROMA
PEOPLE MOVER
To Stazione Marittima (Main Cruise Ship Dock) & Tronchetto (Parking)
SAN
SAN POLO
FRARI
PALAZZO CAPPELLO-LAYARD
SCUOLA SAN ROCCO
SAN TOMÀ
PALAZZO BARBARIGO
PALAZZO GIUSTINIANI
Sant' Angelo
PALAZZO BALBI
San Tomà
FIRE STATION
PALAZZO MOCENIGO
PALAZZO VECCHIA
CA' FOSCARI
PALAZZO MORO LIN
PALAZZO GIUSTINIAN
PALAZZO GRASSI
CA' REZZONICO
Ca' Rezzonico
PALAZZO MALIPIERO-CAPPELLO
PALAZZO LOREDAN
PALAZZO FALIER
PALAZZO CONTARINI DEGLI SCRIGNI
PALAZZO GIUSTINIAN LOLIN
Accademia
PALAZZO QUERINI
PALAZZO BARBARO
Grand
ACCADEMIA BRIDGE & GALLERY
PALAZZO BARBARIGO
Vaporetto Stops
1 Ferrovia
2 Riva de Biasio
3 San Marcuola
4 San Stae
5 Ca' d'Oro
6 Mercato Rialto
7 Rialto
8 San Silvestro
9 Sant'Angelo
10 San Tomà
11 Ca' Rezzonico
12 Accademia
13 Santa Maria del Giglio
14 Salute
15 San Marco
16 San Zaccaria

PALAZZO MARCELLO
PALAZZO MOLIN
PALAZZO ZULLAN
PALAZZO BARBARIGO
200 Meters
200 Yards
Fondamenta Nove
FONDAMENTE NOVE
To San Michele, Murano, Burano & Torcello
Lagoon
CANNAREGIO
San Stae
SAN STAE
PALAZZO FONTANA
PALAZZO GIUSTI
STRADA NOVA
PAL. DONÀ
CA' D'ORO
PALAZZO SAGREDO
CA' PESARO
PAL. FAVRETTO
PALAZZO MICHIEL COLONNE
PAL. BRANDOLIN
Ca d'Oro
PALAZZO VALMARANA
PALAZZO CORNER DELLA REGINA
FISH MARKET
PALAZZO CA' DA MOSTO
Mercato Rialto
HOSPITAL
PRODUCE MARKET
PALAZZO CIVRAN
SANTI GIOVANNI E PAOLO (SAN ZANIPOLO)
POLO
GERMAN EXCHANGE (FORMER POST)
RIALTO BRIDGE
PALAZZO PAPADOPOLI
Rialto
SAL. S. LIO
S. MARIA FORMOSA
PALAZZO BARZIZZA
PALAZZO DOLFIN-MANIN
PALAZZO DONÀ
San Silvestro
PALAZZO BEMBO
MERCERIE
PALAZZO BERNARDO
PALAZZO GRIMANI
PALAZZO FARSETTI-DANDOLO
CASTELLO
PALAZZO BENZON
PAL. CORNER-CONTARINI
MERCERIE
FABBRI
PALAZZO CORNER-SPINELLI
PALAZZO MARTINENGO
CLOCK TOWER
ST. MARK'S BASILICA
SAN ZACCARIA
CAMPANILE
BRIDGE OF SIGHS
SAN MARCO
SAN MARCO
DOGE'S PALACE
TOUR ENDS
CALLE LARGA XXII MARZO
SAN MARCO & SAN THEODORE COLUMNS
San Zaccaria
HARRY'S AMERICAN BAR
To Lido
CA' GRANDE
GRITTI PALACE HOTEL
PALAZZO FLANGINI
San Marco
St. Mark's Basin
Santa Maria del Giglio
Salute
Canal
To San Giorgio Maggiore & Giudecca
PEGGY GUGGEN.
PAL. GENOVESE
LA SALUTE CHURCH
PUNTA DELLA DOGANA MUSEUM (CUSTOMS HOUSE)

THE TOUR BEGINS

❶ Ferrovia

The **Santa Lucia train station,** one of the few modern buildings in town, was built in 1954. It's been the gateway into Venice since 1860, when the first station was built. "F.S." stands for "Ferrovie dello Stato," the Italian state railway system.

More than 20,000 people a day commute in from the mainland, making this the busiest part of Venice during rush hour. The **Calatrava Bridge** (✪ see page 146), just upstream, was built in 2008 to alleviate some of the congestion.

Opposite the train station, atop the green dome of **San Simeon Piccolo** church, St. Simeon waves *ciao* to whoever enters or leaves the "old" city. The pink church with the white Carrara-marble facade, just beyond the train station, is the **Church of the Scalzi** (Church of the Barefoot, named after the shoeless Carmelite monks), where the last doge (Venetian ruler) rests. It looks relatively new because it was partially rebuilt after being bombed in 1915 by Austrians aiming (poorly) at the train station.

❷ Riva de Biasio

Venice's main thoroughfare is busy with all kinds of **boats:** taxis, police boats, garbage boats, ambulances, construction cranes, and even brown-and-white UPS boats. Somehow they all manage to share the canal in relative peace.

About 25 yards past the Riva de Biasio stop, you'll look left down the broad **Cannaregio Canal** to see what was the **Jewish Ghetto** (✪

Ferrovia, a.k.a. Santa Lucia train station

The Grand Canal, lined with grand buildings

described on page 144). The twin, pale-pink, eight-story "skyscrapers"—the tallest buildings you'll see at this end of the canal—are reminders of how densely populated the community was. Founded in 1516 near a copper foundry, this segregated community gave us our word "ghetto."

❸ San Marcuola

At this stop, facing a tiny square just ahead, stands the unfinished church of San Marcuola, one of only five churches fronting the Grand Canal. Centuries ago, this canal was a commercial drag of expensive real estate in high demand by wealthy merchants. About 20 yards ahead on the right stands the stately gray **Turkish "Fondaco" Exchange,** one of the oldest houses in Venice. Its horseshoe arches and roofline of triangles and dingleballs are reminders of its Byzantine heritage. Turkish traders in turbans docked here, unloaded their goods into the warehouse on the bottom story, then went upstairs for a home-style meal and a place to sleep. Venice in the 1500s was very cosmopolitan, welcoming every religion and ethnicity, so long as they carried cash. (Today the building contains the city's Museum of Natural History—and Venice's only dinosaur skeleton.)

Just 100 yards ahead on the left, Venice's **Casinò** is housed in the palace where German composer Richard *(The Ring)* Wagner died in 1883. See his distinct, strong-jawed profile in the white plaque on the brick wall. In the 1700s, Venice was Europe's Vegas, with casinos and prostitutes everywhere. *Casinòs* ("little houses" in Venetian dialect) have long provided Italians with a handy escape from daily life. Today they're run by the state to keep Mafia influence at bay. Notice the fancy front porch, rolling out the red carpet for high rollers arriving by taxi or hotel boat.

Turkish "Fondaco" Exchange

San Stae Church

❹ San Stae

The San Stae Church sports a delightful Baroque facade. Opposite the San Stae stop is a little canal opening—on the second building to the right of that opening, look for the peeling plaster that once made up **frescoes** (you can barely distinguish the scant remains of little angels on the lower floors). Imagine the facades of the Grand Canal at their finest. Most of them would have been covered in frescoes by the best artists of the day. As colorful as the city is today, it's still only a faded, sepia-toned remnant of a long-gone era, a time of lavishly decorated, brilliantly colored palaces.

Just ahead, jutting out a bit on the right, is the ornate white facade of **Ca' Pesaro** (which houses the International Gallery of Modern Art—✪ see page 143). *"Ca'"* is short for *casa* (house). Because only the house of the doge (Venetian ruler) could be called a palace (palazzo), all other Venetian palaces are technically *"Ca'."*

In this city of masks, notice how the rich marble facades along the Grand Canal mask what are generally just simple, no-nonsense brick buildings. Most merchants enjoyed showing off. However, being smart businessmen, they only decorated the side of the buildings that would be seen and appreciated. But look back as you pass Ca' Pesaro. It's the only building you'll see with a fine side facade. Ahead, on the left, is Ca' d'Oro with its glorious triple-decker medieval arcade (just before the next stop).

❺ Ca' d'Oro

The lacy **Ca' d'Oro** (House of Gold) is the best example of Venetian Gothic architecture on the canal. Its three stories offer different variations on balcony design, topped with a spiny white roofline. Venetian Gothic mixes

Ca' Pesaro—this "ca" houses modern art

Ca' d'Oro—textbook Venetian Gothic

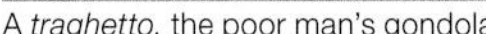

A *traghetto,* the poor man's gondola

Mercato Rialto hosts the fish market.

traditional Gothic (pointed arches and round medallions stamped with a four-leaf clover) with Byzantine styles (tall, narrow arches atop thin columns), filled in with Islamic frills. Like all the palaces, this was originally painted and gilded to make it even more glorious than it is now. Today the Ca' d'Oro is an art gallery.

Look at the Venetian chorus line of palaces in front of the boat. On the right is the arcade of the covered **fish market,** with the open-air **produce market** just beyond. It bustles in the morning but is quiet the rest of the day. This is a great scene to wander through—even though European Union hygiene standards have made it cleaner but less colorful than it once was.

Find the ***traghetto*** gondola ferrying shoppers—standing like Washington crossing the Delaware—back and forth. There are seven *traghetto* crossings along the Grand Canal, each one marked by a classy low-key green-and-black sign. Driving a *traghetto* isn't these gondoliers' normal day jobs. As a public service, all gondoliers are obliged to row the *traghetto* a few days a month. Make a point to use them. At €2 a ride, *traghetti* offer the cheapest gondola rides in Venice (but at this price don't expect them to sing to you).

❻ Mercato Rialto

Boats stop here (but only between 8:00 and 20:00) to serve the busy market. The long and officious-looking building at this stop is the Venice courthouse. Straight ahead in the distance, rising above the huge post office, is the tip of the Campanile (bell tower), crowned by its golden angel at St. Mark's Square, where this tour will end. The **German Exchange** (100 yards directly ahead, on left side) was the trading center for German

Rialto Bridge, with its 160-foot single span, marks Venice's traditional commercial neighborhood.

metal merchants in the early 1500s (once a post office, it will soon be a shopping center).

You'll cruise by some trendy and beautifully situated wine bars on the right, but look ahead as you round the corner and see the impressive Rialto Bridge come into view.

A major landmark of Venice, the **Rialto Bridge** is lined with shops and tourists. Constructed in 1588, it's the third bridge built on this spot. Until the 1850s, this was the only bridge crossing the Grand Canal. With a span of 160 feet and foundations stretching 650 feet on either side, the Rialto was an impressive engineering feat in its day. Earlier Rialto Bridges could open to let big ships in, but not this one. When this new bridge was completed, much of the Grand Canal was closed to shipping and became a canal of palaces.

When gondoliers pass under the fat arch of the Rialto Bridge, they take full advantage of its acoustics: *"Volare, oh, oh..."*

7 Rialto

Rialto, a separate town in the early days of Venice, has always been the commercial district, while San Marco was the religious and governmental center. Today, a winding street called the Mercerie connects the two, providing travelers with human traffic jams and a mesmerizing gauntlet of shopping temptations. This is the only stretch of the historic Grand Canal with landings upon which you can walk. They unloaded the city's basic necessities here: oil, wine, charcoal, iron. Today, the quay is lined with tourist-trap restaurants.

Venice's sleek, black, graceful **gondolas** are a symbol of the city (for more on gondolas, ✪ see page 204). With about 500 gondoliers joyriding amid the churning *vaporetti,* there's a lot of congestion on the Grand Canal. Pay attention—this is where most of the gondola and vaporetto accidents take place. While the Rialto is the highlight of many gondola rides, gondoliers understandably prefer the quieter small canals. Watch your vaporetto driver curse the better-paid gondoliers.

Ahead 100 yards on the left, two gray-colored **palaces** stand side by side (the City Hall and the mayor's office). Their horseshoe-shaped, arched windows are similar and their stories are the same height, lining up to create the effect of one long balcony.

❽ San Silvestro

We now enter a long stretch of important **merchants' palaces,** each with proud and different facades. Because ships couldn't navigate beyond the Rialto Bridge, the biggest palaces—with the major shipping needs—line this last stretch of the navigable Grand Canal.

Palaces like these were multifunctional: ground floor for the warehouse, offices and showrooms upstairs, and the living quarters above the offices on the "noble floors" (with big windows designed to allow in maximum light). Servants lived and worked on the top floors (with the smallest

Merchant's palace with water-level entries

Docking posts painted the family colors

windows). For fire-safety reasons, the kitchens were also located on the top floors. Peek into the noble floors to catch a glimpse of their still-glorious chandeliers of Murano glass.

⑨ Sant'Angelo

Notice how many buildings have a foundation of waterproof white stone *(pietra d'Istria)* upon which the bricks sit high and dry. Many canal-level floors are abandoned as the rising water level takes its toll.

The **posts**—historically painted gaily with the equivalent of family coats of arms—don't rot underwater. But the wood at the waterline, where it's exposed to oxygen, does. On the smallest canals, little blue gondola signs indicate that these docks are for gondolas only (no taxis or motorboats).

⑩ San Tomà

Fifty yards ahead, on the right side (with twin obelisks on the rooftop) stands **Palazzo Balbi,** the palace of an early 17th-century captain general of the sea. These Venetian equivalents of five-star admirals were honored with twin obelisks decorating their palaces. This palace, like so many in the city, flies three flags: Italy (green-white-red), the European Union (blue with ring of stars), and Venice (a lion on a field of red and gold). Today it houses the administrative headquarters of the regional government.

Just past the admiral's palace, look immediately to the right, down a side canal. On the right side of that canal, before the bridge, see the traffic light and the **fire station** (the 1930s Mussolini-era building with four arches hiding fireboats parked and ready to go).

The impressive **Ca' Foscari,** with a classic Venetian facade (on the corner, across from the fire station), dominates the bend in the canal. This is the main building of the University of Venice, which has about 25,000 students. Notice the elegant lamp on the corner—needed in the old days to light this intersection.

The grand, heavy, white **Ca' Rezzonico,** just before the stop of the same name, houses the Museum of 18th-Century Venice (✪ described in the Ca' Rezzonico Tour chapter). Across the canal is the cleaner and leaner **Palazzo Grassi,** the last major palace built on the canal, erected in the late 1700s. It was purchased by a French tycoon and now displays a contemporary art collection.

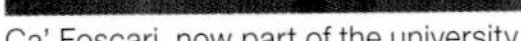
Ca' Foscari, now part of the university

Ca' Rezzonico evokes 18th-century luxury.

⑪ Ca' Rezzonico

Up ahead, the Accademia Bridge leads over the Grand Canal to the **Accademia Gallery** (right side), filled with the best Venetian paintings. The bridge was put up in 1934 as a temporary structure. Locals liked it, so it stayed. It was rebuilt in 1984 in the original style.

⑫ Accademia

From here, look through the graceful bridge and way ahead to enjoy a classic view of **La Salute Church,** topped by a crown-shaped dome supported by scrolls. This Church of Saint Mary of Good Health was built to thank God for delivering Venetians from the devastating plague of 1630 (which had killed about a third of the city's population).

The low, white building among greenery (100 yards ahead, on the right, between the Accademia Bridge and the church) is the **Peggy Guggenheim Collection.** The American heiress "retired" here, sprucing up a palace that had been abandoned mid-construction. Peggy willed the city her fine collection of modern art.

As you approach the next stop, notice on the right how the fine line of higgledy-piggledy palaces evokes old-time Venice. Two doors past the Guggenheim, Palazzo Dario has a great set of characteristic **funnel-shaped chimneys.** These forced embers through a loop-the-loop channel until they were dead—required in the days when stone palaces were surrounded by humble, wooden buildings, and a live spark could make a merchant's workforce homeless. Notice this early Renaissance building's flat-feeling facade with "pasted-on" Renaissance motifs. Three doors later is the **Salviati building,** which once served as a glassworks. Its fine

Accademia Bridge—great viewpoint and gateway to the art-filled Dorsoduro neighborhood

mosaic, done by Art Nouveau in the early 20th century, features Venice as a queen being appreciated by the big shots of society.

⑬ Santa Maria del Giglio

Back on the left stands the fancy **Gritti Palace hotel.** Hemingway and Woody Allen both stayed here (but not together).

Take a deep whiff of Venice. What's all this nonsense about stinky canals? All I smell is my shirt. By the way, how's your captain? Smooth dockings? To get to know him, stand up in the bow and block his view.

⑭ Salute

The huge **La Salute Church** towers overhead as if squirted from a can of Catholic Reddi-wip. Like Venice itself, the church rests upon pilings. To build the foundation for the city, more than a million trees were piled together, reaching beneath the mud to the solid clay. Much of the surrounding countryside was deforested by Venice. Trees were imported and consumed locally—to fuel the furnaces of Venice's booming glass industry, to build Europe's biggest merchant marine, to form light and flexible beams for nearly all of the buildings in town, and to prop up this city in the mud.

La Salute Church—its towering dome is topped with a statue of "Our Lady of Health"

As the Grand Canal opens up into the lagoon, the last building on the right with the golden ball is the 17th-century **Customs House,** which now houses the Punta della Dogana Museum of Contemporary Art. Its two bronze Atlases hold a statue of Fortune riding the ball. Arriving ships stopped here to pay their tolls.

⓯ San Marco

Up ahead on the left, the green pointed tip of the Campanile marks **St. Mark's Square,** the political and religious center of Venice...and the final destination of this tour. You could get off at the San Marco stop and go straight to St. Mark's Square. But I'm staying on the boat for one more stop, just past St. Mark's Square (it's a quick walk back).

Survey the lagoon. Opposite St. Mark's Square, across the water, the ghostly white church with the pointy bell tower is **San Giorgio Maggiore,** with great views of Venice. Next to it is the residential island Giudecca, stretching from close to San Giorgio Maggiore past the Venice youth hostel (with a nice view, directly across) to the Hilton Hotel (good nighttime view, far right end of island).

Still on board? If you are, as we leave the San Marco stop, prepare for a drive-by view of St. Mark's Square. First comes the bold white facade of the old mint (marked by a tiny cupola, where Venice's golden ducat, the "dollar" of the Venetian Republic, was made) and the library facade. Then come the twin columns, topped by St. Theodore and St. Mark, who've welcomed visitors since the 15th century. Between the columns, catch a glimpse of two giant figures atop the **Clock Tower**—they've been whacking their clappers every hour since 1499. The domes of **St. Mark's Basilica** are soon eclipsed by the lacy facade of the **Doge's Palace.** Next you'll see the **Bridge of Sighs** (leading from the palace to the prison—check out the maximum security bars), many gondolas with their green breakwater buoys, and then the grand harborside promenade—the **Riva.**

Follow the Riva with your eye, past elegant hotels to the green area in the distance. This is the largest of Venice's few **parks,** which hosts the annual Biennale festival (✪ see page 150). Much farther in the distance is the **Lido,** the island with Venice's beach. Its sand and casinos are tempting, but its car traffic disrupts the medieval charm of Venice.

⑯ San Zaccaria

OK, you're at your last stop (likely San Zaccaria-Danieli or San Zaccaria-M.V.E.). Quick—muscle your way off this boat! (If you don't, you'll eventually end up at the Lido.)

At San Zaccaria, you're right in the thick of the action. A number of other *vaporetti* depart from here (✪ see page 196). Otherwise, it's a short walk back along the Riva to St. Mark's Square. Ahoy!

St. Mark's Square Tour

Piazza San Marco

Venice was once Europe's richest city, and Piazza San Marco was its center. As middleman in the trade between Asia and Europe, wealthy Venice profited from both sides. In 1450, Venice had 180,000 citizens and a gross "national" product that exceeded that of entire countries.

The rich Venetians taught the rest of Europe about the good life—silks, spices, and jewels from the East, crafts from northern Europe, good food and wine, fine architecture, music, theater, and laughter. Venice was a vibrant city full of painted palaces, glittering canals, and impressed visitors. Five centuries after its power began to decline, Venice still has all of these, with the added charm of romantic decay. In this tour, we'll spend an hour in the heart of this Old World superpower.

ORIENTATION

Getting There: Signs all over town point to *San Marco*—meaning both the square and the basilica—located where the Grand Canal spills out into the lagoon. Vaporetto stops: San Marco or San Zaccaria.

Information: There's a TI in the southwest corner of the square.

Audio Tour: You can download this chapter as a free Rick Steves audio tour (✪ see page 199).

Services: Handy public WCs (€1.50) are behind the Correr Museum and also at the waterfront park, Giardinetti Reali (near San Marco-Vallaresso vaporetto dock).

Eating: Cafés with live music provide an engaging soundtrack for St. Mark's Square (✪ see "Cafés on St. Mark's Square" sidebar, later). The Correr Museum (at the end of the square opposite the basilica) has a quiet coffee shop overlooking the crowded square. For a list of restaurants in the area, ✪ see page 172.

Necessary Eyesores: Expect scaffolding and advertising billboards on monuments as a necessary part of long-term renovation projects.

Cardinal Points: The square is aligned (roughly) east-west. So, facing the basilica, north is to your left.

Starring: Byzantine domes, Gothic arches, Renaissance arches...and the wonderful, musical space they enclose.

Mark's winged lion appears everywhere.

St. Mark's Square makes the spirit soar.

St. Mark's Square
To Rialto
To Rialto
CALLE D. FABBRI
CALLE FIUBERA
MARZARIA OROLOGIO
SPADARIA
C. ANGELO
ATENEO SAN BASSO
Piazzetta dei Leoni
C. CANONICA
RUGA G. APOLLONIA
C. FIGHER
C. D. CHIESA
To S. M. Formosa
Campo Santi Filippo & Giacomo
SAN GALLO
FOND. SAN GALLO
C. CAVALETTO
Bacino Orseolo
ORSEOLO
Rio de le Procuratie
OLD OFFICES
CLOCK TOWER
ST. MARK'S BASILICA
Rio de la Palazzo
DIOCESAN MUSEUM
C. D. ALBANESI
C. DE LE RASSE
Rio del Vin
RAMO SALVA
TETRARCHS
Piazza San Marco
CAMPANILE
BRIDGE OF SIGHS
CORRER MUSEUM
7TH COLUMN
DOGE'S PALACE
PRISON
NAPOLEON'S WING
Piazzetta
PONTE DE PAGLIA
POST
FREZZERIA
C. LARGA DE L'ASCENCION
NEW OFFICES
RIVA DEGLI SCHIAVONI
To Accademia
WC
SAL. SAN MOISÈ
SAN MARCO COLUMN
SAN THEODORE COLUMN
San Zaccaria-Danieli
SAN MOISÈ
C. DEL RIDOTO
C. VALLARESSO
Giardinetti Reali
To Lido
WC
HARRY'S AMERICAN BAR
San Marco-Giardinetti
San Marco-Vallaresso
Grand Canal
St. Mark's Basin
To Accademia
PUNTA DOGANA (CUSTOMS HOUSE)
100 Meters
100 Yards
Eateries & Entertainment
1 Caffè Florian
2 Gran Caffè Quadri
3 Gran Caffè Lavena; Galleria San Marco Glassblowing
4 Gran Caffè Chioggia
5 Eden Bar
6 Caffè Aurora
Other
7 Il Merletto Lace Shop
8 Libreria Studium Bookstore
9 Oltrex Change & Travel
10 St. Mark's Basilica Bag Check

THE TOUR BEGINS

▶ *For an overview of this grand square, view it from the west end of the square (away from St. Mark's Basilica).*

The Piazza

St. Mark's Basilica dominates the square with its Eastern-style onion domes and glowing mosaics. Mark Twain said it looked like "a vast warty bug taking a meditative walk." (I say it looks like tiara-wearing ladybugs copulating.) To the right of the basilica is its 325-foot-tall Campanile. Between the basilica and the Campanile, you can catch a glimpse of the pale-pink Doge's Palace. Lining the square are the former government offices *(procuratie)* that managed the treasury of St. Mark's, back when the church and state were one, and administered the Venetian empire's vast network of trading outposts, which stretched all the way to Turkey.

The square is big, but it feels intimate with its cafés and dueling orchestras. By day, it's great for people-watching and pigeon-chasing. By night, under lantern light, it transports you to another century, complete with its own romantic soundtrack. The piazza draws Indians in saris, English nobles in blue blazers, and Nebraskans in shorts. Napoleon called the piazza "the most beautiful drawing room in Europe." Napoleon himself added to the intimacy by building the final wing, opposite the basilica, that encloses the square.

For architecture buffs, here are three centuries of styles, bam, side by side, *uno-due-tre,* for easy comparison:

1. On the left side (as you face the basilica) are the "Old" offices, built about 1500 in solid, column-and-arch Renaissance style.

2. The "New" offices (on the right), in a High Renaissance style from a century later (c. 1600), are a little heavier and more ornate. This wing mixes arches, the three orders of columns from bottom to top—Doric, Ionic, and Corinthian—and statues in the Baroque style.

3. Napoleon's wing, at the opposite end from the basilica, is later (c. 1800) and designed to fit in. The dozen Roman emperors decorating the parapet were once joined by Napoleon in the middle, but today the French emperor is gone.

The arcade ringing the square, formerly lined with dozens of fine cafés, still provides an elegant promenade—complete with drapery that is dropped when necessary to provide relief from the sun.

Imagine this square full of water, with gondolas floating where people now sip cappuccinos. That happens every so often at very high tides *(acqua alta),* a reminder that Venice and the sea are intertwined. (Now that one is sinking and the other is rising, they are more intertwined than ever.)

Venice became Europe's richest city from its trade with northern Europeans, Ottoman Muslims, and Byzantine Christians. Here in St. Mark's Square, the exact center of this East-West axis, we see both the luxury and the mix of Eastern and Western influences.

Watch out for pigeon speckle. The pigeons are not indigenous to Venice (they were imported by the Habsburgs) nor loved by residents. In fact, Venetians love seagulls because they eat pigeons. In 2008, Venice outlawed the feeding of pigeons, so their days may be numbered. There are now fewer pigeons, but they're still here. Vermin are a problem on this small island, where it's said that each Venetian has two pigeons and four rats. (The rats stay hidden, except when high tides flood their homes.)

► *Now approach the basilica. If it's hot and you're tired, grab a shady spot at the foot of the Campanile.*

The piazza is magnificent whether floodlit or flooded—as it occasionally is at *acqua alta.*

Cafés on St. Mark's Square

In the Venetian culture, coffee was huge. It was said that the freedoms a gentleman could experience in Venice went far beyond what any one person could actually indulge in. But one extravagance all could enjoy was the ritual of coffee's public consumption: showing off with an affordable luxury, participating in something new and trendy, sharing the ideas of the Enlightenment.

Exotic coffee was made to order for the fancy café scene. Traders introduced coffee, called the "wine of Islam," from the East. The first coffeehouses opened in the 17th century, and by 1750 there were dozens of cafés lining Piazza San Marco and 200 operating in Venice.

Today, several fine old cafés survive and still line the square. Those with live music feature similar food, prices, and a three- to five-piece combo playing a selection of classical and pop hits, from Brahms to "Bésame Mucho." If you sit outside and get just a drink, expect to pay €12-20, including a €6 cover charge when the orchestra is playing (no cover charge otherwise). A coffee—your cheapest option—costs about €6 if you sit at an outside table, plus the €6 cover charge when the music plays, bringing it to €12 total (even at the venerable Caffè Florian). It's perfectly acceptable to nurse a cappuccino for an hour—you're paying for the music with the cover charge. The price for a coffee enjoyed inside at the bar is reasonable, thanks to a city law regulating coffee prices.

Caffè Florian (on the right as you face the church) is the most famous Venetian café and one of the first places in Europe to serve coffee

St. Mark's Basilica

The facade is a wild mix of East and West, with round, Roman-style arches over the doorways, golden Byzantine mosaics, a roofline ringed with pointed Gothic pinnacles, and Muslim-shaped onion domes (wood, covered with lead) on the roof. The brick-structure building is blanketed in marble that came from everywhere—columns from Alexandria, capitals from Sicily, and carvings from Constantinople. The columns flanking the doorways show the facade's variety—purple, green, gray, white, yellow,

(daily 10:00-24:00, shorter hours in winter). It's been a popular spot for a discreet rendezvous in Venice since 1720. The orchestra here plays a more classical repertoire than at the other cafés. The outside tables are the main action, but do walk inside through the richly decorated, old-time rooms where Casanova, Lord Byron, Charles Dickens, and Woody Allen have all paid too much for a drink.

Gran Caffè Quadri, opposite the Florian, has an equally illustrious roster of famous clientele, including the writers Stendhal and Dumas, and composer Richard Wagner.

Gran Caffè Lavena, near the Clock Tower, is newer and less storied. Drop in to check out its dazzling but politically incorrect chandelier.

Gran Caffè Chioggia, on the Piazzetta facing the Doge's Palace, charges slightly less, with one or two musicians, usually a pianist, playing cocktail jazz.

Eden Bar and **Caffè Aurora** are less expensive and don't have live music.

some speckled, some striped horizontally, some vertically, some fluted—all topped with a variety of different capitals.

What's amazing isn't so much the variety as the fact that the whole thing comes together in a bizarre sort of harmony. St. Mark's remains simply the most interesting church in Europe, a church that (to paraphrase Goethe) "can only be compared with itself."

For more on the basilica, inside and out, see the ✪ St. Mark's Basilica Tour chapter.

▸ *Facing the basilica, turn 90 degrees to the left to see the...*

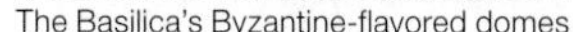

The Basilica's Byzantine-flavored domes

The Clock Tower's statues chime the hours.

Clock Tower (Torre dell'Orologio)

Any proper Renaissance city wanted to have a fine, formal entry and a clock tower. In Venice's case, its entry was visible from the sea and led from the big religious and governmental center to the rest of the city. The Clock Tower retains some of its original blue-and-gold pigments, a reminder that, in centuries past, this city glowed with bright color.

Two bronze "Moors" stand atop the Clock Tower (built originally to be Caucasian giants, they only switched their ethnicity when their metal darkened over the centuries). At the top of each hour they swing their giant clappers. The clock dial shows the 24 hours, the signs of the zodiac, and in the blue center, the phases of the moon—important information, as a maritime city with a shallow lagoon needs to know the tides. Above the dial is the world's first digital clock, which changes every five minutes.

An alert winged lion, the symbol of St. Mark and the city, looks down on the crowded square. He opens a book that reads *"Pax Tibi Marce,"* or "Peace to you, Mark." As legend goes, these were the comforting words that an angel spoke to the stressed evangelist, assuring him he would find serenity here on the island. Eventually, St. Mark's body found its final resting place inside the basilica, and now his winged-lion symbol is everywhere. (Find four in 20 seconds. Go.)

Venice's many lions express the city's various mood swings through history—triumphant after a naval victory, sad when a favorite son has died, hollow-eyed after a plague, and smiling when the soccer team wins. The pair of lions squatting between the Clock Tower and basilica have probably been photographed being ridden by every Venetian child born since the dawn of cameras.

Campanile

The original Campanile (cam-pah-NEE-lay, bell tower) was an observation tower and a marvel of medieval and Renaissance architecture—until 1902, when it toppled into the center of the piazza. It had groaned ominously the night before, sending people scurrying from the cafés. The next morning... crash! The golden angel on top landed right at the basilica's front door, standing up.

The Campanile was rebuilt 10 years later complete with its golden archangel Gabriel, who always faces the breeze. You can ride a lift to the top for the best view of Venice. It's crowded at peak times, but well worth it (for Campanile hours, ✪ see page 131).

You may see construction work around the Campanile's base. Hoping to prevent a repeat of the 1902 collapse, they've wrapped the underground foundations with a titanium girdle to shore up a crack that appeared in 1939.

Because St. Mark's Square is the first place in town to start flooding, there are tide gauges at the outside base of the Campanile (near the exit, facing St. Mark's Square) that show the current sea level *(livello marea).* Find the stone plaque (near the exit door) that commemorates the high-water 77-inch level from the disastrous floods of 1966. In December 2008, Venice suffered another terrible high tide, cresting at 61 inches.

If the tide is mild (around 20 inches), the water merely seeps up through the drains. But when there's a strong tide (around 40 inches), it looks like someone's turned on a faucet down below. The water bubbles upward and flows like a river to the lowest points in the square, which can be covered with a few inches of water in an hour or so. When the water

Many generations have struck the same pose.

The Basilica's bell tower, or Campanile

Escape from St. Mark's Square

Crowds getting to you? Here are some relatively quiet areas on or near St. Mark's Square.

Correr Museum: Sip a cappuccino in the café of this uncrowded history museum in a building that overlooks St. Mark's Square (enter at the far end of the piazza). ✪ See page 129.

Giardinetti Reali: The small park is along the waterfront, west of the Piazzetta (facing the water, turn right—it's next to the TI and the only place for a legal picnic).

San Giorgio Maggiore: This is the fairy-tale island you see from the Piazzetta (catch vaporetto #2 from the San Zaccaria-M.V.E. stop, past the Bridge of Sighs). ✪ See page 132.

Il Merletto: This lace shop is in a small, decommissioned chapel near the northwest corner of St. Mark's Square (daily 10:00-17:00, go through Sotoportego del Cavalletto and across the little bridge on the right). Ask for the sheet in English explaining the history of Venetian lace.

La Salute Church: This cool church in a quiet neighborhood is a short hop on vaporetto #1 from the San Marco-Vallaresso stop; or you can ride the nearby *traghetto*. ✪ See page 138.

Caffè Florian: The plush interior of this luxurious 18th-century café, located on St. Mark's Square, is generally quiet and nearly empty. A coffee here can be a wonderful break (✪ see "Cafés on St. Mark's Square," earlier).

level rises one meter above mean sea level, a warning siren sounds, and it repeats if a serious flood is imminent.

Many doorways have three-foot-high wooden or metal barriers to block the high water *(acqua alta),* but the seawater still seeps in through floors and drains, rendering the barriers nearly useless.

You might see stacked wooden benches in the square; during floods, the benches are placed end-to-end to create elevated sidewalks. If you think the square is crowded now, when it's flooded it turns into total grid-lock, as all the people normally sharing the whole square jostle for space on the narrow wooden walkways.

In 2006, the pavement around St. Mark's Square was taken up, and the entire height of the square was raised by adding a layer of sand, and then replacing the stones. If the columns along the ground floor of the Doge's Palace look stubby, it's because this process has been carried out many times over the centuries, buying a little more time as the sea slowly swallows the city.

▸ *The small square between the basilica and the water is the...*

Piazzetta

This "Little Square" is framed by the Doge's Palace on the left, the library on the right, and the waterfront of the lagoon. In former days, the Piazzetta was closed to the public for a few hours a day so that government officials and bigwigs could gather in the sun to strike shady deals.

The pale-pink Doge's Palace is the epitome of the style known as Venetian Gothic. Columns support traditional, pointed Gothic arches, but with a Venetian flair—they're curved to a point, ornamented with a trefoil (three-leaf clover), and topped with a round medallion of a quatrefoil (four-leaf clover). The pattern is found on buildings all over Venice and on the formerly Venetian-controlled Croatian coast, but nowhere else in the world (except Las Vegas).

The two large 12th-century columns near the water were looted from Constantinople. Mark's winged lion sits on top of one. The lion's body (nearly 15 feet long) predates the wings and is more than 2,000 years old. The other column holds St. Theodore (battling a crocodile), the former patron saint who was replaced by Mark. I guess stabbing crocs in the back

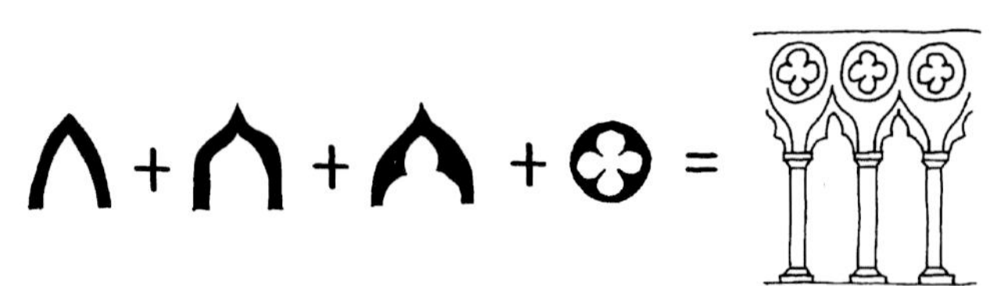

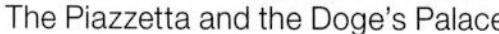
The Piazzetta and the Doge's Palace

Venetian Gothic—arches and medallions

isn't classy enough for an upwardly mobile world power. Criminals were executed by being hung from these columns in the hopes that the public could learn its lessons vicariously.

Venice was the "Bride of the Sea" because she depended on sea trading for her livelihood. This "marriage" was celebrated annually by the people on Ascension Day. The doge, in full regalia, boarded a ritual boat (his Air Force One) here at the edge of the Piazzetta and sailed out into the lagoon. There a vow was made, and he dropped a jeweled ring into the water to seal the marriage.

In the distance, on an island across the lagoon, is one of the grandest views in the city, of the Church of San Giorgio Maggiore. With its four tall columns as the entryway, the church, designed by the late-Renaissance architect Andrea Palladio, influenced the appearance of future government and bank buildings around the world.

Palladio's sober classical lines are pure and intellectual, but with their love of extravagance, Venetians wanted something more exuberant. More to local taste was the High Renaissance style of Jacopo Sansovino, who (around 1530) designed the library (here on the Piazzetta) and the delicate Loggetta at the base of the Campanile (destroyed by the collapse of the tower in 1902 and then pieced back together).

Tetrarchs and the Doge's Palace's Seventh Column

Where the basilica meets the Doge's Palace is the traditional entrance to the palace, decorated with four small Roman statues—the Tetrarchs. No one knows for sure who they are, but I like the legend that says they're the scared leaders of a divided Rome during its fall, holding their swords and each other as all hell breaks loose around them. Some believe that they are the leaders of the Eastern and Western empires (the bearded ones) with their chosen successors (the clean-shaven, younger ones). Whatever the legend, these statues—made of precious purple porphyry stone—are symbols of power. They were looted, likely from Constantinople, and then placed here proudly as spoils of war. How old are they? They've guarded the palace entrance since the city first rose from the mud.

The Doge's Palace's seventh column (the seventh from the water) tells a story of love, romance, and tragedy in its carved capital: 1) In the first

The Bridge of Sighs connects the rich Doge's Palace (left) with its notorious prisons (right).

scene (the carving facing the Piazzetta), a woman on a balcony is wooed by her lover, who says, "Babe, I want *you!*" 2) She responds, "Why, little ol' *me?*" 3) They get married. 4) Kiss. 5) Hit the sack—pretty racy for 14th-century art. 6) Nine months later, guess what? 7) The baby takes its first steps. 8) And as was all too common in the 1300s...the child dies.

For more on the Doge's Palace, see the ✪ Doge's Palace Tour chapter.

▸ *At the waterfront in the Piazzetta, turn left and walk (east) along the water. At the top of the first bridge, look inland at the...*

Bridge of Sighs

In the Doge's Palace (on your left), the government doled out justice. On your right are the prisons. (Don't let the palatial facade fool you—see the bars on the windows?) Prisoners sentenced in the palace crossed to the prisons by way of the covered bridge in front of you. This was called the Prisons' Bridge until the Romantic poet Lord Byron renamed it in the 19th century. From this bridge, the convicted got their final view of sunny, joyous Venice before entering the black and dank prisons. According to the Romantic legend, they sighed.

Venice has been a major tourist center for four centuries. Anyone who's ever come here has stood on this very spot, looking at the Bridge of Sighs. Lean on the railing leaned on by everyone from Casanova to Byron to Hemingway.

I stood in Venice, on the Bridge of Sighs,
a palace and a prison on each hand.
I saw, from out the wave, her structures rise,
as from the stroke of the enchanter's wand.
A thousand years their cloudy wings expand
around me, and a dying glory smiles
o'er the far times, when many a subject land
looked to the Winged Lion's marble piles,
where Venice sat in state, throned on her hundred isles!

—from Lord Byron's *Childe Harold's Pilgrimage*

St. Mark's Basilica Tour

Basilica di San Marco

Among Europe's churches, St. Mark's is peerless. From the outside, it's a riot of domes, columns, and statues, completely unlike the towering Gothic churches of northern Europe or the heavy Baroque of much of the rest of Italy. Inside is a decor of mosaics, colored marbles, and oriental treasures that's rarely seen elsewhere. The Christian symbolism is unfamiliar to Western eyes, done in the style of Byzantine icons and even Islamic designs. Older than most of Europe's churches, it feels like a remnant of a lost world.

This is your best chance in Italy (outside of Ravenna) to glimpse a forgotten and somewhat mysterious part of the human story—Byzantium.

ORIENTATION

Cost: Entering the church is free. Three separate, optional sights inside require paid admission: the Treasury (€3, includes audioguide), Golden Altarpiece (€2), and San Marco Museum (€5, skip the €3.50 audioguide).

Hours: The church and its museums are open Mon-Sat 9:45-17:00, Sun 14:00-17:00 (Sun until 16:00 Nov-March). The interior and its mosaics are brilliantly lit daily from 11:30 to 12:30.

Dress Code: Modest dress (no bare knees or bare shoulders) is strictly enforced, even for kids. Shorts are OK if they cover the knees.

Information: Tel. 041-270-8311, www.basilicasanmarco.it.

Tours: Free, hour-long English tours (heavy on the mosaics' religious symbolism) are offered many days at 11:00 (meet in atrium). You can download this chapter as a free Rick Steves audio tour (✪ see page 199).

Length of This Tour: Allow one hour.

Avoiding Lines: There's almost always a long line to get in, and once inside, there can be shoulder-to-shoulder crowds. Avoid crowds by going early or late. Those who have a (large) bag to check get to skip the line. Read on.

Bag Check (and Skipping the Line): Bags larger than a small purse or shoulder-slung bag are not allowed inside. Check them for free for up to one hour at Ateneo San Basso church, 30 yards to the left of the basilica, down narrow Calle San Basso (✪ see map facing page; daily 9:30-17:00). Note that you can't check small bags that would be allowed inside.

Those with a bag to check actually get to skip the line, as do their companions (up to three or so). Just present your claim tag to the guard (enter to the left of the railing where the line forms), and he'll let you in.

WC: Inside the San Marco Museum.

Theft Alert: Watch for pickpockets in the jostling crowds.

Mass: Full services are outside of visiting hours (e.g., daily at 8:00 or 18:30; see www.basilicasanmarco.it for full schedule). Enter through the "worship only" door around the left side of the basilica.

Photography: Forbidden inside the church; allowed on the view balcony.

Starring: St. Mark, Byzantium, mosaics, and ancient bronze horses.

St. Mark's Basilica

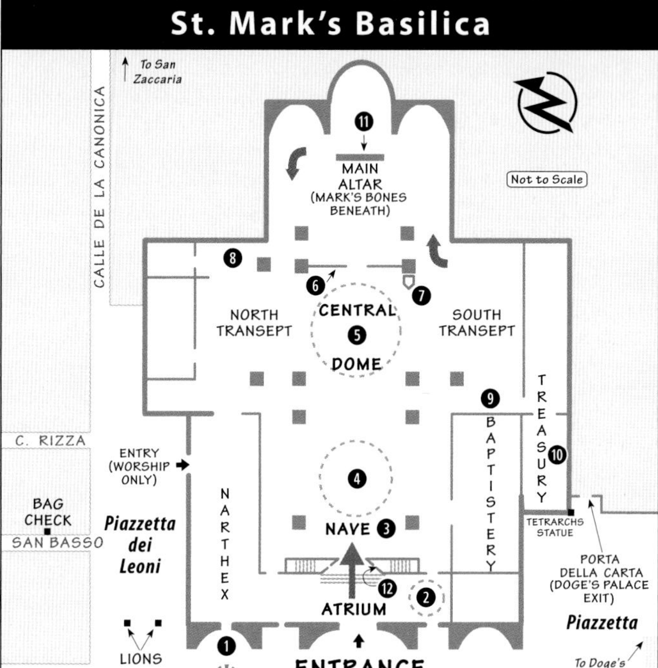

1. Exterior – Mosaic of Mark's Relics
2. Atrium – Mosaic of Noah's Ark & the Great Flood
3. Nave – Mosaics & Greek-Cross Floor Plan
4. Pentecost Mosaic
5. Central Dome – Ascension Mosaic
6. Rood Screen
7. Doge's Pulpit
8. Nicopeia Icon
9. Discovery of Mark Mosaic
10. Treasury
11. Golden Altarpiece
12. Stairs up to Loggia: San Marco Museum & Bronze Horses

THE TOUR BEGINS

❶ Exterior—Mosaic of Mark's Relics

▸ *Start outside in the square, far enough back to take in the whole facade. Then zero in on the details.*

St. Mark's Basilica is a treasure chest of booty that was looted during Venice's glory days. That's most appropriate for a church built on the stolen bones of a saint.

The **mosaic over the far left door** shows the theft that put Venice on the pilgrimage map. Two men (in the center, with crooked staffs) enter the church bearing a coffin with the body of St. Mark, who looks pretty grumpy from the long voyage.

St. Mark was the author of one of the Gospels, the four Bible books telling the story of Jesus' life (Matthew, Mark, Luke, and John). Eight centuries after his death, his holy body was in Muslim-occupied Alexandria, Egypt. In A.D. 828, two visiting merchants from Venice "rescued" the body from the "infidels," hid it in a pork barrel (which was unclean to Muslims), and spirited it away to Venice.

The merchants presented the body—not to a pope or bishop—but to the doge (with white ermine collar, on the right) and his wife, the dogaressa (with entourage, on the left), giving instant status to Venice's budding secular state. They built a church here over Mark's bones and made him the patron saint of the city. You'll see his symbol, the winged lion, all over Venice.

The original church burned down in A.D. 976, Today's structure was begun in 1063. The mosaic, from 1260, shows that the church hasn't

St. Mark's—a church unlike any other

Mark's body is carried into the church.

changed much since then—you can see the onion domes and famous bronze horses on the balcony.

St. Mark's was modeled after a great fourth-century church in Constantinople (Istanbul), giving upstart Venice an aura of tradition. In subsequent centuries, the church was encrusted with materials looted from buildings throughout the Venetian empire—bronze horses, plundered columns, and so on. The architectural style of St. Mark's has been called "Early Ransack."

▶ *Enter the atrium (entrance hall) of the basilica, through a sixth-century, bronze-paneled Byzantine door—which likely once swung in Constantinople's Hagia Sophia church. Immediately after being admitted by the dress-code guard, look up and to the right into an archway decorated with mosaics.*

❷ Atrium—Mosaic of Noah's Ark and the Great Flood

These are some of the oldest (13th century), finest, and most accessible mosaics in the church.

In the scene to the right of the entry door, Noah and sons are sawing logs to build a boat. Venetians—who were great ship builders—related to the story of Noah and the Ark. At its peak, Venice's Arsenale warship-building plant employed several thousand. Below that are three scenes of Noah putting all species of animals into the Ark, two by two. (Who's at the head of the line? Lions.) Another scene shows the Flood in full force, drowning the wicked. Noah sends out a dove twice to see whether there's any dry land where he can dock. He finds it, leaves the Ark with a gorgeous rainbow overhead, and offers a sacrifice of thanks to God.

Atrium mosaic—Noah loads the ark

After the Flood, Noah releases a dove.

The nave—golden mosaics (on the ceiling), rood screen (midway down), and altar (far end)

Christ as Pantocrator

Most Eastern Orthodox churches have at least one mosaic or painting of Christ in a standard pose—as "Pantocrator," a Greek word meaning "Ruler of All." St. Mark's features several images of Christ as Pantocrator (especially the one in the central dome). The image, so familiar to Orthodox Christians, may be a bit foreign to Protestants, Catholics, and secularists.

As King of the Universe, Christ sits (usually on a throne) facing directly out, with penetrating eyes. He wears a halo divided with a cross. In his left hand is a Bible, while his right hand blesses, with the fingers forming the Greek letters chi and rho, the first two letters of "Christos." The thumb touches the fingers, symbolizing how Christ unites both his divinity and his humanity. On either side of Christ's head are the Greek letters "IC XC," short for "IesuC XristoC."

▸ *Rejoin the slow flow of people. Notice the entrance to the San Marco Museum (Loggia dei Cavalli), which we'll visit later. Now climb seven steps, pass through the doorway, and enter the nave. Loiter somewhere just inside the door (crowd permitting) and let your eyes adjust.*

❸ The Nave—Mosaics and Greek-Cross Floor Plan

The initial effect is dark and unimpressive (unless they've got the floodlights on). But as your pupils slowly unclench, notice that the entire upper part is decorated in mosaic—nearly 5,000 square yards (imagine paving a football field with contact lenses). These golden mosaics are in the Byzantine style, though many were designed by artists from the Italian Renaissance and later. The often-overlooked lower walls are covered with green-, yellow-, purple-, and rose-colored marble slabs, cut to expose the grain, and laid out in geometric patterns. Even the floor is mosaic, with mostly geometrical designs. It rolls like the sea. Venice is sinking and shifting, creating these cresting waves of stone.

The church is laid out with four equal arms, topped with domes, radiating out from the center to form a Greek cross (+). The Greek-cross floor plan symbolizes perfection, rather than the more common Latin cross of the crucifixion (emphasizing man's sinfulness).

Mosaics

St. Mark's mosaics are designs or pictures made with small cubes of colored stone or glass pressed into wet plaster. Ancient Romans paved floors, walls, and ceilings with them. When Rome "fell," the art form died out in the West but was carried on by Byzantine craftsmen. They perfected the gold background effect by baking gold leaf into tiny cubes of glass called *tesserae* (tiles). The surfaces of the tiles are purposely cut unevenly to capture light and give off a shimmering effect. The reflecting gold mosaics helped to light thick-walled, small-windowed, lantern-lit Byzantine churches, creating a golden glow that symbolized the divine light of heaven.

St. Mark's mosaics tell the entire Christian history from end to beginning— from the Apocalypse near the entrance to Christ's Old Testament origins near the altar. At either end are images of Christ— the beginning and the end, the Alpha and Omega of the Christian universe.

Those familiar with Eastern Orthodox churches will find familiar elements in St. Mark's: a central floor plan, domes, mosaics, and iconic images of Mary and Christ as Pantocrator—ruler of all things. As your eyes adjust, the mosaics start to give off a "mystical, golden luminosity," the atmosphere of the Byzantine heaven. The air itself seems almost visible, like a cloud of incense. It's a subtle effect, one that grows on you as the filtered light changes. There are more beautiful, bigger, more overwhelming, and even holier churches, but none is as stately.

► *Find the chandelier near the entrance doorway (in the shape of a Greek cross cathedral space station), and run your eyes up the support chain to the dome above.*

❹ Pentecost Mosaic

In a golden heaven, the dove of the Holy Spirit shoots out a pinwheel of spiritual lasers, igniting tongues of fire on the heads of the 12 apostles below, giving them the ability to speak other languages without a Rick Steves phrase book. You'd think they'd be amazed, but their expressions are as solemn as...icons. One of the oldest mosaics in the church (c. 1125), it has distinct "Byzantine" features: a gold background and apostles with halos, solemn faces, almond eyes, delicate blessing hands, and rumpled robes, all facing forward.

This is art from a society still touchy about the Bible's commandment against making "graven images" of holy things. The Byzantine style emphasizes otherworldliness rather than literal human detail.

▶ *Shuffle along with the crowds up to the central dome.*

❺ Central Dome—Ascension Mosaic

Gape upward to the very heart of the church. Christ—having lived his miraculous life and having been crucified for man's sins—ascends into the starry sky on a rainbow. He raises his right hand and blesses the universe.

Ascension Mosaic—12 Apostles and Mary ring the dome beneath Christ in heaven

This isn't the dead, crucified, mortal Jesus featured in most churches, but a powerful, resurrected god, the ruler of all.

Christ's blessing radiates, rippling down to the ring of white-robed apostles below. They stand amid the trees of the Mount of Olives, waving good-bye as Christ ascends. Mary is with them, wearing blue with golden Greek crosses on each shoulder and looking ready to play pattycake. From these saints, goodness descends, creating the Virtues that ring the base of the dome between the windows. In Byzantine churches, the window-lit dome represented heaven, while the dark church below represented earth—a microcosm of the hierarchical universe.

Beneath the dome at the four corners, the four Gospel writers ("Matev," "Marc," "Luca," and "Ioh") thoughtfully scribble down the heavenly events. This wisdom flows down like water from the symbolic Four Rivers below them, spreading through the church's four equal arms (the "four corners" of the world), and baptizing the congregation with God's love. The church building is a series of perfect circles within perfect squares—the cosmic order—with Christ in the center solemnly blessing us. God's in his heaven, saints are on earth, and all's right with the world.

Look around at the church's furniture and imagine a service here. The ❻ **rood screen,** topped with 14 saints, separates the congregation from the high altar, heightening the "mystery" of the Mass. The ❼ **pulpit on the right** was reserved for the doge, who led prayers and made important announcements.

The Venetian church service is a theatrical multimedia spectacle, combining words, music, images (mosaics), costumes (priests' robes), props (candles, incense), set design (rood screen), and even stage direction (processionals through the crowd). Coincidentally or not, the first modern opera—also a multimedia theatrical experience—was written by St. Mark's *maestro di cappella,* Claudio Monteverdi (1567-1643).

North Transept

In the north transept (the arm of the church to the left of the altar), today's Venetians pray to a painted wooden icon of Mary and Baby Jesus known as ❽ **Nicopeia,** or "Our Lady of Victory." It's on the east wall of the north transept, a small painting crusted over with a big stone canopy. In its day, this was the ultimate trophy—the actual icon used to protect the Byzantine army in war, looted by the Crusaders. Supposedly painted by the evangelist Luke, it was once enameled with bright paint and precious stones,

Byzantium, the Fourth Crusade, and Venice

The Byzantine Empire was the eastern half of the ancient Roman Empire that *didn't* "fall" in A.D. 476. It remained Christian, Greek-speaking, and enlightened for another thousand years.

In A.D. 330, Constantine, the first Christian emperor, moved the Roman Empire's capital to the newly expanded city of Byzantium, which he humbly renamed Constantinople. Venice had strong ties with Byzantium from its earliest days. Venetian merchants were granted trading rights to Byzantine ports in the Adriatic and eastern Mediterranean. They traded raw materials from Western Europe for luxury goods from the East. As Venice grew more powerful, they wanted still more access to Byzantium's wealth. In the year 1204, they saw their chance. They joined the pope's Crusade to "save" the Holy Land from Muslim influence. But along the way, the ships diverted to Constantinople. The doge-led Crusaders sacked the Byzantine capital and brought the booty home to Venice. In St. Mark's Basilica, you can see these treasures: the bronze horses, bronze doors of Hagia Sophia, Golden Altarpiece enamels, the Treasury's treasures, the Nicopeia icon, and much of the marble that now covers the (brick) church.

Mosaics, like this Last Supper, use gold backgrounds to reflect light in the dim church interior.

and Mary was adorned with a crown and necklace of gold and jewels (now on display in the Treasury). Now the protector of Venetians, this Madonna has helped the city persevere through plagues, wars, and crucial soccer games.

► *In the south transept (to the right of the main altar), find the dim mosaic high up on the west wall.*

9 Discovery of Mark Mosaic

It's 1094, the church is nearly complete (see the domes shown in cutaway fashion), and they're all set to re-inter Mark's bones under the new altar. There's just one problem: During the decades of construction, they forgot where they'd stored his body!

So (in the left half of the mosaic), all of Venice gathers inside the church to bow down and pray for help finding the bones. The doge (from the Latin *dux,* meaning leader) leads them. Soon after (the right half), the patriarch (far right) is inspired to look inside a hollow column where he finds the relics. Everyone turns and applauds, including the womenfolk (left side of scene), who stream in from the upper-floor galleries. The relics were soon placed under the altar in a ceremony that inaugurated the current structure.

Nearby, the door under the rose window, with the green curtain, leads directly from the Doge's Palace. On important occasions, the doge entered the church through here, ascended the steps of his pulpit, and addressed the people.

▶ *The two-room Treasury is in the south transept.*

⑩ Treasury (Tesoro)

The Treasury holds an amazing collection of precious items, most of them stolen from Constantinople: Byzantine chalices, silver reliquaries, monstrous monstrances (for displaying the Communion wafer), and icons done in gold, silver, enamels, gems, and semiprecious stones. As Venice thought of itself as the granddaughter of Rome and the daughter of Byzantium, Venetians consider these treasures not stolen, but inherited. This is marvelous handiwork, but all the more marvelous for having been done when Western Europe was still mired in mud.

▶ *Enter the main room, to the right. Start with the large glass case in the center of the room.*

Main Room: In the display case, the hanging lamp with the protruding fish features fourth-century Roman rock crystal framed in 11th-century Byzantine metalwork. In fact, several Treasury items represent the fruits of labor by different civilizations over a thousand-year period.

Just behind the lamp, a black bucket, carved with scenes of satyrs chasing nymphs, epitomizes the pagan world that was fading as Christianity triumphed. Also in the case are blue-and-gold lapis lazuli icons of the Crucifixion and of the Archangel Michael—standing like an action hero, ready to conquer evil in the name of Christ. See various chalices made of onyx, agate, and rock crystal, and an incense burner shaped like a domed church.

As this mosaic over the church door shows, St. Mark's looks today much as it did 800 years ago.

The Legend of St. Mark

Mark (died c. A.D. 68) was a Jewish-born Christian, and he might have actually met Jesus. He traveled with fellow convert Paul, eventually settling in Alexandria as the city's first Christian bishop. On a trip to Rome, Peter—Jesus' right-hand man—asked him to write down the events of Jesus' life. This became the Gospel of Mark.

During his travels, Mark stopped in the lagoon (in Aquileia on the north coast of the Adriatic), where he dreamed of a Latin-speaking angel who said, *"Pax tibi Marce, evangelista meus"* ("Peace to you, Mark, my evangelist"), promising him rest after death. Back in Alexandria, Mark was attacked by an anti-Christian mob. They tied him with ropes and dragged his body through the streets until he died.

Eight centuries later, his body lay in an Alexandrian church that was about to be vandalized by Muslim fanatics. Two Venetian traders on a business trip saved the relics from desecration by hiding them in a pork barrel—a meat considered unclean by Muslims—and quickly setting sail. The perilous voyage home was only completed after many more miracles. The doge received the body, and in 828 they built the first church of St. Mark's to house it. During construction of the current church (1094), Mark's relics were temporarily lost, and it took another miracle to find them, hidden inside a column. Today, Venetians celebrate Mark on the traditional date of his martyrdom, April 25.

▸ *Along the walls, find the following displays (working counterclockwise around the room).*

The first three glass cases have bowls and urns from the three medieval cultures that cross-pollinated in the Eastern Mediterranean: Venetian, Byzantine, and Islamic. Next, on a wooden pedestal, comes the Urn of Artaxerxes I (middle of the right wall), an Egyptian-made object that once held the ashes of the great Persian king who ruled 2,500 years ago (r. 465-425 B.C.). The next cases hold religious paraphernalia used for High Mass, including the 600-year-old crosier (shepherd staff) still used today on holy days.

Next is the small marble Ciborio di Anastasia (far left corner). It may be a gift from "Anastasia," the name carved on it in Greek. She was a lady-in-waiting in the court of the Byzantine emperor Justinian (483-565). Legend has it she was so beautiful that Justinian (a married man) pursued her amorously, so she had to dress like a monk and flee to a desert monastery.

Moving to the next wall, you'll see two large golden altarpiece panels, flanked by two golden candlesticks with amazing detail—from the smiling angels on top all the way down to the roots. Continuing counterclockwise, notice how the granite column extends below current floor level, as things have settled over the last 1,000 years.

Continue into the relics room. The glass case over the glowing alabaster altar contains a reliquary showing Christ being whipped (from 1125). It holds a stone (supposedly) from the column he was tied to.

▸ *The Golden Altarpiece is located behind the main altar. Join the line to pay, and then go through the turnstile.*

⑪ Golden Altarpiece (Pala d'Oro)

Under the green marble canopy, supported by four intricately carved alabaster columns, sits the high altar. Inside the altar is an urn (not visible) with the mortal remains of Mark, the Gospel writer. (Look through the grate of the altar to read *Corpus Divi Marci Evangelistae,* or "Body of the Evangelist Mark.") He rests in peace, as an angel had promised him. Shh.

The Golden Altarpiece is a stunning golden wall made of 250 blue-backed enamels with religious scenes, all set in a gold frame and studded with 15 hefty rubies, 300 emeralds, 1,500 pearls, and assorted sapphires, amethysts, and topaz. The Byzantine-made enamels were part of the Venetians' plunder of 1204, subsequently pieced together by Byzantine

The San Marco Museum offers this view down the church nave, with its Pentecost mosaic.

craftsmen specifically for St. Mark's high altar. It's a bit much to take in all at once, but get up close and find several details you might recognize:

In the center of it all, Jesus sits on a golden throne, with a halo of pearls and jewels. Like a good Byzantine Pantocrator, he dutifully faces forward and gives his blessing while stealing a glance offstage at Mark ("Marcus") and the other saints.

Along the bottom row, Old Testament prophets show off the books of the Bible they've written. With halos, solemn faces, and elaborately creased robes, they epitomize the Byzantine icon style.

Mark's story is depicted in the panels along the sides. In the bottom left panel, Mark meets Peter (seated) at the gates of Rome, to receive his call. In the bottom right panel, the two Venetian merchants return by ship, carrying Mark's coffin here to be laid to rest.

Byzantium excelled in the art of cloisonné enameling: A piece of gold leaf is stamped with a design, then filled in with pools of enamel paint, which are baked on. Some saints even have pearl crowns or jewel collars pinned on. This kind of craftsmanship—and the social infrastructure that could afford it—made Byzantium seem like an enchanted world during Europe's dim Middle Ages.

After you've looked at some individual scenes, back up as far as this small room will let you and just let yourself be dazzled by the whole picture—this "mosaic" of Byzantine greatness. This magnificent altarpiece sits on a swivel (as you can see) and is swung around on festival Sundays so the entire congregation can enjoy it, as Venetians have for so many centuries.

⑫ San Marco Museum (Museo di San Marco)—Mosaics, Bronze Horses, View of the Piazza, and More

▶ *The staircase up to the museum is in the atrium near the main entrance. The sign says* Loggia dei Cavalli, Museo. *Ascend the steps, buy your ticket, and enter. In the first room, you'll see several models of the church at various stages of its history. Notice how the original domes, once squat, were made taller in the 13th century, leaving today's church with a dome-within-a-dome structure.*

Next are the museum's three highlights: view of the interior (right), view of the square (out the door to the left), and bronze horses (directly ahead). Belly up to the stone balustrade (on the right) to survey the interior.

View of Church Interior

Scan the church, with its thousands of square meters of mosaics, then take a closer look at the Pentecost mosaic (first dome above you, described earlier). The unique design at the very top signifies the Trinity: throne (God), Gospels (Christ), and dove (Holy Spirit). The couples below the ring of apostles are the people of the world (I can find Asia, Judaea, and Cappadocia), who, despite their different languages, still understood the Spirit's message.

If you were a woman in medieval Venice, you'd enjoy this same close-up view. The balcony was for women, the nave for men, and the altar for the priests. Back then the rood screen (the fence with the 15 figures on it) separated the priest from the public. Appreciate the patterns of the mosaic floor—one of the finest in Italy—that covers the floor like a Persian carpet.

▶ *From here, the museum loops you to the far (altar) end of the church, then back to the bronze horses. Along the way, you'll see...*

Mosaic Fragments

These mosaics once hung in the church, but when they became damaged or aesthetically old-fashioned, they were replaced by new and more fashionable mosaics. You'll see mosaics from the church's earliest days (and most "Byzantine" style, c. 1070) to more recent times (1700s, more realistic and detailed). Many are accompanied by small photos that show how the remaining fragment once fit into a larger scene.

The mosaics—made from small cubes of stone or colored glass pressed into wet clay—were assembled on the ground, then cemented onto the walls. Artists draw the pattern on paper, lay it on the wet clay, and slowly cut the paper away as they replace it with cubes.

▶ *Continuing on, down a set of stairs, you'll catch glimpses of the interior of the church from the north transept. Here you get a close-up view of the Tree of Jesse mosaic, showing Jesus' distant ancestor at the root and his mom at the top. Continue on to the Sala dei Banchetti (WCs near the room's entrance).*

Sala dei Banchetti

This large, ornate room—once the doge's banquet hall—is filled with religious objects, tapestries and carpets that once adorned the church, Burano-made lace vestments, illuminated music manuscripts, a doge's throne, and much more. In the center of the hall stands the most prestigious artwork here, the Pala Feriale, by Paolo Veneziano (1345), with scenes from Mark's life.

▶ *Now double back toward the museum entrance, through displays of stone fragments from the church, finally arriving at...*

The Bronze Horses (La Quadriga)

Stepping lively in pairs and with smiles on their faces, they exude energy and exuberance. Art historians don't know how old they are—they could be from ancient Greece (fourth century B.C.) or from ancient Rome, during its Fall (fourth century A.D.). Professor Carbon Fourteen says they're from around 175 B.C. Originally, the horses pulled a chariot driven by an emperor, *Ben-Hur* style.

These bronze statues were not hammered and bent into shape by metalsmiths, but were cast from clay molds by using the lost-wax technique. The heads are detachable and adjustable—even swappable. The

One of the treasures of the ancient world, this group has inspired Caesars, kings, and doges.

bronze is high quality, with 97 percent copper. Originally gilded, they still have some streaks of gold. Long gone are the ruby pupils that gave the horses the original case of "red eye." While four-horse statues were once relatively common, this is the only intact group of four horses to survive from ancient times. That they survived at all is amazing, as bronze work like this almost always ends up being smelted down by conquerors.

Megalomaniacs through the ages have coveted these horses not only for their artistic value, but because they symbolize Apollo, the Greco-Roman god of the sun...and of secular power. Legend says they were made in the time of Alexander the Great, then taken by Nero to Rome. Constantine took them to his new capital in Constantinople to adorn the chariot racecourse. The Venetians then stole them from their fellow Christians when they sacked the city in 1204 and brought them here to St. Mark's in 1255. The church's atrium was built as a pedestal for the horses. The doge spoke to his people standing between the horses when they graced the balcony atop the church's facade (where the copies—which you'll see next—stand today).

What goes around comes around, and Napoleon came around and

The Bronze Horse copies enjoy a stunning view of the Piazza, as part of the San Marco Museum.

took the horses when he conquered Venice in 1797. They stood atop a triumphal arch in Paris until Napoleon's empire was "blown-aparte" and they were returned to their "rightful" home. Their expressive faces seem to say, "Oh boy, Wilbur, have we done some travelin'."

In 1975, the horses were again removed from their spot when they were attacked by their most dangerous enemy yet—the threat of oxidation from pollution, that sent them galloping for cover inside the church.

▸ *The visit ends outside on the balcony overlooking St. Mark's Square.*

The Loggia and View of St. Mark's Square

You'll be drawn repeatedly to the viewpoint of the square, but remember to look at the facade to see how cleverly all the looted architectural elements blend together. Ramble among the statues of water-bearing slaves that serve as drain spouts. The horses are modern copies (note the 1978 date on the hoof of the horse to the right).

Be a doge, and stand between the bronze horses overlooking St. Mark's Square—under the gilded lion of St. Mark, in front of the four great Evangelists, and flanked by the four glorious horses. Admire the mesmerizing, commanding view of the city, which so long ago was Europe's only superpower, and today is just a small town with a big history.

Doge's Palace Tour

Palazzo Ducale

Venice is a city of beautiful facades—palaces, churches, carnival masks—that can cover darker interiors of intrigue and decay. The Doge's Palace, with its frilly pink exterior, hides the fact that the "Most Serene Republic" (as Venice called itself) was far from serene in its heyday.

The Doge's Palace housed the fascinating government of this rich and powerful empire. It also served as the home for the Venetian ruler known as the doge (pronounced "dohzh"), or duke. For four centuries (about 1150-1550), this was the most powerful half-acre in Europe. The doges wanted their palace to reflect the wealth and secular values of the Republic, impressing visitors and serving as a reminder that the Venetians were Number One in Europe.

ORIENTATION

Cost: €16 combo-ticket also includes the Correr Museum.

Hours: Daily April-Oct 8:30-18:30, Nov-March 8:00-17:30, last entry one hour before closing.

Crowd Control: Avoid the long peak-season line at the Doge's Palace by buying your combo-ticket (or Museum Pass) at the uncrowded Correr Museum. This lets you enter the Doge's Palace at the "prepaid tickets" entrance. You can also get prepaid tickets 48 hours in advance at http://palazzoducale.visitmuve.it. To minimize crowds, visit at about 17:00.

Getting There: The palace is next to St. Mark's Basilica, on the lagoon waterfront, and just off St. Mark's Square. Vaporetto stops: San Marco or San Zaccaria.

Information: Tel. 041-271-5911, http://palazzoducale.visitmuve.it.

Tours: The audioguide (€5, must leave ID) is dry but informative. The fine 1.25-hour Secret Itineraries guided tour lets you skip the line and covers rooms not included in the general admission price (€20, wise to reserve ahead: from the US dial 011-39-041-4273-0892, within Italy call 848-082-000, book online at http://palazzoducale.visitmuve.it, or book directly at the Doge's Palace ticket desk).

Length of This Tour: Allow 1.5 hours.

Services: WCs are in the courtyard and halfway up the stairs to balcony level. Bags bigger than a large purse must be checked (free).

Photography: Not allowed.

Cuisine Art: A sandwich-and-salad café is in the palace courtyard

Starring: Big rooms bare of furnishings but crammed with history, Tintoretto masterpieces, and the doges.

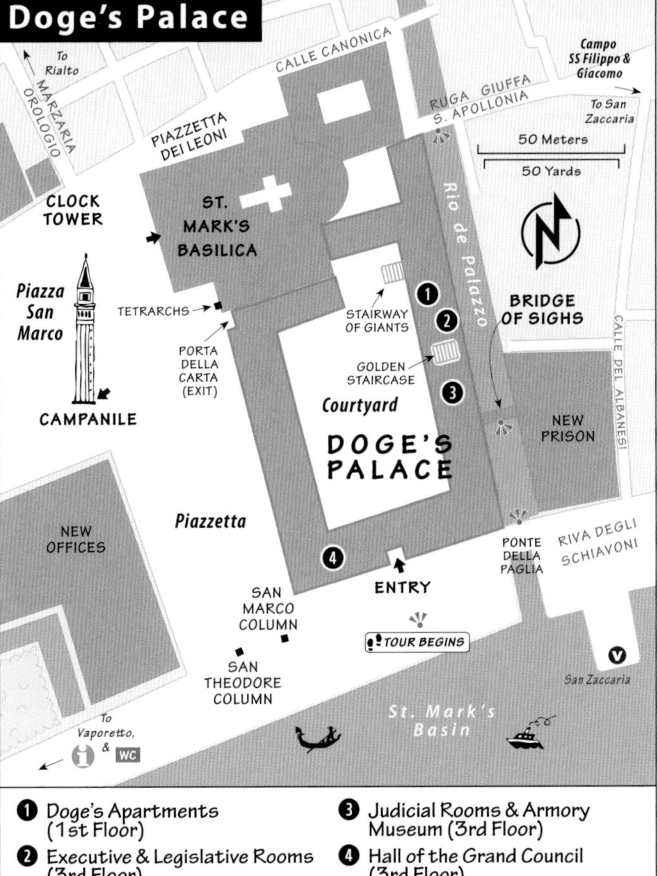

❶ Doge's Apartments (1st Floor)

❷ Executive & Legislative Rooms (3rd Floor)

❸ Judicial Rooms & Armory Museum (3rd Floor)

❹ Hall of the Grand Council (3rd Floor)

THE TOUR BEGINS

Exterior

"The Wedding Cake," "The Tablecloth," or "The Pink House" is also sometimes known as the Doge's Palace. The style is called Venetian Gothic—a fusion of Italian Gothic with a delicate Islamic flair. The columns originally had bases on the bottoms, but these were covered over as the columns sank through the centuries.

The palace was originally built in the 800s, but most of what we see came after 1300, as it was expanded to meet the needs of the empire. Each doge wanted to leave his mark on history with a new wing.

If you compare this lacy, top-heavy structure with the massive fortress palaces of Florence, you realize the wisdom of building a city in the middle of the sea—you have no natural enemies except gravity. This unfortified palace in a city with no city wall was the doge's way of saying, "I am an elected and loved ruler. I do not fear my own people."

► *Enter the Doge's Palace from along the waterfront. After you pass through the turnstile, ignore the signs and cross to the far side of the courtyard. Stand at the foot of the grand staircase topped by two statues.*

The Courtyard and the Stairway of Giants (Scala dei Giganti)

Imagine yourself as a foreign dignitary on business to meet the doge. In the courtyard, you look up a grand staircase topped with two nearly nude statues of, I think, Moses and Paul Newman (more likely, Neptune and Mars, representing Venice's prowess at sea and at war). The doge and his aides would be waiting for you at the top, between the two statues

Lacy, unfortified home of the doge

Grand entrance guarded by Neptune and Mars

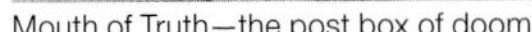
Mouth of Truth—the post box of doom

Golden Staircase with a 24-carat ceiling

and beneath the winged lion. No matter who you were—king, pope, or emperor—you'd have to hoof it up. The powerful doge would descend the stairs for no one.

Many doges were crowned here, between the two statues. The doge was something like an elected king—which makes sense only in the dictatorial republic that was Venice. Technically, he was just a noble selected by other nobles to carry out their laws and decisions. Many doges tried to extend their powers and rule more as divine-right kings. Many others just put on their funny hats and accepted their role as figurehead and ceremonial ribbon-cutter.

The palace is attached to the church, symbolically welding church and state. Both buildings have ugly brick behind a painted-lady veneer of marble. In this tour, we'll see the similarly harsh inner workings of an outwardly serene, polished republic.

▶ *Cross back to near the entrance and follow the signs up the tourists' staircase to the first-floor balcony (loggia). Midway along the balcony, you'll find a face in the wall, the...*

Mouth of Truth

This fierce-looking androgyne opens his/her mouth, ready to swallow a piece of paper, hungry for gossip. Letterboxes like this (some with lions' heads) were scattered throughout the palace. Originally, anyone who had a complaint or suspicion about anyone else could accuse him anonymously *(denontie secrete)* by simply dropping a slip of paper in the mouth. This set the blades of justice turning inside the palace.

▶ *Toward Paul Newman is the entrance to the...*

Paintings by Titian, Veronese, and Tintoretto

The doge had only the top Venetian painters decorate his palace. While the palace was once rich in Titians, fires in the late 1500s destroyed nearly all the work by the greatest Venetian master. As the palace was reconstructed, the Titians were replaced with works by Veronese and Tintoretto. Most are canvases—not murals or frescoes—painted in workshops and hung on the walls.

Veronese used the best pigments available—from precious stones, sapphires, and emeralds—and his colors have survived vividly. These Veronese paintings are by his hand and are fine examples of his genius. Tintoretto, on the other hand, didn't really have his heart in these commissions, and the pieces here were done by his workshop.

The paintings of the Doge's Palace are a study of old Venice, with fine views of the old city and its inhabitants. The extravagant women's gowns in the paintings by Veronese show off a major local industry—textiles. While the paintings are not generally of masterpiece quality, they're historically interesting. They prove that in the old days, Venice had no pigeons.

Golden Staircase (Scala d'Oro)

The palace was architectural propaganda, designed to impress visitors. This 24-karat gilded-ceiling staircase was something for them to write home about. As you ascend the stairs, look back at the floor below and marvel at its 3-D pattern.

▶ *Start up the first few steps of the Golden Staircase. Midway up, at the first landing, turn right, which takes you up into the...*

Doge's Apartments (Appartamento del Doge)

The dozen or so rooms on the first floor are where the doge actually lived. The blue-and-gold-hued Sala dei Scarlatti (room 5) is typical of the palace's interior decoration: gold-coffered ceiling, big stone fireplace, silky walls with paintings, and a speckled floor. There's very little original furniture, as doges were expected to bring their own. Despite his high office, the doge had to obey several rules that bound him to the city. He couldn't leave the palace unescorted, he couldn't open official mail in private, and he and his family had to leave their own home and live in the Doge's Palace.

The large room 6, the Sala dello Scudo (Shield Hall), is full of maps and globes. The main map illustrates the reach of Venice's maritime realm, which stretched across most of the eastern Mediterranean. With the maps in this room you can trace the eye-opening trip across Asia—from Italy to Greece to Palestine, Arabia, and "Irac"—of local boy Marco Polo (c. 1254-1325). Finally, he arrived at the other side of the world. This last map (at the far end of the room) is shown "upside-down," with south on top, giving a glimpse of the Venetian worldview circa 1550. It depicts China, Taiwan (Formosa), and Japan (Giapan), while America is a nearby island with California and lots of Terre Incognite.

In room 7, the Sala Grimani, are several paintings of the lion of St. Mark, including the famous one by Vittore Carpaccio of a smiling lion (on the long wall). The lion holds open a book with these words, *"Pax Tibi Marce..."* ("Peace to you, Mark"), which according to legend were spoken by an angel welcoming St. Mark to Venice. In the background is the Doge's Palace and the Campanile.

▶ *After browsing the dozen or so private rooms of the Doge's Apartments, continue up the Golden Staircase to the third floor, which was the "public" part of the palace. The first room at the top of the stairs is the...*

Square Room (Atrio Quadrato)

The ceiling painting, ***Justice Presenting the Sword and Scales to Doge Girolamo Priuli,*** is by Tintoretto. (Stand at the top of the painting for the full 3-D effect.) As you'll soon see, this palace is wallpapered with Titians, Tintorettos, and Veroneses. Many have the same theme you see here: a doge, in his ermine cape, gold-brocaded robe, and funny one-horned hat with earflaps, kneeling in the presence of saints, gods, or mythological figures.

▶ *Enter the next room.*

Executive & Legislative Rooms

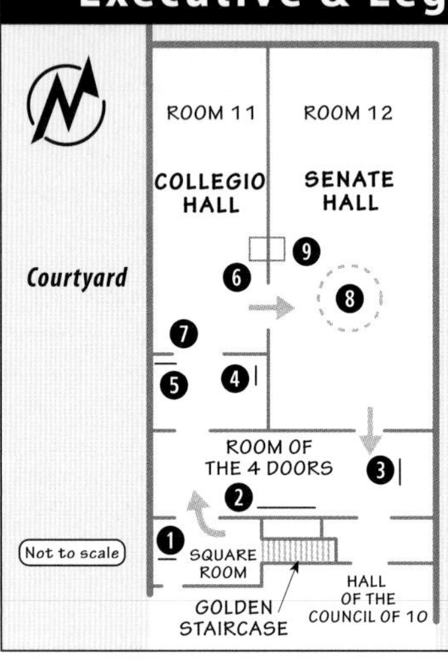

1. TINTORETTO – *Justice Presenting the Sword and Scales*
2. TITIAN – *Doge Kneeling*
3. TIEPOLO – *Venice Receiving Neptune*
4. VERONESE – *The Rape of Europa*
5. TINTORETTO – *Bacchus and Ariadne*
6. VERONESE – *Discussion*
7. VERONESE – *Mars and Neptune with Campanile and Lion*
8. TINTORETTO – *Triumph of Venice*
9. *Clocks*

Room of the Four Doors (Sala delle Quattro Porte)

This was the central clearinghouse for all the goings-on in the palace. Visitors presented themselves here and were directed to their destination—the courts, councils, or the doge himself. The room was designed by Andrea Palladio, the architect who did the impressive Church of San Giorgio Maggiore, across the Grand Canal from St. Mark's Square. On the intricate stucco ceiling, notice the feet of the women dangling down below the edge (above the windows), extending the illusion.

On the wall to the left of the door you entered from is a painting by Titian, showing a **doge kneeling** with great piety before a woman embodying Faith holding the Cross of Jesus. Notice old Venice in the misty distance under the cross. This is one of many paintings you'll see of doges in uncharacteristically humble poses—paid for, of course, by the doges themselves.

G. B. Tiepolo's well-known ***Venice Receiving Neptune*** is now displayed on an easel, but it was originally hung on the wall above the windows where they've put a copy. The painting shows Venice as a woman—Venice

G. B. Tiepolo's *Venice Receiving Neptune*—the city personified by a sensual woman

is always a woman to artists—reclining in luxury, dressed in the ermine cape and pearl necklace of a doge's wife (dogaressa). Crude Neptune, enthralled by the First Lady's beauty, arrives bearing a seashell bulging with gold ducats. A bored Venice points and says, "Put it over there with the other stuff."

▶ *Enter the small room with the big fireplace and several paintings.*

Ante-Collegio Hall (Sala dell'Anticollegio)

It took a big title or bribe to get in to see the doge. Once accepted for a visit, you would wait here before you entered, combing your hair, adjusting your robe, popping a breath mint, and preparing the gifts you'd brought. While you cooled your heels and warmed your hands at the elaborate fireplace, you might look at some of the paintings—among the finest in the palace, worthy of any museum in the world.

The Rape of Europa (on the wall opposite the fireplace), by Paolo Veronese, most likely shocked many small-town visitors with its risqué subject matter. Here Zeus, the king of the Greek gods, appears in the form of a bull with a foot fetish, seducing a beautiful earthling while cupids spin playfully overhead.

Tintoretto's ***Bacchus and Ariadne*** (to the right of the fireplace) is another colorful display of Venice's sensual tastes. The God of Wine seeks a threesome, offering a ring to the mortal Ariadne, who's being crowned with stars by Venus, who turns slowly in zero gravity. The ring is the center of a spinning wheel of flesh, with the three arms like spokes.

Veronese's *Rape of Europa* greeted palace visitors with a glimpse into the city's risqué tastes.

► *But wait, the doge is ready for us. Let's go in. Enter the next room and approach your imaginary doge.*

Collegio Hall (Sala del Collegio)

Flanked by his cabinet of six advisers—one for each Venetian neighborhood—the doge would sit on the wood-paneled platform at the far end to receive ambassadors, who laid their gifts at his feet and pleaded their countries' cases. All official ceremonies, such as the ratification of treaties, were held here.

At other times, it was the "Oval Office" where the doge and his cabinet (the executive branch) met privately to discuss proposals to give to the legislature, pull files from the cabinets (along the right wall), or rehearse a meeting with the pope. The wooden benches around the sides (where they sat) are original. The clock on the wall is a backward-running 24-hour clock with Roman numerals and a sword for hands.

The ceiling is 24-karat gold, framing paintings by Veronese. These are not frescoes (painting on wet plaster), like those in the Sistine Chapel, but actual canvases painted in Veronese's studio and then placed on the ceiling. Within years, Venice's humidity would have melted frescoes like mascara.

The T-shaped painting of the woman with the spider web (on the ceiling, opposite the big window) represents the Venetian symbol of ***Discussion.*** You can imagine the webs of truth and lies woven in this room by the doge's scheming advisers. In ***Mars and Neptune with Campanile and Lion*** (the ceiling painting near the entrance), Veronese presents four symbols of the Republic's strength—military, sea trade, city, and government (plus a cherub about to be circumcised by the Campanile).

▸ *Enter the large Senate Hall.*

Senate Hall (Sala del Senato)

While the doge presided from the stage, senators mounted the podium (middle of the wall with windows) to address their 120 colleagues. The legislators, chaired by the doge, debated and passed laws in this room.

Venice prided itself on its self-rule (independent of popes, kings, and tyrants), with most power placed in the hands of these annually elected men. Which branch of government really ruled? All of them. It was an elaborate system of checks and balances to make sure no one rocked the gondola, no one got too powerful, and the ship of state sailed smoothly ahead.

Tintoretto's large ***Triumph of Venice*** on the ceiling (central painting, best viewed from the top) shows the city in all its glory. Lady Venice is up in

Mars and Neptune with Campanile and Lion

Triumph of Venice oversees the Senate.

heaven with the Greek gods, while barbaric lesser nations swirl up to give her gifts and tribute. Do you get the feeling the Venetian aristocracy was proud of its city?

On the wall are two large **clocks,** one of which has the signs of the zodiac and phases of the moon. And there's one final oddity in this room, in case you hadn't noticed it yet. In one of the wall paintings (above the entry door), there's actually a doge...not kneeling.

▸ *Exiting the Senate Hall, pass again through the Room of the Four Doors, then around the corner into a hall with a semicircular platform at the far end.*

Hall of the Council of Ten (Sala del Consiglio dei Dieci)

By the 1400s, Venice had a worldwide reputation for swift, harsh, and secret justice. The dreaded Council of Ten—10 judges, plus the doge and his six advisers—met here to dole out punishment to traitors, murderers, and "morals" violators. Note the 17 wood panels where they presided.

This secret council eventually had their own security force of guards, spies, informers, and assassins. It seemed no one was safe from the spying eye of the "Terrible Ten." You could be accused anonymously (by a letter dropped into a Mouth of Truth), swept off the streets, tried, judged, and thrown into the dark dungeons in the palace for the rest of your life without so much as a Miranda warning.

It was in this room that the Council decided who lived or died, and who was decapitated, tortured, or merely thrown in jail. The small, hard-to-find **door** leading off the platform (the fifth panel to the right of center) leads through secret passages to the prisons and torture chambers.

The large, central, oval ceiling painting by Veronese (a copy of the original stolen by Napoleon and still in the Louvre) shows ***Jupiter Descending from Heaven to Strike Down the Vices,*** redundantly informing the accused that justice in Venice was swift and harsh. Though the dreaded Council of Ten was eventually disbanded, today their descendants enforce the dress code at St. Mark's Basilica.

▸ *Pass through the next room, turn right, and head up the stairs to the Armory Museum.*

Armory Museum (L'Armeria)

The aesthetic of killing is beyond me, but I must admit I've never seen a better collection of halberds, falchions, ranseurs, targes, morions, and

Judicial Rooms

1. Secret Door to Prisons
2. VERONESE – Copy of Jupiter Descending
3. Stairs up to Armory Museum
4. Armory Museum (on Mezzanine)
5. Stairs down to Hall of the Grand Council

Not to scale

ROOM OF THE 4 DOORS
GOLDEN STAIRCASE
HALL OF THE COUNCIL OF 10
SALA DELLA BUSSOLA
BARRIER
ARMORY MUSEUM
Courtyard

brigandines in my life. The weapons in these three rooms make you realize the important role the military played in keeping the East-West trade lines open.

Room 1: In the glass case on the right, you'll see the suit of armor worn by the great Venetian mercenary general, Gattamelata (far right, on horseback), as well as "baby's first armor" (how soon they grow up!). A full suit of armor could weigh 66 pounds. Before gunpowder, crossbows (look up) were made still more lethal by turning a crank on the end to draw the bow with extra force.

Room 2: In the thick of battle, even horses needed helmets. The hefty broadswords were brandished two-handed by the strongest and bravest soldiers who waded into enemy lines. Suspended from the ceiling is a large triangular banner captured from the Ottoman Turks at the Battle of Lepanto (1571).

Room 3: At the far (left) end of the room is a very, very early (17th-century) attempt at a 20-barrel machine gun. On the walls and weapons, the "C-X" insignia means that this was the private stash of the "Council of Ten."

Room 4: In this room, rifles and pistols enter the picture. Don't miss the glass case in the corner, with a tiny crossbow, some torture devices (including an effective-looking thumbscrew), the wooden "devil's box" (a clever item that could fire in four directions at once), and a nasty, two-holed chastity belt. These disheartening "iron breeches" were worn by the devoted wife of the Lord of Padua.

► *Exit the Armory Museum. Go downstairs, turn left, and pass through the long hall with a wood-beam ceiling. Now turn right and open your eyes as wide as you can to see the...*

Hall of the Grand Council (Sala del Maggiore Consiglio)

It took a room this size to contain the grandeur of the Most Serene Republic. This huge room (175 by 80 feet) could accommodate up to 2,600 people at one time. The engineering is remarkable. The ceiling is like the deck of a ship—its hull is the rooftop, creating a huge attic above that.

The doge presided from the raised dais, while the nobles—the backbone of the empire—filled the center and lined the long walls. Nobles were generally wealthy men over 25, but the title had less to do with money than with long bloodlines. In theory, the doge, the Senate, and the Council of Ten were all subordinate to the Grand Council of nobles who elected them.

On the wall over the doge's throne is Tintoretto's monsterpiece, ***Paradise,*** the largest oil painting in the world. At 570 square feet, it could be sliced up to wallpaper an apartment with enough left over for placemats.

Christ and Mary are at the top of heaven, surrounded by 500 people. It's rush hour in heaven, and all the good Venetians made it. Tintoretto worked on this in the last years of his long life. On the day it was finished, his daughter died. He got his brush out again and painted her as saint number 501. She's dead center with the blue skirt, hands clasped, getting sucked up to heaven. (At least that's what an Italian tour guide told me.)

Veronese's ***The Apotheosis of Venice*** (on the ceiling at the

Tintoretto's *Paradise*—500-plus figures

Siege of Constantinople—Venice triumphs

Hall of the Grand Council

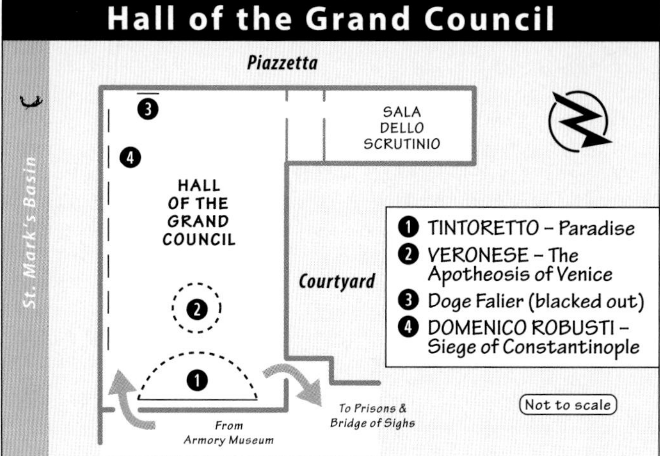

Tintoretto end—view it from the top) is a typically unsubtle work showing Lady Venice being crowned a goddess by an angel.

Ringing the hall are portraits, in chronological order, of the first 76 doges. The one at the far end that's blacked out is the notorious **Doge Marin Falier,** who opposed the will of the Grand Council in 1355. He was tried for treason, beheaded, and airbrushed from history.

Along the entire wall to the right of Paradise, the ***Siege of Constantinople*** (by Tintoretto's son, Domenico) shows Venice's greatest military (if not moral) victory, the conquest of the fellow-Christian city of Constantinople during the Fourth Crusade (✪ see sidebar on page 55). The sneaky Venetians (in the fifth painting) attacked the mighty city from the water. They cozied their galleys right up to the dock and scooted across the masts to the city walls. The gates open, the Byzantine emperor parades out to surrender, and tiny Doge Dandolo says, "Let's go in and steal some bronze horses."

But soon Venice would begin its long slide into historical oblivion. The rising Ottoman Turks gobbled up Venice's trading outposts. New trade routes to the East and America broke Venice's monopoly on trade. The once-mighty empire was reduced to little more than the city itself, a tourist town with a reputation for decadence. Finally, in 1797, the French general

Napoleon marched into town shouting *"Liberté, egalité, fraternité."* The Most Serene Republic was overthrown, and the last doge was deposed in the name of modern democracy.

▸ *Consider reading about the prisons here in the Grand Council Hall, where there are more benches and fewer rats.*

To reach the prisons, exit the Grand Hall by squeezing through the door to the left of Tintoretto's monsterpiece. Follow signs for Prigioni/Ponte dei Sospiri, *passing through several rooms. In room 31, pause at four fascinating paintings by Hieronymus Bosch showing sinners tortured in hell by genetic mutants and* Wizard of Oz *monkeys. In a room adjoining room 31, you'll find a narrow staircase going down, following signs to the prisons. (Don't miss it, or you'll miss the prisons altogether and end up at the bookshop near the exit.) Then cross the covered Bridge of Sighs over the canal to the prisons. Start your visit in the cells to your left.*

Prisons

The palace had its own dungeons. In the privacy of his own home, a doge could oversee the sentencing, torturing, and jailing of political opponents. By the 1500s, the dungeons were full of political prisoners, so new prisons were built across the canal connected with a covered bridge.

Circle the cells. Medieval justice was harsh. The cells consisted of cold stone with heavily barred windows, a wooden plank for a bed, a shelf, and a bucket. (My question: What did they put on the shelf?) You can feel the cold and damp. Notice the carvings made by prisoners—from olden days up until 1930—on some of the stone windowsills of the cells, especially in the far corner of the building.

Explore the rest of the prisons. You can descend lower to the notorious cells known as "the wells"—so-called because they were deep, wet, and cramped. Or stay on this floor, where there's a room displaying ceramic shards found in archaeological digs. Adjoining that are more cells, including the farthest cell, where you can see the bored prisoners' compelling and sometimes artistic graffiti.

▸ *Wherever you roam, you'll end up where you entered. Now re-cross...*

The Bridge of Sighs

According to romantic legend, criminals were tried and sentenced in the palace, then marched across the canal here to the dark prisons. On this bridge, they got one last look at Venice. They gazed out at the sky, the water, and the beautiful buildings.

▶ *Cross back over the Bridge of Sighs, pausing to look through the marble-trellised windows at all of the tourists and the heavenly Church of San Giorgio Maggiore. Heave one last sigh and leave the palace.*

It's a romantic scene today, but the "sighs" from this bridge once came from condemned prisoners.

Frari Church Tour

Basilica di Santa Maria Gloriosa dei Frari

For me, this church offers the best art-appreciation experience in Venice, because so much of its great art is in situ—right where it was designed to be seen, rather than hanging in museums.

The church was built (and consecrated in 1492) by the Franciscan order. They were inspired by St. Francis of Assisi (c. 1182-1226), who dedicated himself to a non-materialistic lifestyle. The spirit of St. Francis of Assisi warms both the church of his "brothers" *(frari)* and the art that decorates it. The Franciscan love of all of creation—Nature and Man—later inspired Renaissance painters to capture the beauty of the physical world and human emotions, showing worshippers the glory of God in human terms.

ORIENTATION

Cost: €3.

Hours: Mon-Sat 9:00-18:00, Sun 13:00-18:00, last entry 30 minutes before closing.

Information: Tel. 041-272-8618, www.basilicadeifrari.it.

Dress Code: Modest dress is recommended.

Getting There: It's near the San Tomà vaporetto and *traghetto* stops. From the dock, follow signs to *Scuola Grande di San Rocco.* For a pleasant stroll from the Rialto Bridge, ✪ take the Rialto to Frari Church Walk.

Audioguides: €2. Or you can download this chapter as a free Rick Steves audio tour (✪ see page 199).

Length of This Tour: Allow one hour.

Photography: Prohibited.

Eating: The church square is ringed with small, simple, reasonably priced cafés.

Nearby: For efficient sightseeing, combine your visit with the nearby Scuola San Rocco and the Ca' Rezzonico, a seven-minute walk away.

Starring: Titian, Giovanni Bellini, Paolo Veneziano, and Donatello.

THE TOUR BEGINS

▶ *Enter the church and find a spot with a good view down the long nave toward the altar.*

❶ Church Interior and Choir (1250-1443)

The simple, spacious (110-yard-long), well-lit Gothic church—with rough wood crossbeams and a red-and-white color scheme—is truly a remarkable sight in a city otherwise crammed with exotic froufrou. Because Venice's spongy ground could never support a real stone Gothic church (such as those you'd find in France), the Frari is made of light and flexible brick. Traditionally, churches in Venice were cross-shaped, but this T-shaped footprint featured a long, lofty nave—flooded with light and suited to large gatherings—where common people heard sermons.

The wooden choir area in the center of the nave allowed friars to hold smaller, more intimate services. From the early 16th century, as worshippers entered the church and looked down the long nave to the altar, they were greeted by Titian's glorious painted altarpiece—then, as now, framed by the arch of the choir entrance.

Walk prayerfully toward the Titian, stopping in the finely carved 1480s choir. Notice the fine inlay above the chairs, showing the Renaissance enthusiasm for Florentine-style depth and perspective.

▸ *Approach Titian's heavenly vision.*

❷ Titian (Tiziano Vecellio)—*The Assumption of the Virgin* (1516-1518)

Glowing red and gold like a stained-glass window, this altarpiece sets the tone of exuberant beauty found in this church. At the end of her life (though looking 17 here), Mary was miraculously "assumed" into heaven. As cherubs lift her up to meet a Jupiter-like God, the stunned apostles on earth reach up to touch the floating bubble of light.

Look around. The church is littered with chapels and tombs "made possible by the generous financial support" of rich people who donated to the Franciscans for the good of their souls (and usually for tomb-topping statues of themselves, as well).

For the altar, they hired the new whiz artist, Titian, to create a dramatic painting. Unveiled in 1518, the work scandalized a Venice accustomed to simpler, more contemplative church art. The rich colors, twisting poses, and mix of saccharine angels with blue-collar apostles were unheard of. Most striking, this Virgin is fully human, not a stiff icon on a throne. The Franciscans thought this Mary aroused excitement rather than spirituality. They agreed to pay Titian only after the Holy Roman Emperor offered to buy the altar if they refused.

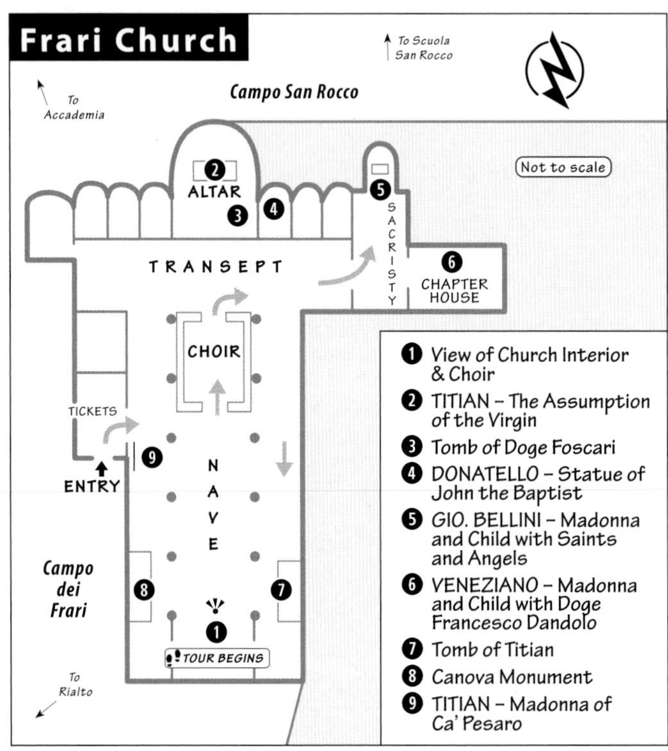

In a burst of youthful innovation, Titian (1488-1576) had rewritten the formula for church art, hinting at changes to come with the Mannerist and Baroque styles. He energized the scene with a complex composition, overlapping a circle (Mary's bubble) and a triangle (draw a line from the apostle reaching up to Mary's face and down the other side) on three horizontal levels (God in heaven, Man on earth, Mary in between). Together, these elements draw our eyes from the swirl of arms and legs to the painting's focus—the radiant face of a triumphant Mary, "assumed body and soul into heaven."

Titian's *Assumption*—as she rises to heaven, Mary radiates spirituality through physical beauty

▸ *Flanking the painting are marble tombs lining the walls. On the wall to the right of the altar is the...*

❸ Tomb of Doge Foscari (15th Century)

This heavy, ornate tomb marks the peak of Venice's worldly power. Doge Francesco Foscari (1373-1457) assumed control of the city's powerful seafaring empire and then tried to expand it onto the mainland, battling Milan in a 31-year war of attrition that swept through northern Italy. Meanwhile, on the unprotected eastern front, the Ottomans took Constantinople (1453) and scuttled Venice's trade. Venice's long slide into historical oblivion had begun. Financially drained city fathers forced Foscari to resign, turn in his funny hat, and hand over the keys to the Doge's Palace.

▸ *In the first chapel to the right of the altar, you'll find...*

❹ Donatello—*Statue of John the Baptist* (1438)

In the center of the altarpiece, the cockeyed prophet of the desert—emaciated from his breakfast of bugs 'n' honey and dressed in animal skins—freezes mid-rant when he spies something in the distance. His jaw goes slack, and he twists his face and raises his hand to announce the coming of...the Renaissance.

Florentine expatriates living in Venice commissioned Donatello to make this wooden statue, and it reflects their tastes. The Renaissance began in the Florence of the 1400s, where Donatello (1386-1466) created realistic statues with a full range of human emotions. This warts-and-all John the Baptist is harshly realistic, with muted colors. By contrast, Venetian art is generally soft-focus and beautiful, with bright colors.

Donatello's bold *John the Baptist* (center)

Bellini's *Madonna* in an illusory niche

▶ *Enter the sacristy through the door at the far end of the right transept. You'll bump into an elaborate altar crammed with reliquaries. Opposite that (near the entrance door) is a clock, intricately carved from a single piece of wood. At the far end of the room, you'll find Bellini's glowing altarpiece.*

❺ Giovanni Bellini—*Madonna and Child with Saints and Angels* (1488)

The Pesaro family, who negotiated an acceptable price and place for their family tomb, funded this delightful chapel dominated by a Bellini masterpiece.

Mary sits on a throne under a half-dome, propping up Baby Jesus (who's just learning to stand), flanked by saints and serenaded by musician angels. Giovanni Bellini (c. 1430-1516), the father of the Venetian Renaissance, painted fake columns and a dome to match the real ones in the gold frame, making the painting seem to be an extension of the room. He completes the illusion with glimpses of open sky in the background. Next, he fills the artificial niches with symmetrically posed, thoughtful saints—left to right, find Saints Nicholas, Peter, Mark, and Sean Connery (Benedict).

Bellini combined the meditative poses of the Venetian Byzantine tradition with Renaissance improvements in modern art. He made the transition from painting with medieval tempera (egg yolk-based) to painting in oil (pigments dissolved in vegetable oil). Oils allowed a subtler treatment of colors because artists could apply them in successive layers. And because darker colors aren't so muddy when painted in oil, they "pop," effectively giving the artist a brighter palette.

Bellini virtually invented the formula (later to be broken by his precocious pupil, Titian) for Venetian altarpieces. This type of holy conversation *(Sacra Conversazione)* between saints and Mary can also be seen in Venice's Accademia and Church of San Zaccaria.

Renaissance humanism demanded Madonnas and saints that were accessible and human. Bellini delivers, but places them in a physical setting so beautiful that it creates its own mood of serene holiness. The scene is lit from the left, but nothing casts a harsh shadow—Mary and the babe are enveloped in a glowing aura of reflected light from the golden dome. The beauty is in the details, from the writing in the dome, to the red brocade backdrop, to the swirls in the marble steps, to the angels' dimpled legs.

Veneziano's *Madonna*—solemn, icon-like faces and a neutral background show Byzantine roots

▶ *In the adjoining room, find a painting in the shape of a Gothic arch.*

⑥ Paolo Veneziano—*Madonna and Child with Doge Francesco Dandolo* (c. 1339)

Bellini's Byzantine roots can be traced to Paolo Veneziano (literally, "Paul the Venetian"), the first "name" artist in Venice, who helped shape the distinctive painting style of his city. Veneziano paints Byzantine icons, then sets them in motion. Baby Jesus turns to greet a kneeling Doge Dandolo, while Mary turns to acknowledge the doge's wife. None other than St. Francis presents "Francis" (Francesco) Dandolo to the Madonna. Both he and St. Elizabeth (on the right) bend at the waist and gesture as naturally as 14th-century icons can.

▶ *Return to the nave and head left, toward the far end. Turn around and face the altar. The Tomb of Titian is in the second bay on your right.*

⑦ Tomb of Titian (1852)

The enormous carved marble monument is labeled "Titiano Ferdinandus MDCCCLII." The tomb celebrates both the man and his famous paintings (depicted in the background reliefs).

Titian (c. 1488/90-1576) sits center stage, with a beard and crown of laurels. Titian was the greatest Venetian painter, excelling equally in inspirational altarpieces, realistic portraits, joyous mythological scenes, and erotic female nudes.

As a young man, he studied as a mosaic-maker and then a painter under Giovanni Bellini and Giorgione. Soon he established his own bold style, which featured teenage Madonnas, like the Frari altarpiece (see a relief of *The Assumption* behind Titian). He became wealthy and famous, traveling Europe to paint stately portraits of kings and nobles, and colorful, sexy works for their bedrooms. But he always returned to his beloved Venice (see winged lion on top)...and favorite Frari Church.

In his old age, Titian painted dark, tragic masterpieces. His *Pietà* (see relief in upper left) was intended for his tomb but ended up in the Accademia (✪ see page 135). Nearing 90, he labored to finish the *Pietà* as the plague enveloped Venice. One in four people died, including Titian's son. Heartbroken, Titian died soon afterward. The cause of death was probably the plague, although his death was officially chalked up to influenza to keep his body from being burned—a requirement for plague victims. His tomb was built three centuries later to remember and honor this great Venetian.

▶ *On the opposite side of the nave is the pyramid-shaped...*

❽ Canova Monument (1827)

Antonio Canova (1757-1822, see his portrait above the door) was Venice's greatest sculptor. He created gleaming white, highly polished statues of

Titian's tomb—Venice's greatest painter

Canova Monument—its greatest sculptor

beautiful Greek gods and goddesses in the Neoclassical style. (✪ See several of his works at the Correr Museum, page 129.)

The pyramid shape is timeless, suggesting pharaohs' tombs and the Christian Trinity. Mourners, bent over with grief, shuffle up to pay homage to the master artist. Even the winged lion is choked up.

Follow me here. Canova himself designed this pyramid-shaped tomb, not for his own use, but as the tomb of an artist he greatly admired: Titian. But the Frari picked another design for Titian's tomb, so Canova used the pyramid for an Austrian princess in Vienna. After his death, Canova's pupils copied the design here to honor their master. In fact, Canova isn't buried here—he lies in southern Italy. But inside the tomb's open door, you can (barely) see an urn, which contains his heart.

▸ *Head back toward the altar. Halfway up the left wall is...*

⑨ Titian—*Madonna of Ca' Pesaro* (1519-1526)

Titian's second altarpiece for the Frari Church displays all his many skills. Following his teacher Bellini, he puts Mary (seated) and baby (standing) on a throne, surrounded by saints having a holy conversation. And, like Bellini, he paints fake columns that echo the church's real ones.

But wait. Mary is off-center, Titian's idealized saints mingle with Venetians sporting five o'clock shadows, and the stairs run diagonally away from us. Mary sits not on a throne, but on a pedestal. Baby Jesus is restless. The precious keys of St. Peter seem to dangle unnoticed. These things upset traditional Renaissance symmetry, but they turn a group of figures into a true scene. St. Peter (center, in blue and gold, with book) looks down at Jacopo Pesaro, who kneels to thank the Virgin for his recent naval victory over the Ottomans (1502). A flag-carrying lieutenant drags in a turbaned captive. Meanwhile, St. Francis talks to Baby Jesus while gesturing down to more members of the Pesaro family. The little guy looking out at us (lower right) is the Pesaro descendant who administered the trust fund to keep prayers coming for his dead uncle.

Titian combines opposites: a soft-focus Madonna with photo-realist portraits, chubby winged angels with a Muslim prisoner, and a Christian cross with a battle flag. In keeping with the spirit of St. Francis' humanism, Titian lets mere mortals mingle with saints. And we're right there with them.

▸ *While this church is a great example of art in situ, in a sense, all of Venice is art in situ. Explore some back lanes and lonely canals here in the meditative side of town.*

Madonna of Ca' Pesaro—saints mingle with Venetians, making the heavenly seem real

HOTEL
ASTORIA

St. Mark's to Rialto Loop Walk

Two rights and a left (simple!) can get you from St. Mark's Square to the Rialto Bridge via a completely different route from the one most tourists take. Along the way, take in some lesser sights and appreciate the reality of Venice today.

Venice's population is half what it was just 30 years ago. Sad, yes, but imagine raising a family here: Apartments are small, high up, and expensive. Home-improvement projects involve miles of red tape. Running a simple errand can mean crossing arched bridges while pushing a child in a stroller and carrying a day's worth of groceries.

On the other hand, those who stay couldn't think of living anywhere else. This walk may help you understand why.

ORIENTATION

Length of This Walk: Allow one hour for a leisurely walk.
San Moisè Church: Free, Mon-Sat 9:30-12:30, Sun Mass only at 11:00, tel. 041-296-0630.
La Fenice Opera House: €8 for dry 45-minute audioguide tour, generally open daily 9:30-13:30, theater box office open daily 9:30-18:00.
Rialto Market: The souvenir stalls are open daily; the produce market is closed on Sunday; and the fish market is closed on Sunday and Monday. The market is lively only in the morning.

THE WALK BEGINS

Start at St. Mark's Square

▸ *From the square, walk to the waterfront and turn right. You're walking on recently raised Venice—in 2006, the stones were taken up and six inches of extra sand put down, to minimize flooding. Continue along the water toward the white TI pavilion.*

Along the waterfront, you'll see the various boats that ply Venice's waters. Hiring a gondola here is often more expensive than elsewhere in Venice. Classic wooden motorboats operating as water taxis are pricey (about €60 from here to the train station), but they are a classy splurge if you split the fare with others. Hotel shuttle boats bring guests here from distant, $700-a-night hotels.

Run the gauntlet of souvenir stands to the entrance to the Giardinetti Reali (Royal Gardens, once the site of a huge grain-storage depot that was destroyed by Napoleon). The grounds offer some precious greenery in a city built of stone on mud. Nearby is a TI in a cute 18th-century former coffeehouse pavilion. From atop the bridge by the TI, look across the mouth of the Grand Canal to view the big dome of La Salute Church, and the guy balancing a bronze ball on one foot on top of the old Customs House, which is now a contemporary art museum (the Punta della Dogana).

▸ *Twelve steps down and 20 yards ahead on the right is...*

❶ Harry's American Bar

Hemingway put this bar on the map by making it his hangout in the late 1940s. If Brad and Angelina are in town, this is where they'll be. If they're

St. Mark's to Rialto Loop Walk

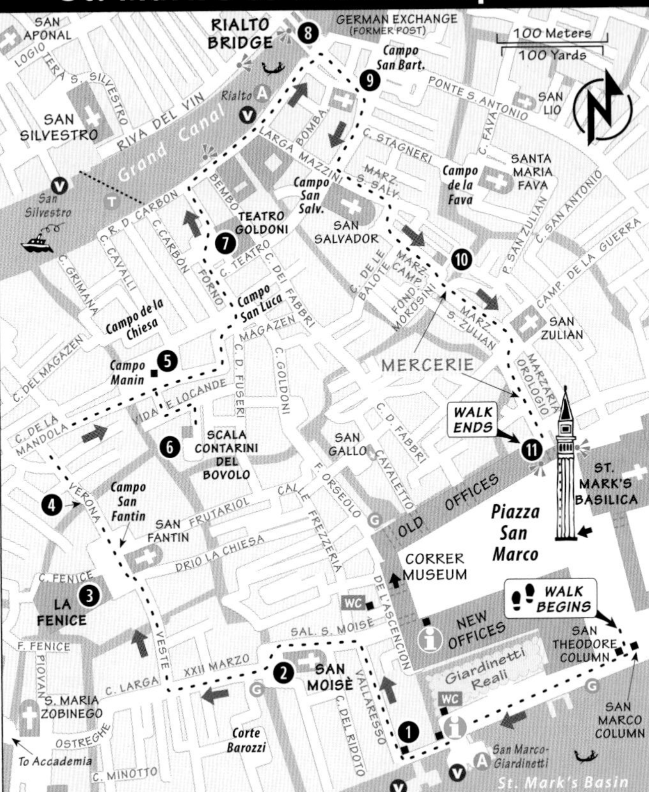

1. Harry's American Bar
2. San Moisè Church
3. La Fenice Opera House
4. Ponte de la Verona
5. Daniele Manin Statue
6. Scala Contarini del Bovolo
7. Teatro Goldoni
8. Rialto Bridge
9. Campo San Bartolomeo
10. Casino
11. Clock Tower

The waterfront by St. Mark's Square

Harry's Bar—overpriced "celebrity" haunt

not, you'll see plenty of dressed-up Americans looking around for celebrities. The discreet (and overpriced) restaurant upstairs is where the glitterati hang out. The street-level bar is for gawkers. If you wear something a bit fancy (or artsy bohemian), you can pull up a stool at the tiny bar by the entrance and pay too much for a Bellini (Prosecco and peach puree), which was invented right here.

► *Head inland down Calle Vallaresso, one of Venice's most exclusive streets, past fancy boutiques such as Pucci, Gucci, and Roberto Cavalli. At the T intersection, turn left and head west on Salizada San Moisè (which becomes Calle Larga XXII Marzo). Continue to the first bridge and a square dominated by the fancy facade of a church. Climb the bridge, and against a soundtrack of tourists negotiating with hustling gondoliers, look back at the ornate...*

❷ San Moisè Church

This is the parish church for St Mark's; because of tourist crowds at the basilica, this is where the community actually worships. While it's one of Venice's oldest churches, dating from the 10th century (note the old tower on the right), its busy facade is 17th-century Baroque. The big shot who funded the project has his bust in the center of the facade, while Moses (Moisè) caps it.

Inside, the altarpiece depicts Mount Sinai, with Moses (kneeling) receiving the two tablets with the Ten Commandments. The alcove to the left of the altar has Tintoretto's 16th-century *Christ Washing the Disciples' Feet*.

The modern building nearby is the ritzy, five-star Bauer Hotel, originally an 18th-century palace. In the 1940s, the owners added this Fascist-deco wing, defying Italian historical-preservation codes. Its facade still gives locals the Mussolini-creeps. You can take a few minutes to wander through the hotel for a James Bond-meets-Mussolini architectural experience.

▶ *Continue past the bridge, down Calle Larga XXII Marzo, a big street that seems too wide and large for Venice. It was created during the 19th century by filling in a canal. You can make out the outline of the sidewalks that once flanked the now-gone canal. Pass by the Vivaldi look-alikes selling concert tickets and (mostly Senegalese) immigrants illegally selling knockoffs of Prada bags.*

Halfway down the street, turn right on tiny Calle del Sartor da Veste. Go straight, crossing a bridge. At the next square, you'll find...

❸ La Fenice Opera House (Gran Teatro alla Fenice)

Venice's famed opera house, built in 1792 (read the *MDCCXCII* on the facade), was started as a business venture by a group of nobles who recognized that Venice was short on entertainment opportunities for the well-heeled set.

La Fenice was reduced to a hollowed-out shell by a disastrous fire in 1996. After a vigorous restoration campaign, "The Phoenix"—true to its name—has risen again from the ashes. La Fenice resumed opera productions in 2004, opening with *La Traviata.* The theater is usually open daily to the public (for information, ✪ see page 132).

Venice is one of the cradles of the multimedia art form known as opera. Some of the great operas were first performed here in this luxurious setting. Verdi's *Rigoletto* (1851) and *La Traviata* (1853) were actually commissioned by La Fenice. The man who put words to some of Mozart's

San Moisè Church and Bauer Hotel

"The Phoenix," a classic opera house

View from Ponte de la Verona—a slice of everyday life that's both charming and crumbling

opera tunes was a Venetian, Lorenzo da Ponte, who drew inspiration from the city's libertine ways and joie de vivre. In recent years, La Fenice's musical standing was overshadowed by its reputation as a place for the wealthy to parade in furs and jewels.

► *Continue north along the same street (though its name is now Calle de la Verona), to a small bridge over a quiet canal.*

❹ Ponte de la Verona

Pause atop this bridge, where reflections can make you wonder which end is up. Looking above you, see bridges of stone propping up leaning buildings, and there's a view of the "Leaning Tower" of San Stefano.

People actually live in Venice. Notice their rooftop gardens, their laundry, their plumbing, electricity lines snaking into their apartments, and the rusted iron bars and bolts that hold their crumbling homes together. On one building, find centuries-old relief carvings—a bearded face and a panel of an eagle with its prey. People once swam freely in the canals. Find the sign that reads *Divieto di Nuoto* ("swimming not allowed").

You may see some private boats. Italian law stipulates that a luxury tax is levied on all boats—except in Venice, where they're considered a necessity. Calling a taxi? A boat comes. Going to the hospital to have a baby? Take an ambulance boat. Garbage day? You put your bag on the canal edge, and a garbage boat mashes it and takes it away. While many Venetians own (and love) their own boats, parking is a huge problem. If you take your boat to run errands, you either know a friend nearby with a grandfathered parking space, or your partner has to "circle the block" while you shop.

While many Venetians own a car for driving on the isle of Lido or the mainland, they admit, "We're not very much beloved on the road."

► *Continue north. At the T intersection, turn right on Calle de la Mandola. You'll cross over a bridge into a spacious square dominated by a statue and an out-of-place modern building.*

❺ Campo Manin

The centerpiece of the square is a statue of Daniele Manin (1804-1857), Venice's fiery leader in the battle for freedom from Austria and eventually a united Italy (the Risorgimento). The statue faces the red house Manin lived in.

▸ *Scala Contarini del Bovolo is a block south of here, with yellow signs pointing the way. Facing the Manin statue, turn right and exit the square down an alley. Follow yellow signs to the left, then immediately to the right, into a courtyard with one of Venice's hidden treasures...*

⑥ Scala Contarini del Bovolo

The Scala is a cylindrical brick tower with five floors of spiral staircases faced with white marble banisters (probably closed for renovation during your visit).

Built in 1499, it was the external staircase of a palace (external stairs saved interior space for rooms). Architecture buffs admire the successful blend of a Gothic building with a Renaissance staircase.

If the tower is open, you can pay a small fee to wind your way up the "snail shell" (*bovolo* in the local dialect). It's 113 steps to the top, where you're rewarded with views of the Venetian skyline.

▸ *Unwind and return to the Manin statue. Continue east, circling around the big Cassa di Risparmio bank, marveling at its Modernist ugliness. At Campo San Luca, turn left (north) on Calle del Forno. Note the 24-hour pharmacy vending machine that dispenses shower gel, Band-Aids, bug repellant, toothbrushes, condoms, and other after-hours necessities. Heading north, glance 20 yards down the street to the right at the flag-bedecked...*

⑦ Teatro Goldoni

Though this theater dates from the 1930s, there's been a theater here since the 1500s, when Venice was at the forefront of secular entertainment.

Daniele Manin, 19th-century patriot

The photogenic Scala Contarini del Bovolo

Many of Carlo Goldoni's (1707-1793) groundbreaking comedies—featuring real-life situations of the new middle class—got their first performances here. Today, Teatro Goldoni is still a working theater of mainly Italian productions.

► *Continue north on Calle del Forno. You're very close to the Grand Canal. Keep going north, jogging to the right at the small square (Corte del Teatro), then left down a teeny-tiny alleyway. Pop! You emerge on the Grand Canal, about 150 yards downstream from the...*

8 Rialto Bridge

Of Venice's more than 400 bridges, only four cross the Grand Canal. Rialto was the first among these four.

The original Rialto Bridge, dating from 1180, was a platform supported by boats tied together. It linked the political side (Palazzo Ducale) of Venice with the economic center (Rialto). Rialto, which takes its name from *riva alto* (high bank), was one of the earliest Venetian settlements. When

The Rialto Bridge, lined with shops, is the geographic "heart" of fish-shaped Venice.

Venice was Europe's economic superpower, this was where bankers, brokers, and merchants conducted their daily business.

Rialto Bridge II was a 13th-century wooden drawbridge. It was replaced in 1588 by the current structure, with its bold single arch (spanning 160 feet) and arcades on top designed to strengthen the stone span. Its immense foundations stretch 650 feet on either side. Heavy buildings were then built atop the foundations to hold everything in place. The Rialto remained the only bridge crossing the Grand Canal until 1854.

Marking the geographical center of Venice (midway down the Grand Canal), the Rialto is the most sensible location for retail shops. The government built it with the (accurate) expectation that it'd soon pay for itself with rent from the shops built into it. Like the (older) Ponte Vecchio in Florence, the Rialto was originally lined with luxury gold and jewelry shops. The bridge is cleverly designed to generate maximum rent: three lanes, two rows of twelve shops each, with a warehouse area above each shop under the lead-and-timber roof.

Reliefs of the Venetian Republic's main mascots, St. Mark and St. Theodore, crown the arch. Barges and *vaporetti* run the busy waterways below, and merchants vie for tourists' attention on top.

The Rialto has long been a symbol of Venice. Aristocratic inhabitants built magnificent palaces just to be near it. The poetic Lord Byron swam to it all the way from Lido Island. And thousands of marriage proposals have been sealed right here, with a kiss, as the moon floated over La Serenissima.

▸ *From here, you could cross the bridge to check out the fish and produce market. Or continue even farther along my ✪ Rialto to Frari Church Walk (the next chapter). But this walk returns along the main tourist route to St. Mark's Square. From the base of the Rialto Bridge (on the near side), go 100 yards directly to...*

⑨ Campo San Bartolomeo

This square is one of the city's main crossroads. Locals routinely meet at the statue of playwright Carlo Goldoni. The pharmacy on this square (marked by a green cross) keeps an electronic counter in its window, ticking down the population of Venice as it shrinks.

▸ *Head to the right 100 yards, down Via 2 Aprile, setting your sights on the green-and-red umbrellas on the corner. They mark a stretch of town*

Playwright Carlo Goldoni

Stucco work adorns this casino.

once famous for selling umbrellas and handbags. From there, turn left and follow the crowds 100 yards more along the...

Mercerie

The high-rent Mercerie (or "Marzarie," in Venetian dialect) is a string of connecting streets lined mostly with big-name chain and luxury stores. Much of the "Venetian" glass displayed here is actually made in China (always look for the Murano symbol). The Caputo shop—behind the Rolex shop, down an alley and on the left—is handy for phone and camera needs.

▶ *When you get to the yellow two-way arrow "directing" you to San Marco, head right and then follow the flow left another 100 yards until you reach a bridge, which makes for a fun gondola viewing perch. At the top of the bridge, belly up to the railing on the left. Above the arcade on your left is the fancy little balcony of the city's best-preserved...*

⑩ Casino

If the windows are open, spy the lacy pastel and stucco ceilings inside. Though only a few of Venice's casinos still exist, the city once had several hundred of these "little houses"—city-center retreats for the palazzo-dwelling set. For many patricians, they served as 17th-century man caves, used for entertaining, gambling, and/or intimate encounters. For well-to-do women, casinos provided a different kind of escape: Inspired by Madame de Pompadour (Louis XV's mistress), ladies would hold court with writers, artists, and avant-garde types.

▶ *Cross the bridge and continue straight for 100 yards along Marzaria San Zulian. On the way, notice the metal two-foot-high flood barrier braces at shop doors—and how merchandise is elevated in anticipation of high water (local insurance doesn't cover floods).*

When you hit the next schizophrenic Per S. Marco *arrow, go right a few steps, then left onto Marzaria dell'Orologio, a street named for where you're heading: the Clock Tower. The Renaissance* ⓫ ***Clock Tower*** *was built when it was considered important that cities have a proper main gate with a grand clock. Pass through "Venice's front door" and into its grand courtyard—St. Mark's Square.*

Rialto to Frari Church Walk

Cross the Rialto Bridge, and dive headlong into Venice's thriving market area. Smell the fresh-caught fish, ogle the produce, and rub shoulders with Venetian shoppers following the same rhythm of life that's gone on here for generations. Home to a number of colorful *cicchetti* pubs, the area's a great place for lunch. From the market, we'll continue on another 20 minutes through the less-touristed San Polo neighborhood—a place where "real" Venetians live. We'll pass workaday stores, neighborhood squares, and one of Venice's best mask shops. Finally, we'll spill out at Tintoretto's Scuola San Rocco (✪ see page 141), and the subject of a previous chapter—the art-filled Frari Church.

ORIENTATION

Length of This Walk: Allow a leisurely hour.

When to Go: The markets are lively only in the morning. The produce market is closed on Sunday, and the fish market is closed on Sunday and Monday.

Church of San Polo: €3, Mon-Sat 10:00-17:00, closed Sun.

Tragicomica Mask Shop: Daily 10:00-19:00, at Calle dei Nomboli 2800, tel. 041-721-102. The owners are generally happy to show their workshop to visitors who've called ahead.

Eateries: Many pubs and restaurants in the Rialto area are recommended in the Eating chapter.

THE WALK BEGINS

▸ *From the top of the Rialto Bridge, walk down the bridge (heading away from the St. Mark's side) and about 50 yards onward until you see an old square on your right. Go to its fountain.*

❶ Campo San Giacomo

The square looks like it did in the 16th century. After a fire devastated the area, this High Renaissance square was built, in 1520—or "MDXX," as it says on the arcade. The church, which escaped the fire, has one of the oldest facades in town, with a clock that predates minute hands.

Notice that the square slopes toward the center. Originally, rainwater flowed to the center, filtered down through limestone, where it was collected in an underground cistern. Several thousand cisterns like this provided the city with its drinking water up until 1886, when an aqueduct was built (paralleling the railroad bridge) to bring in water from nearby mountains.

Back when the Rialto Bridge was a drawbridge (until the 1590s), big ships would dock here to unload their spices, oil, wine, and jewels. The line of buildings between Campo San Giacomo and the canal was once a strip of banks—the Bancogiro. Today it's a line of popular eateries (✪ described on page 170). Behind today's trashy jewelry stands are real jewelry shops, which have thrived here for more than 500 years.

Opposite the church, find the granite hunchback supporting steps leading to a column. Back when this prosperous neighborhood was Europe's "Wall Street," the column was its "*Wall Street Journal.*" A man climbed the stair each noon, stood atop the column, and read aloud the daily news from the doge: which ships had docked, which foreign ambassadors were in town, the price of pepper, and so on.

Walk along the left side of the church and turn left, to the canal's edge. Look back at the large white building behind the church (the city's fiscal administration building). Notice how it tilts out, probably because the bridge's huge foundation is compressing the mud beneath it.

Now walk along the canal to a little canalside dead-end that's as close as you can get to the Rialto Bridge. Take in the great view of the bridge. The former post office (directly across from you) was originally the German merchants' hall (see the seal). It's about to be reincarnated as a Benetton-owned shopping center.

You're standing under a former prison. Study the iron grills over the windows. Notice the interlocking pipes with alternating joints—you couldn't cut just one and escape.

► *From the prison, walk back along the canal, through the triple archway, cross the square, and enter the square named Casaria (for the historic cheese market). Today, this is Venice's...*

❷ Produce Market (Erberia)

Colorful stalls offer fresh fruit and vegetables, some quite exotic. Nothing is grown on the island of Venice, so everything is shipped in daily from the mainland. The Mercato Rialto vaporetto stop is a convenient place for boats to unload their wares, here in the heart of fish-shaped Venice.

Cross the Rialto Brigde into less-touristed Venice.

Campo San Giacomo, near the Rialto Market

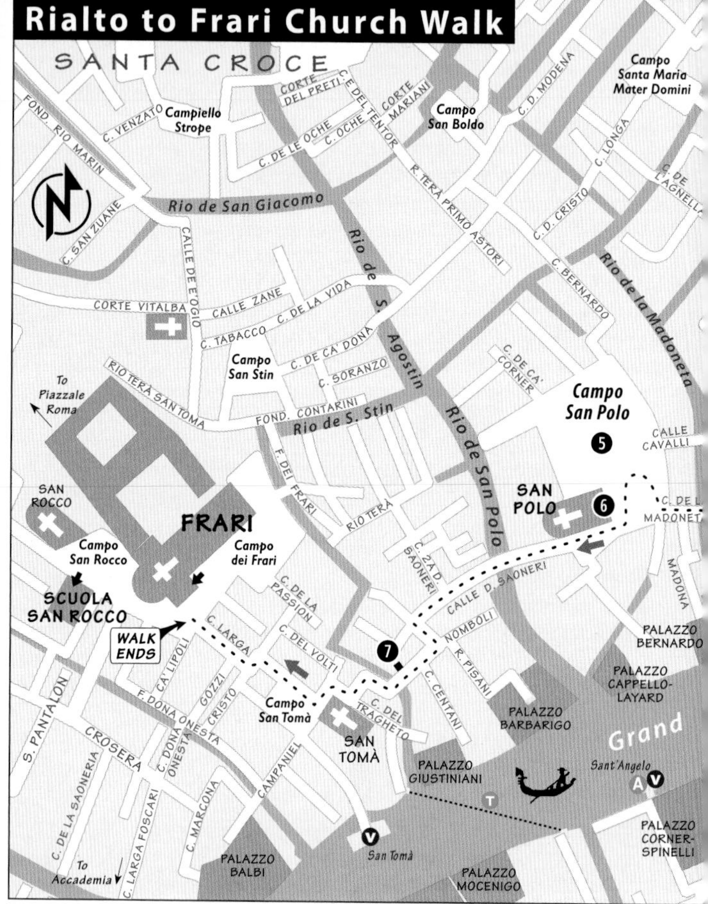
Rialto to Frari Church Walk
SANTA CROCE
Campiello Strope
Campo San Boldo
Campo Santa Maria Mater Domini
Rio de San Giacomo
Rio de S. Agostin
Rio de la Madoneta
Campo San Stin
Rio de S. Stin
Rio de San Polo
Campo San Polo
SAN POLO
FRARI
Campo San Rocco
Campo dei Frari
SCUOLA SAN ROCCO
SAN ROCCO
WALK ENDS
Campo San Tomà
SAN TOMÀ
PALAZZO BARBARIGO
PALAZZO CAPPELLO-LAYARD
PALAZZO BERNARDO
PALAZZO GIUSTINIANI
PALAZZO BALBI
PALAZZO MOCENIGO
PALAZZO CORNER-SPINELLI
Grand
Sant'Angelo
San Tomà
To Piazzale Roma
To Accademia
CALLE ZANE
CORTE VITALBA
C. TABACCO
C. DE LA VIDA
C. DE CA' DONÀ
C. SORANZO
FOND. CONTARINI
RIO TERÀ SAN TOMÀ
F. DEI FRARI
RIO TERÀ
CALLE D. SAONERI
C. 2A D. SAONERI
NOMBOLI
R. PISANI
C. CENTANI
C. DEL TRAGHETO
C. DEL VOLTI
C. DE LA PASSION
C. LARGA
CA' LIPOLI
GOZZI
CRISTO
F. DONÀ ONESTA
C. DONÀ ONESTA
CROSERA
S. PANTALON
C. DE LA SAONERIA
C. LARGA FOSCARI
C. MARCONA
CAMPANIEL
CALLE CAVALLI
C. DE LA MADONETA
MADONA
C. BERNARDO
C. DE CA' CORNER
C. D. CRISTO
C. LONGA
C. DE L'AGNELLA
C. D. MODENA
CORTE MARIANI
R. TERÀ PRIMO ASTORI
C. DEL TENTOR
C. OCHE
C. DE LE OCHE
CORTE DEL PRETI
C. VENZATO
FOND. RIO MARIN
C. SAN ZUANE
CALLE DE L'OGIO
5
6
7

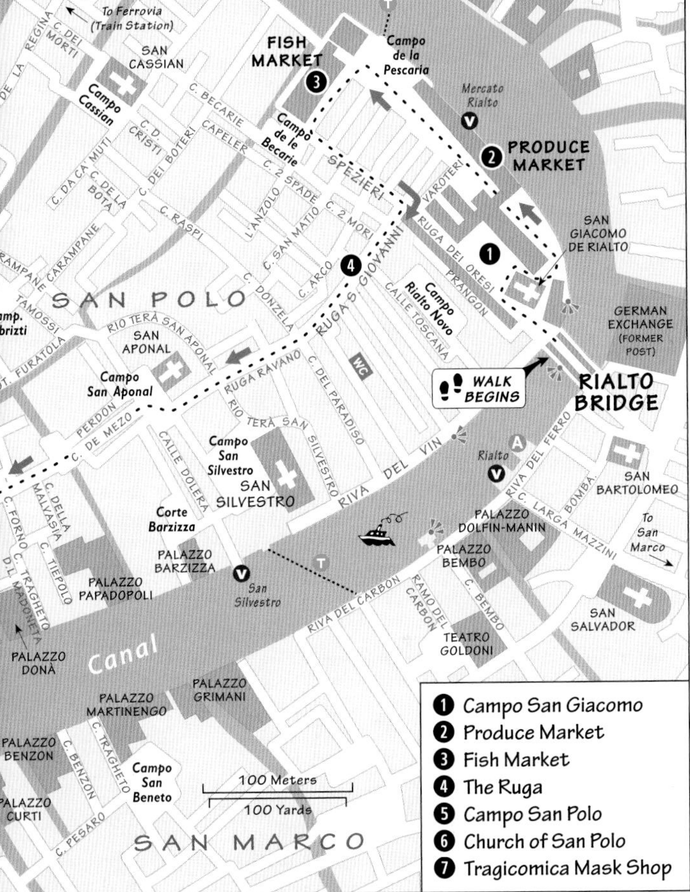
To Ferrovia (Train Station)
FISH MARKET
Campo de la Pescaria
SAN CASSIAN
Campo Cassian
Campo de le Becarie
Mercato Rialto
PRODUCE MARKET
SAN GIACOMO DE RIALTO
SAN POLO
Campo Rialto Novo
SAN APONAL
Campo San Aponal
GERMAN EXCHANGE (FORMER POST)
RIALTO BRIDGE
WALK BEGINS
Campo San Silvestro
SAN SILVESTRO
Corte Barzizza
PALAZZO BARZIZZA
PALAZZO PAPADOPOLI
San Silvestro
Rialto
SAN BARTOLOMEO
PALAZZO DOLFIN-MANIN
PALAZZO BEMBO
To San Marco
SAN SALVADOR
TEATRO GOLDONI
PALAZZO DONÀ
Canal
PALAZZO GRIMANI
PALAZZO MARTINENGO
PALAZZO BENZON
Campo San Beneto
PALAZZO CURTI
100 Meters
100 Yards
SAN MARCO
RUGA S. GIOVANNI
RUGA DEI ORESI
RUGA RAVANO
RIVA DEL VIN
RIVA DEL CARBON
RIVA DEL FERRO
SPEZIERI
C. LARGA MAZZINI
1 Campo San Giacomo
2 Produce Market
3 Fish Market
4 The Ruga
5 Campo San Polo
6 Church of San Polo
7 Tragicomica Mask Shop

At #203-204, the shop called Macelleria Equina sells horse and donkey *(asino)* meat. Continue along the canal, exploring all the produce stalls.

► *Follow your nose straight ahead (passing six alleyways on your left) until you see* Mercato del Pesce *on the brick wall of the open-air arcade that houses the...*

❸ Fish Market (Pescaria)

This market is especially vibrant and colorful in the morning. The open-air stalls have the catch of the day—Venice's culinary specialty. Find eels, scallops, crustaceans with five-inch antennae, and squid destined for tonight's risotto soaking in their own ink. This is the Venice that has existed for centuries: Workers toss boxes of fish from delivery boats while shoppers step from the *traghetto* into the action. It's a good peek at workaday Venice. Shoppers are exacting and expect to know if the fish is fresh or frozen, farmed or wild. Local fish are small and considered particularly tasty because of the high concentration of salt at this end of the Adriatic. Any salmon you see are farmed, mostly from northern Europe. It's not unusual to pay €30 per kilo (about 2.2 pounds) for the best fish.

In the courtyard between market buildings, locate a square white Istrian stone on the wall between two arches. It lists the minimum length permitted for a fish to be sold. Sardines must be seven centimeters; *peocio* (mussels) must be three centimeters. (Below that, someone has added a penis joke.)

Now turn left and walk away from the water to the end of the fish market. You're on Campo de la Becarie (Butchers' Square). Within 40 yards of here (find Calle de le Do Spade) are several of my favorite local *cicchetti*

Many Venetians shop daily in this market.

The Ruga cuts through the San Polo area.

bars (✪ see page 166). Or for fish hors d'oeuvres in the market, try the hole-in-the-wall Pronto Pesce at #319, on Calle de le Becarie o Panataria (✪ see page 170).

When you're ready, follow Ruga dei Spezieri (Spicers' Road) back toward Rialto. Along the way, pop into Antica Drogheria Mascari at #380, which hides a vast *enoteca* holding 600 different Italian wines arranged by region, plus spices and lots of gifty edibles.

▸ *At the end of Ruga dei Spezieri, you'll see a sign for* Ruga Vechia San Giovanni. *Turn right along it.*

❹ The Ruga

This busy street is lined with shops that get progressively less touristy and more practical. As you walk, you'll see fewer trinkets and more clothes, bread, shoes, watches, shampoo, and underwear.

▸ *The Ruga changes names as you go. Just keep heading basically straight (little jogs are OK). When in doubt, follow signs pointing to* Ferrovia *(train station). You'll cross one bridge, then shortly after come to...*

❺ Campo San Polo

One of the largest squares in Venice, Campo San Polo is shaped like an amphitheater, with its church tucked away in the corner (just ahead of you). Antica Birraria la Corte, a fine and family-friendly pizzeria/ristorante, is located at the far side (✪ see page 170). The square's amphitheater shape was determined by a curved canal at the base of the buildings. Today, the former canal is now a *rio terà*—a street made of landfill. A few rare trees grace the square, as do rare benches occupied by grateful locals. In the summer, bleachers and a screen are erected for open-air movies.

▸ *On the square is the...*

❻ Church of San Polo (S. Paolo Apostolo)

This church, one of the oldest in Venice, dates from the ninth century (English description at ticket desk). The wooden, boat-shaped ceiling recalls the earliest basilicas built after Rome's fall. While the church is skippable for many, art enthusiasts visit to see Tintoretto's *Last Supper,* Giovanni Battista Tiepolo's *Virgin Appearing to St. John of Nepomuk* and his son Domenico's *Stations of the Cross,* and Veronese's *Betrothal of the Virgin with Angels*.

Tintoretto's *Last Supper*—one of the less-touristed versions of this scene found in Venice

▶ *From the Church of San Polo, continue about 200 yards (following* Ferrovia *signs). You'll cross a bridge, jog left when you have to, then right, onto Calle dei Nomboli. On the right at #2800, directly across the alley from the Casa Goldoni museum, you'll see the...*

❼ Tragicomica Mask Shop

One of Venice's best mask stores, Tragicomica is also a workshop that offers a glimpse into the process of mask-making. You'll see Walter and Alessandra hard at work.

Venice's masks have always been a central feature of the celebration of Carnevale—the local pre-Lent, Mardi Gras-like blowout. (The translation of Carnevale is "goodbye to meat," referring to the lean days of Lent.) Many masks are patterned after standard characters of the theater style known as commedia dell'arte: the famous trickster Harlequin, the beautiful and cunning Columbina, the country bumpkin Pulcinella (who later evolved into the Punch of marionette shows), and the solemn, long-nosed Doctor *(dottore)*. For more on masks, ✪ see page 202.

▶ *Continuing along, cross the bridge and veer right. You'll soon see purple signs directing you to Scuola Grande di San Rocco (✪ see page 141). Follow these until you bump into the back end of the Frari Church. Here, you can step inside the cool church, take a seat at a pew, and enjoy one of the city's most delightful art experiences. For more on the church, ✪ see the Frari Church Tour chapter on page 85.*

St. Mark's to San Zaccaria Walk

San Zaccaria, one of the oldest churches in Venice, is just a few minutes on foot from St. Mark's Square. The church features a Bellini altarpiece and a submerged crypt that might be the oldest place in Venice. This short walk gets you away from the bustle of St. Mark's, includes a stroll along the waterfront, and brings you right back to where you started.

ORIENTATION

Length of This Walk: Allow about an hour for a leisurely walk (though the actual distance is short), including a stop inside the church.

Church of San Zaccaria: Free, €1 to enter crypt, €0.50 coin to illuminate Bellini's altarpiece, open Mon-Sat 10:00-12:00 & 16:00-18:00, Sun 16:00-18:00 only. Mass is held Mon-Sat at 18:30 and Sun at 10:00 and 12:00.

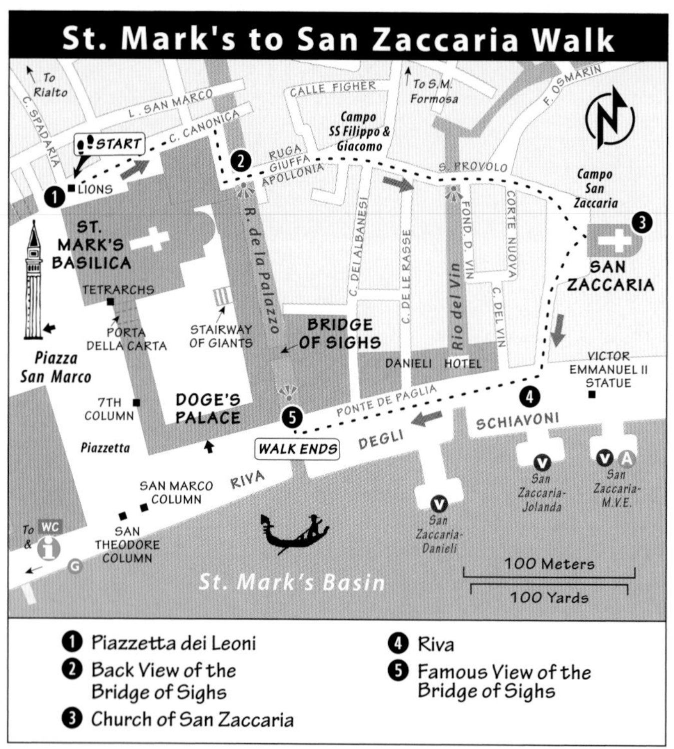

THE WALK BEGINS

❶ Start at St. Mark's—Piazzetta dei Leoni

Facing St. Mark's Basilica, start in the small square to the left of the church (Piazzetta dei Leoni), with the 18th-century stone lions that kids love to play on. See those drains in the pavement? You're standing on a cistern, fed by four drains.

Notice the nicely restored north side of the basilica, with fine 14th-century reliefs. Notice also the worship-only entrance below the exquisite Porta dei Fiori. To the left, high above the tomb of Daniele Manin, the great 19th-century Italian and Venetian patriot, is a statue with Baby Jesus on his shoulder. That's St. Christopher, patron saint of us travelers.

The white Neoclassical building at the far east end of the square (built in 1834, when Venice was under Austrian rule) houses the offices of Venice's "patriarch," the special title given to the local bishop. In the 1950s, this is where the future Pope John XXIII presided as Venice's patriarch and cardinal. The popular, warm-hearted cardinal went on to become the "Sixties Pope," who oversaw major reforms in the Catholic Church (Vatican II). You'll see a plaque dedicated to "Papa Giovanni XXIII," the man locals still refer to as "Il Papa Buono"—the good pope.

▸ *Head east along Calle de la Canonica, past a fine English-language bookstore, circling behind the basilica. Passing some of the sexiest gondoliers in town, you'll reach a bridge with a...*

❷ View of the Bridge of Sighs

This lesser-known view of the Bridge of Sighs also lets you see the tourists

The lions of Piazzetta dei Leoni

Bridge of Sighs with tourists in distance

who are ogling it, with cameras cocked. You can just see the Lady Justice relief (centered above the windows), with her sword and scales—a reminder that the courts were to the right and the prison to the left.

On the near side of the bridge is a common sight in neighborhood Venice: a street-side altarpiece and donation box. As the street signs tell you, the bridge you're on marks the boundary between two traditional neighborhoods, the *sestiere* (district) of San Marco and that of Castello. Throughout this walk, you'll pass relics of a fast-fading era: newspaper stands, public telephones, and a 24-hour cigarette vending machine.

▸ *Continue east. You'll cross another bridge with a view of a "Modern Bridge of Sighs," which connects two wings of the exclusive Danieli Hotel. Continue east another 50 yards, through the Gothic gate of what was once a cloistered Benedictine convent, and into a square where you see the...*

❸ Church of San Zaccaria

Back in the ninth century, when Venice was just a collection of wooden houses and before there was a St. Mark's Basilica, a stone church and convent stood here. This is where the doges worshipped, public spectacles occurred, and sacred relics were kept. Today's structure dates mostly from the 15th century.

The tall facade by Mauro Codussi (who also did the Clock Tower in St. Mark's Square) and others is early Renaissance. The "vertical" effect produced by the four support pillars that rise up to an arched crown is tempered by the horizontal, many-layered stories and curved shoulders.

In the northwest corner of Campo San Zaccaria (near where you entered) is a plaque from 1620 listing all the things that were prohibited "in this square" *(in questo campo),* including games, obscenities, dishonesty, and robbery, all "under grave penalty" *(sotto gravis pene).*

▸ *Enter the church. The second chapel on the right holds the...*

Body of Zechariah (S. Zaccaria)

Of the two bodies in the chapel, the lower one in the glass case is the reputed body of Zechariah, the father of John the Baptist. Back when mortal remains were venerated and thought to bring miracles to the faithful, Venice was proud to own the bones of St. Zechariah ("San Zaccaria," also known as Zacharias).

Bellini's *Madonna* (center) sits in a fake niche that appears to be an extension of the church.

► *The church is blessed with fine art. On the opposite side of the nave (second chapel on the left), you'll find...*

Giovanni Bellini—*Madonna and Child with Saints* (1505)

Mary and the baby, under a pavilion, are surrounded by various saints interacting in a so-called *Sacra Conversazione* (holy conversation), which in this painting is more like a quiet meditation. The saints' mood is melancholy, with lidded eyes and downturned faces. A violinist angel plays a sad solo at Mary's feet.

This is one of the last of Bellini's paintings in the *sacra conversazione* formula, the newer type of altarpiece that liberated the Virgin, Child, and saints from the separate cells of the older triptych style. Compare this to his other variations on this theme in the Accademia (✪ see page 135) and Frari Church (✪ see the Frari Church Tour). The life-size saints stand in an imaginary extension of the church—the pavilion's painted columns match those of the real church. We see a glimpse of trees and a cloudy sky beyond. Bellini establishes a 3-D effect using floor tiles. The four saints pose symmetrically, and there's a harmony in the big blocks of richly colored robes—blue, green, red, white, and yellow. A cool white light envelops the whole scene, creating a holy ambience.

The ever-innovative Bellini was productive until the end of his long life—he painted this masterpiece at age 75. The German artist Albrecht Dürer said of him: "He is very old, and still he is the best painter of them all."

► *On the right-hand side of the nave is the entrance (€1 entry fee) to the...*

Crypt

Before you descend into the crypt, the first room (Chapel of Sant'Atanasio) contains **Tintoretto's *Birth of John the Baptist*** (c. 1560s, on the altar), which tells the backstory of Zechariah. In the background, old Zechariah's wife, Elizabeth, props herself up in bed while nurses hold and coo over her newborn son, little John the Baptist. The birth was a miracle, as she was past childbearing age. On the far right, Zechariah—the star of this church—witnesses the heavens opening up, bringing this miracle to earth.

The five **gold thrones** (displayed in this room or one of the next rooms) were once seats for doges. Every Easter, the current doge would walk from St. Mark's Square to this religious center and thank the nuns of San Zaccaria for giving the land for the square.

The small next room contains religious objects as well as an engraving of the doge parading into Campo San Zaccaria.

Next comes the Chapel of San Tarasio, dominated by an impressive 15th-century prickly gold altarpiece by Antonio Vivarini. The predella (seven small scenes beneath the altarpiece) may be by Paolo Veneziano, the 14th-century grandfather of Venetian painting. Look down through glass in the floor to see the 12th-century mosaic floor from the original church. In fact, these rooms were parts of the earlier churches.

Finally, go downstairs to the **crypt**—the foundation of a church built in the 10th century. The crypt is low and the water table high, so the room is often flooded, submerging the bases of the columns. Venice has battled rising water levels since the fifth century. It's a weird experience, calling up echoes of the Dark Ages.

Flooding (the *acqua alta)* affects parts of Venice about 100 times a year, usually in winter. It occurs when an unusually high tide combines with strong sirocco winds from Africa that push the water toward Venice, causing a surging storm tide. In 2003, the city began construction on a system of underwater gates near the Lido, hoping to block the tidal surge. Still, some worry that—with global warming and rising sea levels—Venice's battle against the sea is not over, and the water seems to be winning.

▸ *Emerge from the Church of San Zaccaria into the small campo. Before leaving the campo, check out the small art gallery on the left (free), the thirst-quenching water fountain, and the pink Carabinieri police station (a former convent), marked by the Italian flag. Then exit the square at the far end, and head south—past that cigarette machine—until you pop out at the waterfront, right on the...*

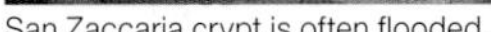
San Zaccaria crypt is often flooded.

Grand hotels along the Riva promenade

❹ Riva

The waterfront promenade known as the "Riva" was built not for tourists but as part of the port of San Marco. Until recently, big ships tied up here. Today it's lined with some of the town's finest hotels and provides a great view of the Church of San Giorgio Maggiore (one stop away on vaporetto #2).

The big equestrian monument depicts Victor Emmanuel II, who helped lead Italy to unification and became the country's first king in 1861. Beyond that (over the bridge) is the four-columned La Pietà Church, where Antonio Vivaldi once directed the music. Five bridges farther along (not visible from here) are the Arsenale and Naval Museum (✪ described on page 147).

The Riva is lined with many of Venice's most famous luxury hotels. For a peek at the *most* famous and luxurious, turn right, cross over one bridge, and nip into the **Danieli Hotel.** Tuck in your shirt, stand tall and aristocratic, and (with all the confidence of a guest) be swept by the revolving door into the sumptuous interior of what was once the Gothic Palazzo Dandolo. As you check out the Danieli's restaurant menu (that's why you're there, isn't it?), admire the lobby, the old-style chandeliers, water-taxi drive-up entrance, and the occasional celebrity. Since 1820, the Neo-Gothic Danieli has been Venice's most exclusive hotel. Exquisite as all this is, it still gets flooded routinely in the winter.

▸ *Facing the water, turn right and head west toward St. Mark's Square. The commotion atop a little bridge marks the...*

❺ Famous View of the Bridge of Sighs

The Bridge of Sighs connects the Doge's Palace (left) with the doge's prison (right). The bridge let justice be very swift indeed, as convicted criminals could, upon sentencing, be escorted directly from the palace's secretive courtroom to prison, without being seen in public.

Notice the beefy bars on the prison. There were no windows, so throughout the year it would alternate between very hot and very cold. The top floor, below the lead roof, was nicknamed "The Oven." While designed for 300 people, the prison routinely held 500.

From this historic bridge (according to romantic legend), prisoners took one last look at Venice before entering the dark and unpleasant prisons. And sighed. Lord Byron picked up on the legend in the early 1800s and gave the bridge its famous nickname, making this sad little span a big stop on the Grand Tour. Look high up on your left—while that rogue Casanova wrote of the bridge in his memoirs, he was actually imprisoned here in the Doge's Palace.

Nowadays, while the bridge is a human traffic jam of gawking tourists during the day, it remains breathtakingly romantic in the lonely late-night hours.

▶ *Your tour's over. (By the way, if you need some quick cash, this is a great place to pick a pocket. There's lots of bumping, and everyone's distracted...)*

Sights

Venice's greatest sight is the city itself. As well as seeing world-class museums and buildings, make time to wander narrow lanes, linger over a meal, glide through the canals on a gondola, or enjoy evening magic on St. Mark's Square.

Remember that some of Venice's biggest sights (marked with a ✪) are described in much more detail in the individual walks and tours chapters. Also, one of Venice's most unique "sights"—a gondola ride—is covered on ✪ page 204.

Use my sightseeing tips to avoid crowds and lines at St. Mark's Square, the Basilica, and the Doge's Palace. A Museum Pass may save you a little money. For more sightseeing tips, ✪ see the Practicalities chapter (page 185).

Venice
To Mestre & Mainland
To Ghetto & Guglie Bridge
SAN GEREMIA
SAN MARCUOLA
SANTA LUCIA STATION (FERROVIA)
LISTA DI SPAGNA
Grand Canal
SCALZI
SAN ZAN DEGOLÀ
BEMBO
To Tronchetto & Mainland
SAN SIMEONE GRANDE
SCALZI BRIDGE
To Stazione Marittima (Main Cruise Dock) & Tronchetto (Parking)
SAN SIMEONE PICCOLO
SAN GIACOMO
PALAZZO MOCENIGO
SANTA CROCE
CALATRAVA BRIDGE
GARAGE
PEOPLE MOVER
Piazzale Roma
BUS STATION
CA' AMAI
SAN NICOLO DA TOLENTINO
TINTORETTO
Campo San Stin
Campo San Polo
SAN POLO
SAN ROCCO
FRARI
SAONERI
SCUOLA SAN ROCCO
SAN TOMÀ
SAN PANTALON
C. LARGA FOSCARI
SANTA MARGARITA
CA' FOSCARI
Campo Santa Margarita
CA' REZZONICO
PALAZZO GRASSI
SANTA MARIA DEI CARMINI
Campo San Barnaba
SAN BARNABA
Campo San Stefano
OGNISSANTI
DORSODURO
ACCADEMIA BRIDGE
TOLETTA
CORFU
SANTA MARTA CRUISE DOCK
SAN TROVASO
ACCADEMIA GALLERY
WC
AGNESE
SAN BASILIO CRUISE DOCK
FOND. ZATTERE AL PONTE LONGO
RIO TERA FOSCARINI
200 Meters
200 Yards
Giudecca Canal
ZATTERE

SANTA MARIA MADALENA
STRADA
SAN FELICE
SAN STAE
CA' D'ORO
CA' PESARO
NOVA
SANTI APOSTOLI
Campo Santi Apostoli
FONDAMENTE NOVE
To San Michele, Murano, Burano & Torcello
Lagoon
FOND. DEI MENDICANTI
HOSPITAL
SAN CANZIAN
FISH MARKET
Campo de le Becarie
SAN CASSIAN
PRODUCE MARKET
POLO
RUGA V. SAN GIO.
RIALTO BRIDGE
Campo San Bartolomeo
COLLEONI STATUE
SANTI GIOVANNI E PAOLO (SAN ZANIPOLO)
Campo San Aponal
SAN SILVESTRO
RIVA DEL VIN
SAN LIO
SAL. SAN LIO
Campo Santa Maria Formosa
SAN LORENZO
2 APRILE
SANTA MARIA FAVA
TEATRO GOLDONI
SAN SALVADOR
MERCERIE
SCUOLA DALMATIA
CASTELLO
Campo San Luca
SAN ZULIAN
Campo Manin
FABBRI
MANDOLA
SCALA CONTARINI DEL BOVOLO
Campo S. Anzolo
ST. MARK'S
BRIDGE OF SIGHS
SAN ZACCARIA
LA PIETA
LA FENICE OPERA HOUSE
CORRER MUSEUM
Piazza San Marco
CAMPANILE
RIVA DEGLI SCHIAVONI
WC
SAN MARCO
DOGE'S PALACE
To Public Gardens & Santa Elena
Campo San Maurizio
22 MARZO
SAN MOISÈ
Campo Santa Maria Zobenigo
SAN MARCO & SAN THEODORE COLUMNS
Grand Canal
St. Mark's Basin
LA SALUTE
PUNTA DELLA DOGANA MUSEUM (CUSTOMS HOUSE)
To Lido
PEGGY GUGGENHEIM COLLECTION
SAN GIORGIO MAGGIORE
SPIRITO SANTO
SAN GIORGIO

And finally, remember that—although Venice can be crowded and stressful—the city itself prides itself on its gentility and grace under pressure. Be flexible.

Near St. Mark's Square

Venice's historic heart stretches north from St. Mark's Square to the Rialto Bridge, east to the Church of San Zaccaria, and west to La Fenice Opera House. The handiest vaporetto stops are San Marco-Vallaresso (100 yards west of the square) and the four docks of San Zaccaria (150 yards east of the square).

This area can be very crowded at midday (10:00-17:00), so try to do your sightseeing here early or late. It's another world altogether at night—lantern-lit magic under a ceiling of stars.

Use two of my walks to lace together sights in this area:

✪ St. Mark's to Rialto Loop Walk
✪ St. Mark's to San Zaccaria Walk

▲▲▲St. Mark's Square (Piazza San Marco)

This grand square is surrounded by splashy, historic buildings and music-filled cafés. By day it's a world of pigeons and tourists. At night, it's your private rendezvous with the romantic Venetian past.

✪ See the St. Mark's Square Tour chapter.

▲▲▲St. Mark's Basilica (Basilica di San Marco)

This one-of-a-kind church is adorned with Byzantine-style domes outside and gold mosaics inside. St. Mark's bones lie under the altar. Three separate museums in the church show off rare treasures, a Golden Altarpiece, and the four bronze horse statues.

✪ See the St. Mark's Basilica Tour chapter.

▲▲▲Doge's Palace (Palazzo Ducale)

The seat of the Venetian government and home of its ruling duke (the doge), this was the most powerful half-acre in Europe for 400 years. Walk through (mostly sparse) rooms wallpapered by great Venetian painters, learn about Venetian government, and finish by crossing the Bridge of Sighs into the notorious prison.

✪ See the Doge's Palace Tour chapter.

Sightseeing in the St. Mark's Square area is especially crowded at midday.

▲Bridge of Sighs

This much-photographed bridge connects the Doge's Palace with the prison. Supposedly, a condemned man would cross this bridge, take one last look at the glory of Venice, and sigh. Though overhyped, the Bridge of Sighs is undeniably tingle-worthy, especially after dark.

For more on the bridge, ✪ see page 119 of the St. Mark's to San Zaccaria Walk chapter and ✪ page 82 of the Doge's Palace Tour chapter.

▲▲Correr Museum (Museo Correr)

A doge's hat, gleaming statues by Canova, and paintings by the illustrious Bellini family—for some people, that's a major museum; for others, an historical bore. This uncrowded museum gives a good overview of Venetian history and art, is a quiet refuge with views over tourist-crowded St. Mark's Square, and is included anyway in your Doge's Palace ticket.

The first few rooms highlight Venice's greatest homegrown sculptor, Antonio Canova (1757-1822). He created high-polished, slender, beautiful figures—often arranged in groups that are interesting from many angles—and combined the cool lines of classicism with the romantic sentiment of Venice. In *Orpheus and Eurydice* (1775-1776), the Greek poet is leading his beloved back from hell when she's suddenly tugged backward. Orpheus smacks his forehead in horror, but he must continue on, leaving an empty space between them.

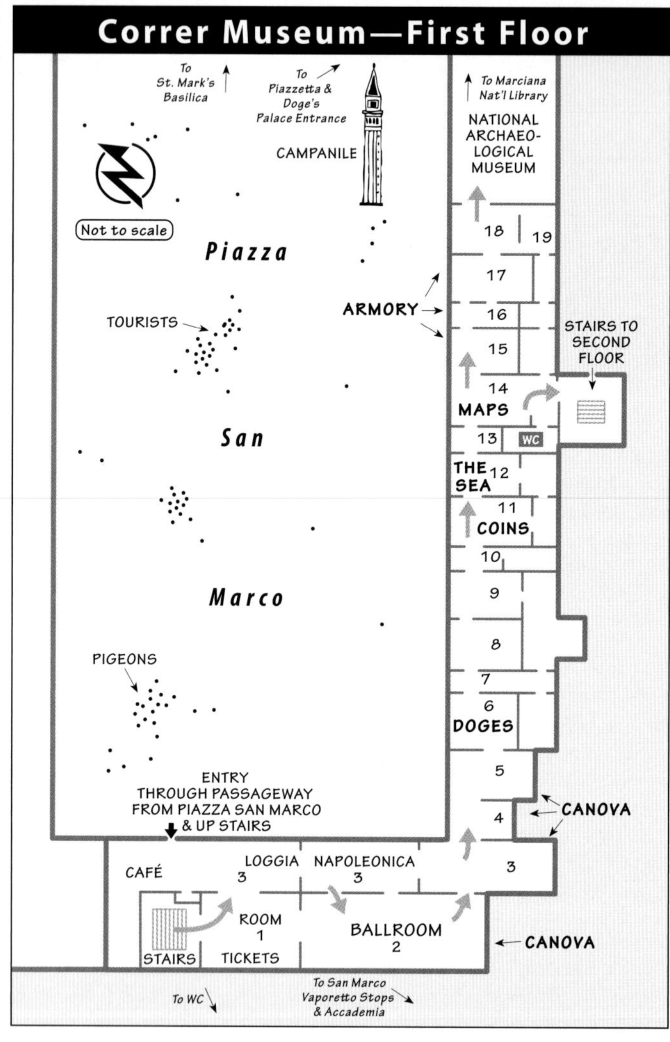

Correr Museum—First Floor
To St. Mark's Basilica
To Piazzetta & Doge's Palace Entrance
CAMPANILE
To Marciana Nat'l Library
NATIONAL ARCHAEO-LOGICAL MUSEUM
Not to scale
Piazza
San
Marco
TOURISTS
PIGEONS
ARMORY
18
19
17
16
15
14
MAPS
STAIRS TO SECOND FLOOR
13
WC
THE SEA 12
11
COINS
10
9
8
7
6
DOGES
5
4
CANOVA
3
ENTRY THROUGH PASSAGEWAY FROM PIAZZA SAN MARCO & UP STAIRS
CAFÉ
LOGGIA 3
NAPOLEONICA 3
ROOM 1
BALLROOM 2
CANOVA
STAIRS
TICKETS
To WC
To San Marco Vaporetto Stops & Accademia

In Rooms 6-14, the world of the doges comes to life with doge portraits and a single-horned doge cap. Room 11 has a Venetian ducat—99 percent pure gold, worth about $1,000—that was once Europe's strongest currency. Room 12 displays models of the sleek, oar- and wind-powered warships that ruled the waves. The Arsenale (Room 13) could crank out a galley a day. Room 14's old maps illustrate how little the city has changed—find your hotel on Barbari's big map from 1500.

Rooms 15-18 display armor and weapons. You can detour into the National Archaeological Museum (so-so classical statues) and the impressive Marciana National Library (globes, manuscripts, and ceiling paintings), both included with admission.

The second floor traces Venetian painting from golden Byzantine icons to Florentine-inspired 3-D to Venice's trademark soft-focus beauty. Room 36 highlights the family that single-handedly brought Venetian painting into the Renaissance—the Bellinis. The famous Giovanni Bellini (c. 1430-1516) specialized in forever-young, pastel-colored Virgins holding rosy-cheeked Baby Jesuses. Finally, in Room 38, Carpaccio's well-known *Two Venetian Gentlewomen* (c. 1490) are surrounded by exotic pets and amusements, absentmindedly awaiting their menfolk. Fascinating stuff, but my eyes—like theirs—are starting to glaze...

▶ *€16 combo-ticket also includes the Doge's Palace. Open daily April-Oct 10:00-19:00, Nov-March 10:00-17:00, last entry one hour before closing. No photos; café has some view tables. Enter at the far end of the square. Tel. 041-240-5211, http://correr.visitmuve.it.*

▲Campanile (Campanile di San Marco)

This dramatic bell tower replaced a shorter tower, part of the original fortress that guarded the entry of the Grand Canal. That tower crumbled into a pile of bricks in 1902, a thousand years after it was built. Today you'll see construction work being done to strengthen the base of the rebuilt tower. Ride the elevator 325 feet up for the best view in Venice (especially at sunset). For an ear-shattering experience, be on top when the bells ring. The golden archangel Gabriel at the top always faces into the wind. Beat the crowds and enjoy the crisp morning air at 9:00 or the cool evening breeze at 18:00.

▶ *€8. Open daily Easter-June and Oct 9:00-19:00, July-Sept 9:00-21:00, Nov-Easter 9:30-16:45. Tel. 041-522-4064, www.basilicasanmarco.it.*

Two of Venice's best views are from the towers of St. Mark's (left) and San Giorgio (right).

For more on the Campanile, ✪ see page 39 of the St. Mark's Square Tour chapter.

La Fenice Opera House (Gran Teatro alla Fenice)

For 200 years, great operas and famous divas debuted here, in one of Europe's most famous opera houses. Then in 1996, an arson fire completely gutted the theater. But La Fenice ("The Phoenix") has risen from the ashes. To see the results at their most glorious, attend an evening performance. The theater box office is open daily 9:30-18:00 (tel. 041-2424, www.teatrolafenice.it).

You can also tour the opera house during the day. All you really see is the theater itself; there's no "backstage" tour of dressing rooms, or an opera museum. However, the auditorium, ringed with box seats, is impressive: pastel blue with sparkling gold filigree, muses depicted on the ceiling, and a starburst chandelier.

For more on the opera house, ✪ see page 101 of the St. Mark's to Rialto Loop Walk chapter.

▸ *€8 tour includes dry audioguide. Generally open daily 9:30-13:30, but can vary wildly, depending on the performance schedule—to confirm, call box office number above or check www.festfenice.com. La Fenice is on Campo San Fantin, 100 yards west of St. Mark's Square.*

▲San Giorgio Maggiore

This is the dreamy church-topped island you can see across the water from St. Mark's Square. It's worth a boat ride there for Palladio's architecture, Tintoretto's *Last Supper,* bell-tower views, and a pleasant escape from tourist-mobbed St. Mark's Square.

Best Views

- The soaring Campanile on St. Mark's Square
- The balcony of St. Mark's Basilica in the San Marco Museum
- Rialto Bridge, with a free, expansive view of the Grand Canal, along with a cooling breeze
- Accademia Bridge, overlooking the Grand Canal and dome of La Salute Church
- The Church of San Giorgio Maggiore's bell tower, with views back at downtown Venice and all around the lagoon
- The swanky bar of the Molino Stucky Hilton Hotel on Giudecca Island (free shuttle boat leaves from near the San Zaccaria-M.V.E. vaporetto dock)

The facade—with its four tall columns topped by a triangular pediment—looks like a Greek temple. The architect Andrea Palladio (1508-1580), with his classical style, was hugely influential on generations of architects in England and America. The bell tower echoes the Campanile in St. Mark's Square.

The interior is white and well-lit by clear glass, with a clarity and mathematical perfection that exudes the classical world.

On the wall to the right of the altar is a *Last Supper* (1592-1594) by Tintoretto. The table stretches diagonally away on a tiled floor, drawing us in. The scene is crowded—servants and cats mingle with wispy angels—and a blazing lamp radiates supernatural light. Your eyes go straight to a well-lit Christ, serving his faithful with both hands. In Tintoretto's *Manna from Heaven,* on the opposite wall, hungry Israelites gather God's heaven-sent bread.

Take the elevator up the bell tower for a stunning view. Looking north is Venice's famous skyline. Facing east across the lagoon, find the long, narrow island of Lido. Facing west is the nearby island of Giudecca. The old flour mill at the far end is now a Hilton Hotel.

Finally, looking up, you see the bells that chime the hours. You're warned.

▸ *Free entry to church, €3 for bell tower. Open May-Sept Mon-Sat 9:30-12:30 & 14:30-18:00, Sun 8:30-11:00 & 14:30-18:00; Oct-April until*

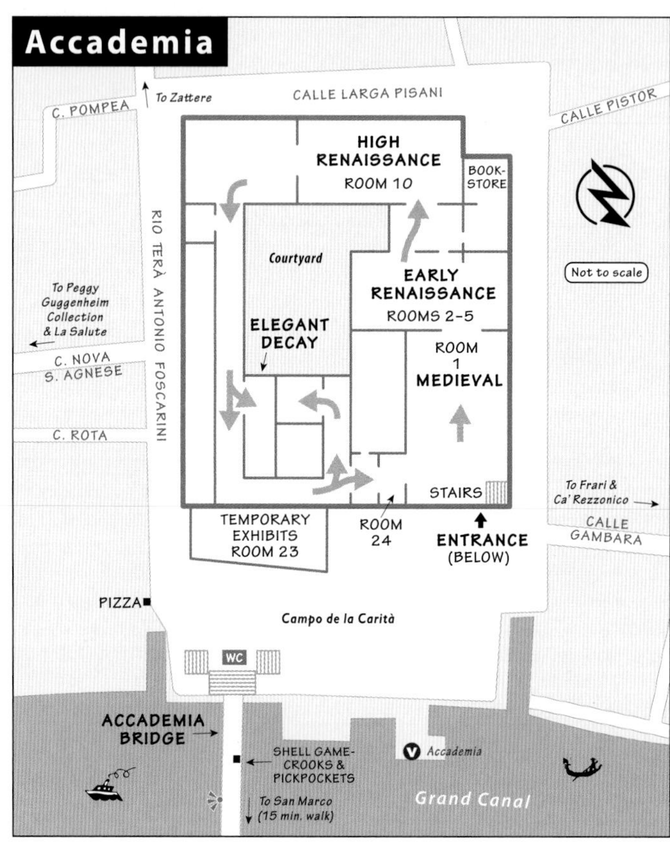

17:00. The bell tower elevator runs from 30 minutes after the church opens until 30 minutes before closing. Bell tower can get crowded at midday. An untouristed harborside café is 150 yards around the left of the church. Get to San Giorgio Maggiore via a five-minute ride on vaporetto #2 from the San Zaccaria-M.V.E dock (€4, direction: Tronchetto, ticket valid one hour).

Accademia and Dorsoduro

The Accademia Bridge, one of the city's key landmarks, is the gateway to the Dorsoduro neighborhood. The Dorsoduro is somewhat less touristed, more intimate, and filled with some of Venice's best art venues. The bridge is a ten-minute walk from St. Mark's Square (vaporetto: Accademia or Zattere).

▲▲Accademia (Galleria dell'Accademia)

Venice's top art museum is a chronological overview of artists whose colorful works are found all over town.

Start with medieval altarpieces in Room 1, whose gold-leaf backgrounds and "icon"-ic faces show Venice's Byzantine roots. In Room 2, Giovanni Bellini's *Enthroned Madonna with Child* (c. 1480) brings Mary down from her golden heaven into the same spacious, 3-D world we inhabit. Bellini created Madonnas with creamy complexions and soft outlines, bathed in his trademark golden haze. In Giorgione's *The Tempest* (c. 1505, Room 4), the serene landscape is about to be shattered by an approaching storm, the center of the composition.

Room 10 features Venetian art at its peak. Veronese's enormous *Feast in the House of Levi* (1573) fills your field of vision with a Venetian party. Everyone's dressed to kill, servants bring on the food, and dogs roam free. The bawdy work was originally called the *Last Supper*, until Veronese was hauled before the Inquisition. Rather than change the painting, he just changed the title.

Veronese's colorful *Feast in the House of Levi* captures Venice's Renaissance-era joie de vivre.

Titian painted his *Pietà* (c. 1573) to hang over his own tomb. The canvas is dark and somber, a mess of rough, proto-"Impressionist" brushstrokes. A dramatic line of motion sweeps up diagonally, culminating in Mary Magdalene, who flings her arm and howls. The kneeling old man is Titian himself. In Tintoretto's *The Removal of St. Mark's Body* (1562-1566), Venetian merchants whisk away the body of St. Mark, seemingly bringing it out the picture frame and into our world.

Rooms 11 and beyond chronicle Venice's elegant years of decline. G. B. Tiepolo (*Discovery of the True Cross,* c. 1745) took Venice's colorful, theatrical style and plastered it on the ceilings of Europe's Baroque palaces. As Venice became Europe's number-one tourist attraction, Venetian artists painted "postcard" scenes for wealthy visitors. Canaletto gave Venice a sharp-focus, wide-lens, camera's-eye perspective, while Guardi sweetened up the city with an Impressionistic haze of messy brushwork.

On your way out (Room 24), don't miss Titian's colorful *Presentation of the Virgin* (1534-1538). Titian painted the work especially for this room; notice how the door on the left, added later, cuts into the masterpiece. The painting sums up the style of the Venetian Renaissance: bright colors, big canvases, 3-D realism, Renaissance architecture, and colorful scenes of everyday life in Venice. Now go out into Venice and enjoy the real thing.

► *€11. Open Mon 8:15-14:00, Tue-Sun 8:15-19:15, last entry 45 minutes before closing. Visit early or late to miss the crowds. Dull audioguide-€5. No photos. Renovation is ongoing, so be flexible. Located next to Accademia Bridge. Tel. 041-522-2247, www.gallerieaccademia.org.*

▲▲Peggy Guggenheim Collection

One of Europe's best early 20th-century modern art museums is housed in the American heiress' former retirement palazzo. Visitors get a glimpse into Peggy's fascinating life, her home, and art by artists she knew personally as friend, lover, and patron.

In 1920, young Peggy Guggenheim (1898-1979) traveled to Paris, where she lived a bohemian life with avant-garde artists. In the 1930s, her friend Marcel Duchamp and boyfriend Samuel *(Waiting for Godot)* Beckett encouraged her to collect modern art. She spent the war years in America, where her New York art gallery inspired a generation. When her memoirs were published, Peggy became a celebrity. She was unconventional and larger than life, with a succession of lovers that made her a female Casanova.

Peggy Guggenheim Collection

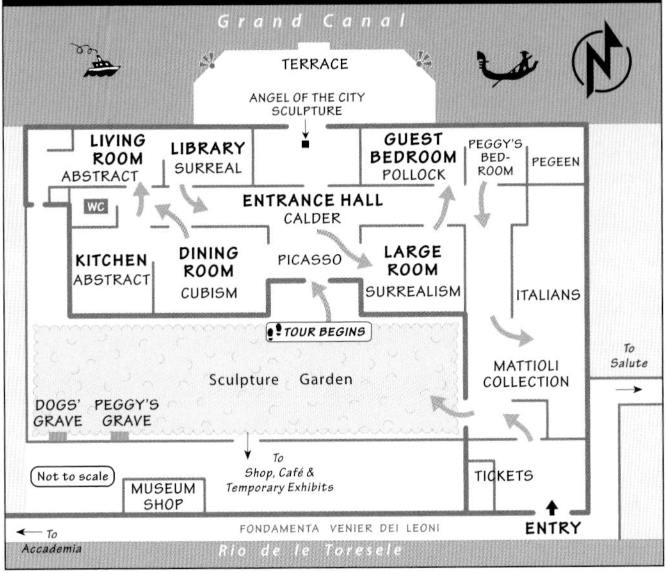

In 1948, Peggy came "home" to Venice, renovating this small palazzo on the Grand Canal. It became a mecca for "Moderns," from composer Igor Stravinsky to actor Marlon Brando to writer Truman Capote to Beatle John Lennon and (Peggy's travel buddy) Yoko Ono.

Today, though most of the furniture is gone, it's easy to get a feel for the place as Peggy's home. The rooms have much the same art as hung here in Peggy's day (as old photos attest). In the entrance hall, you can picture Peggy greeting her guests—standing under the Calder mobile, flanked by Picasso paintings, holding her yapping dogs, and wearing her Mondrian-print dress and "Catwoman" sunglasses. In the dining room, the wood table is original. The bedroom displays the silver headboard by Calder that originally adorned Peggy's bed. Nearby are childlike paintings done by Peggy's daughter, Pegeen.

The collection's strength is in Abstract, Surrealist, and Abstract

Expressionist works. Highlights include Picasso's art-shattering Cubist masterpiece, *The Poet.* Picasso's *On the Beach* was Peggy's favorite painting. Marcel Duchamp's *Nude* is a blurred self-portrait of Peggy's mentor. Abstract works by Kandinsky and Mondrian were highly influential on America's young Abstract Expressionists. You'll see Surrealist works by Yves Tanguy (Peggy's boyfriend) and Max Ernst (her husband). In Ernst's *The Antipope,* the horse-headed nude in red is supposedly a portrait of Peggy. Other Surrealist highlights include an ominous suburban scene by Magritte and a photorealistic dreamscape by Dalí. Jackson Pollock—aka "Jack the Dripper"—became famous largely thanks to Peggy's support. Outside in the sculpture garden, find the graves of Peggy's Lhasa Apso dogs—"Here Lie My Beloved Babies"—with Peggy's ashes buried humbly alongside.

End your visit on the terrace, where Peggy would sip her morning coffee with this incredible view. The exuberant equestrian statue by Marini faces the Grand Canal, spreads his arms wide, and tosses his head back in sheer joy, with an eternal hard-on for the city of Venice.

► *€12, usually includes temporary exhibits. Open Wed-Mon 10:00-18:00, closed Tue. Audioguide-€7. No photos inside, pricey café, art galleries nearby. Easy to reach by vaporetto (Accademia or Salute) or* traghetto. *Tel. 041-240-5411, www.guggenheim-venice.it.*

▲La Salute Church (Santa Maria della Salute)

Where the Grand Canal opens up into the lagoon stands one of Venice's most distinctive landmarks. The white stone church has a steep, crown-shaped dome that rises above an octagonal structure. It's encrusted with

Exuberant modern art at the Guggenheim

La Salute—impressive church, fine art

Baroque scrolls and 125 statues, topped by the Virgin Mary. The church was dedicated to her—Santa Maria della Salute (Our Lady of Health)—by grateful survivors of the 1630 plague.

The architect, Baldassare Longhena (1598-1682), remade Venice in the Baroque style, and La Salute was his crowning achievement. He sank countless pilings (locals claim over a million) into the sandy soil to help support the mammoth dome.

Inside, the church has a bright, healthy glow, well-lit from clear glass windows. The nave is circular, surrounded by chapels. At the main altar, marble statues tell the church's story: The Virgin (center) is approached for help by a kneeling, humble Lady Venice (left). Mary shows compassion and sends an angel baby (right) to drive away Old Lady Plague.

Artwork in the church includes three paintings by Luca Giordano (in the three side chapels to the right of the altar), Titian's *Pentecost* (the chapel to the left of the altar), and works by Tintoretto and Titian in the (not always open) Sacristy.

▶ *Free entry to church, €3 for Sacristy. Open daily 9:00-12:00 & 15:00-17:30. It's a 10-minute walk from the Accademia Bridge, or reach by vaporetto (Salute stop) or* traghetto. *Service with organ music Mon-Fri at 15:30 and Sun at 11:45. No flash photos. Tel. 041-241-1018, www.seminariovenezia.it.*

▲Ca' Rezzonico (Museum of 18th-Century Venice)

Venice in the 1700s was the playground for Europe's aristocrats. Today, the Ca' Rezzonico (ret-ZON-ee-koh)—a palazzo on the Grand Canal—is the best place to experience the luxury-loving spirit of that decadent century. Wander under ceilings by Tiepolo and among Rococo furnishings, enjoying views of the canal and paintings by Guardi, Canaletto, and Longhi.

Start on the first floor, in the 5,600-square-foot Room 1, and imagine a glittering party of masked and powder-wigged dandies, beneath a trompe l'oeil ceiling. Room 2 has the first of several ceiling frescoes by Venice's own G. B. Tiepolo (1696-1770), the renowned decorator of Europe's palaces. Four white horses pull a chariot carrying Rezzonico family newlyweds. Tiepolo's zero-gravity scenes, bright colors, classical motifs, and sheer unbridled imagination made his frescoes blend seamlessly with ornate Rococo furniture. Room 4 has luminous pastel portraits and miniatures by the celebrated Venetian, Rosalba Carriera (1675-1757). Room 5 is decorated with Rococo tapestries, a mirror, and a cabinet door showing an opium smoker on his own little island paradise. Room 6, the Throne Room, has views over the Grand Canal and a Tiepolo ceiling that blows a hole in the roof, allowing angels to descend to honor old man Rezzonico. As the gang returns to heaven, the lady in blue leaves her leg dangling over the "edge" of the fake oval.

Rooms 7-12 have more period furniture, the carved-wood fantasies of Andrea Brustolon (Room 11), and a sedan chair (Room 12) to transport the rich in red-velvet luxury.

The second floor features paintings. Room 13 has two "postcard" scenes of Venice by Canaletto. With a wide-angle lens and photographic clarity, he captures the canals, palaces, and hanging laundry of the city he loved. In Room 14, find scenes (by Tiepolo's son) of the hook-nosed bumpkin Pulcinella partying at Carnevale. Room 17 has a canvas by Guardi where men (wearing the traditional mask, three-cornered hat, and cowl) hit on masked prostitutes. As the 1700s was coming to an end, the decadent gaiety of Venice was giving way to modern democracy and the Industrial Age. Room 18 presents a startling contrast: Tiepolo's lush Rococo fantasy overhead and the straightforward scenes of everyday life by Pietro Longhi (1702-1785).

▸ *€8. Open April-Oct Wed-Mon 10:00-18:00, Nov-March Wed-Mon 10:00-17:00, closed Tue year-round; ticket office closes one hour before museum does. Audioguide-€4. Café, no photos, bag check required and free. Located at Ca' Rezzonico vaporetto stop, a 10-minute walk northwest of Accademia Bridge. Tel. 041-241-0100, http://carezzonico.visitmuve.it.*

▲Punta della Dogana

This museum of contemporary art, housed in the former Customs House at the end of the Grand Canal, features cutting-edge 21st-century art in spacious rooms. This isn't Picasso and Matisse, or even Pollock and Warhol—those guys are ancient history. But if you're into the likes of Jeff Koons, Cy Twombly, Rachel Whiteread, and a host of newer artists, the museum is world-class. The displays change completely about every year, drawn from the museum's large collection. In fact, the art spreads over two locations—the triangular Customs House and Palazzo Grassi (across the Grand Canal, vaporetto: San Samuele).

▸ *€15 for one locale, €20 for both. Open Wed-Mon 10:00-19:00, closed Tue, last entry one hour before closing. Audioguide-€5 or €8 for both museums. Small café. Reach the Punta by vaporetto (Salute stop) or the*

Dogana traghetto *from near St. Mark's Square. Tel. 199-139-139, www .palazzograssi.it.*

Rialto

Rialto is the center of the Venice map and a major stop for vaporetto lines 1 and 2. The bridge is surrounded by tourist services and restaurants with great views and mediocre food. The east side of the bridge—along the busy Mercerie street to St. Mark's Square—is very touristy. The west leads into the less-touristed San Polo neighborhood, with the Frari Church and Scuola San Rocco. North of Rialto, along the Grand Canal, lie a few lesser sights (Ca' Pesaro, Palazzo Mocenigo), easily reached by vaporetto.

▲▲▲Rialto Bridge

One of the world's most famous bridges, this distinctive and dramatic stone structure crosses the Grand Canal with a single confident span. The arcades along the top of the bridge help reinforce the structure...and offer some enjoyable shopping diversions. So does the market (produce, fish, and tourist goods) on the west side of the bridge.

✪ See the St. Mark's to Rialto Loop Walk chapter and the Rialto to Frari Church Walk chapter.

▲▲Frari Church (Basilica di Santa Maria Gloriosa dei Frari)

My favorite art experience in Venice is seeing art in the setting for which it was designed—as it is at the Frari Church. You'll see the work of three great Renaissance masters—Donatello, Giovanni Bellini, and Titian—each showing worshippers the glory of God in human terms.

✪ See the Frari Church Tour chapter.

▲▲Scuola San Rocco

Sometimes called "Tintoretto's Sistine Chapel," this lavish meeting hall has some 50 large, colorful paintings plastered to its walls and ceilings.

Start upstairs in the Albergo Hall (in the left corner of the Great Upper Hall), with scenes of Christ's Passion. In *Christ Before Pilate,* Jesus stands literally head and shoulders above his accusers, radiating innocence. The old man in white is Jacopo Tintoretto himself (1518-1594). The drama culminates in the expansive *Crucifixion.* Workers struggle to hoist crosses, mourners swoon, and riffraff gamble for Christ's clothes. Tintoretto focuses all the painting's lines of sight—the ladder on the ground, the angles of

Scuola San Rocco is wallpapered with Tintoretto's *Crucifixion* and other Bible-themed works.

the crosses, the sloping hillsides—directly to the center, where Christ rises above it all, crucified but ultimately triumphant.

The huge Great Upper Hall has 34 enormous oil canvases in gold frames. They tell biblical history—Old Testament on the ceiling, New Testament along the walls—from Adam and Eve (at the Albergo end) to the Ascension of Christ (at the altar end). Tintoretto painted a staggering 8,500 square feet—like covering a house, inside and out, with a tiny artist's brush. The paintings have Tintoretto's signature sense of drama, elongated bodies, light-dark contrast, diagonal compositions, bright metallic colors, and rough brushwork—creating scenes where the miraculous and the everyday mingle side by side.

The largest ceiling painting is *The Miracle of the Bronze Serpent.* The half-naked Israelites wrestle with snakes and writhe in pain. At the top of the pile, a young woman gestures toward Moses, who points to a bronze serpent that can heal all who gaze upon it. Walk around beneath the painting and it comes alive like a movie. Tintoretto was the Spielberg of his day, making the supernatural seem tangible. Nearby, in *Moses Strikes Water from the Rocks,* the thirsty Israelites scurry to catch the water, while Moses is the calm center of a wheel of activity.

In *The Last Supper* (on the wall to the left of the altar), a dog, a beggar, and a serving girl dominate the foreground, while the apostles dine in darkness. By emphasizing the ordinary elements, Tintoretto confirmed the faith of the San Rocco brotherhood—that God intervenes miraculously into our everyday lives.

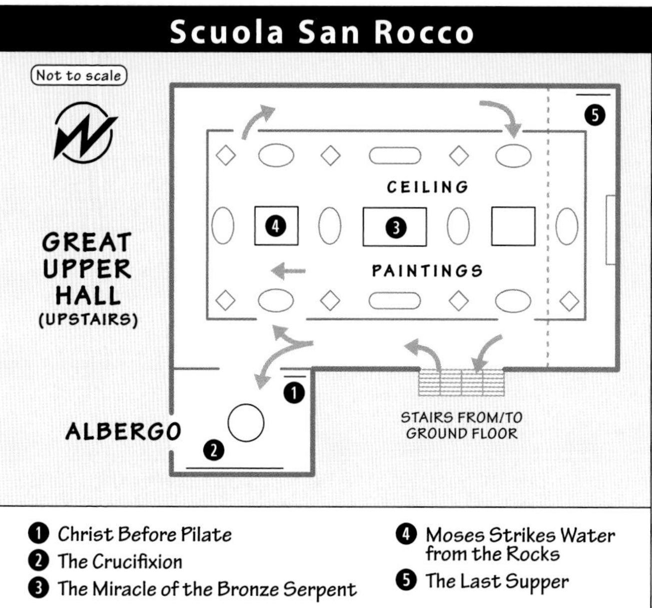

▸ *€8. Open daily 9:30-17:30, last entry 30 minutes before closing. Fine audioguide-€1. Mirrors let you view the neck-breaking splendor. Located next to Frari Church. Get key for WCs from ticket clerk. Tel. 041-523-4864, www.scuolagrandesanrocco.it.*

▲Ca' Pesaro International Gallery of Modern Art

This museum features 19th- and early 20th-century art in a 17th-century canalside palazzo. The highlights are in one large room: Klimt's beautiful/creepy *Judith II,* with eagle-talon fingers; Kandinsky's *White Zig Zags* (plus other recognizable shapes); the colorful *Nude in the Mirror* by Bonnard that flattens the 3-D scene into a 2-D pattern of rectangles; and Chagall's surprisingly realistic portrait of his hometown rabbi, *The Rabbi of Vitebsk.* The adjoining room VII features small-scale works by Matisse, Max Ernst, Mark Tobey, and a Calder mobile.

- *€8. Open Tue-Sun 10:00-18:00, closed Mon, last entry one hour before closing. Two-minute walk from San Stae vaporetto stop. Tel. 041-524-0662, http://capesaro.visitmuve.it.*

Palazzo Mocenigo Costume Museum

Six rooms of a fine 17th-century mansion are filled with period furnishings, family portraits, ceilings painted (c. 1790) with family triumphs (the Mocenigos produced seven doges), Murano glass chandeliers in situ, and a paltry collection of costumes with sparse descriptions.

- *€5. Open Tue-Sun 10:00-17:00, closed Mon, last entry one hour before closing. Located a block inland from San Stae vaporetto stop. Tel. 041-721-798, http://mocenigo.visitmuve.it.*

Near the Train Station (Ferrovia)

Jewish Ghetto

Venice's Jewish population once lived here, segregated from their non-Jewish neighbors. Today, the small neighborhood has centuries of history and a few Jewish-themed sights and eateries.

In medieval times, Jews were grudgingly allowed to do business in Venice, but in 1516, the doge restricted them to this area near the former foundry *(geto)*. In time, the word "ghetto" caught on across Europe as a term for any segregated neighborhood.

Campo de Gheto Novo is the ghetto's center. To get there from the train station, walk five minutes to the Ponte de Guglie bridge that crosses the Cannaregio Canal. Head 50 yards north to find a small covered

Bridge to the once-segregated Jewish Ghetto

Calatrava's bridge to the 21st century

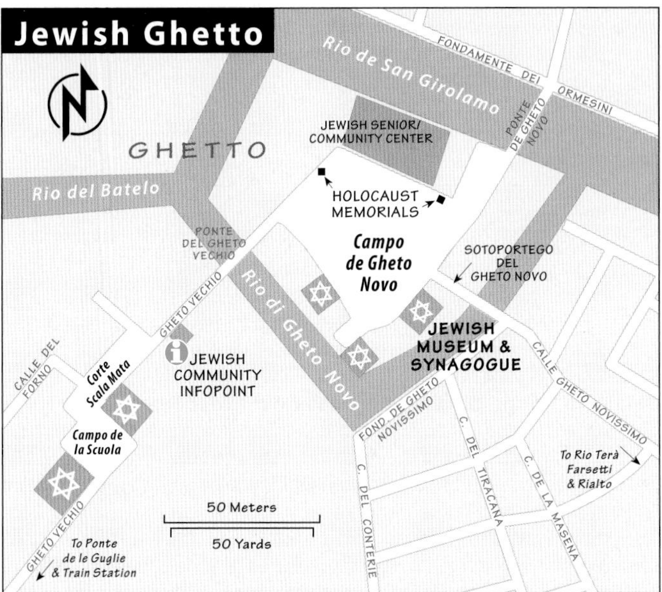

alleyway (Calle del Gheto Vechio) near the Gam-Gam Kosher Restaurant. This street leads to Campo de Gheto Novo.

In the 1600s—the Golden Age of Venice's Jews—the Campo had 70 shops, and 5,000 Jews lived nearby, many packed into the six-story "sky-scrapers" that still surround the square. To save space, the synagogues were built atop these tenements. The ghetto's two bridges were closed at night. In 1797, Napoleon ended the ghetto's isolation, and in the 1860s, the Italian republic granted Jews full citizenship.

Today the square is quiet. Only a few dozen Jews live in the former ghetto, and the Jewish people you may see are likely tourists. The main sight is the Jewish Museum (Museo Ebraico) at #2902b. It has silver menorahs, cloth covers for Torah scrolls, an overview of ghetto history, and guided tours of three old synagogues. From the Campo, you can see two synagogue exteriors (with their five windows) and three cistern wells. The large "Casa Israelitica di Riposo" is a Jewish senior/community center that is becoming a kosher hotel. It's flanked by two different Holocaust memorials, marking where the Nazis rounded up 200 Jews for deportation. Only eight returned.

Backtrack across the bridge you came in on to find the information point at Calle del Gheto Vechio #1222, where Anat Shriki answers questions about ghetto history.

Return to the square and exit through Sotoportego del Gheto Novo. From here, it's easy to gaze on the tall tenement buildings and the easy-to-lock-up bridge, and picture life in the "fortress ghetto."

▸ *Jewish Museum-€3, open June-Sept Sun-Fri 10:00-19:00, Oct-May Sun-Fri 10:00-17:30, closed Jewish holidays and Sat year-round. The €8.50 tours run hourly. Tel. 041-715-359, www.museoebraico.it.*

Calatrava Bridge (a.k.a. Ponte della Costituzione)

This modern bridge (2008) over the Grand Canal, designed by Spanish architect Santiago Calatrava, is just upstream from the train station. Only the fourth bridge over the Canal, it carries foot traffic between the train station and bus terminal at Piazzale Roma.

The bridge draws snorts from Venetians. Its construction was expensive (€11 million total), and the modern design runs counter to Venice's trademark medieval and Renaissance architecture. Adding practical insult to aesthetic injury, critics say the heavy bridge is crushing the centuries-old foundations at either end, threatening nearby buildings.

In the Fish's Tail (East of St. Mark's Square)

Get away from the crowds. Walk along the Riva (the waterfront promenade) or wind your way through back streets behind St. Mark's Basilica. Or take vaporetto line 1 east from San Zaccaria to Arsenale or Giardini. The sights I list are fine enough, but the real "sight" here is Venice's untouristed backyard.

▲Scuola Dalmata di San Giorgio

This little-visited wood-paneled chapel is decorated with the world's best collection of paintings by Vittorio Carpaccio (1465-1526). They tell the story of St. George, who slew a dragon and metaphorically conquered paganism.

Carpaccio cuts right to the climax. In the first panel, George meets the dragon on the barren plain, charges forward, and jams his spear through the dragon's skull, to the relief of the damsel in distress (in red). George gets there just in time—notice half a damsel on the ground. Carpaccio places George and the dragon directly facing each other. Meanwhile, the center of the composition—where George meets dragon—is also the "vanishing point" that draws your eye to the distant horizon. Very clever.

In the next panel, George leads the bedraggled dragon (spear still in his head) before the thankful, wealthy pagan king and queen. Next, they kneel before George (now in red, far right) as he holds a pan of water, baptizing them.

In the last panel (right wall), St. Augustine pauses while writing. He hears something. The dog hears it, too. It's the encouraging voice of St. Jerome, echoing mysteriously through the spacious room.

▶ *€4. Open Mon 14:45-18:00, Tue-Sat 9:15-13:00 & 14:45-18:00, Sun 9:15-13:00, on Calle dei Furlani at #3259a, tel. 041-522-8828.*

The Scuola is located midway between St. Mark's Square and the Arsenale. Go north from Campo San Provolo (by the Church of San Zaccaria), following the street as it changes names from L'Osmarin to St. George to Greci. At the second bridge, turn left on Fondamenta dei Furlani.

Naval Museum and Arsenale

The mighty Republic of Venice was home to a state-of-the-art shipyard that used standardized parts and an assembly line. They could crank out an entire galley in a single day—and did so to intimidate visiting heads of state. While the Arsenale is still a military base and is therefore closed to the public, its massive and evocative gate—the Porta Magna, guarded by impressive stone lions—is worth a look.

Nearby (closer to the waterfront), stands the Naval Museum (Museo Storico Navale). It's very old school but still interesting for maritime buffs. You'll see the evolution of warships, displays on old fishing boats, and gondolas.

▶ *Museum-€2, open Mon-Sat 8:45–13:30, closed Sun, tel. 041-244-1399. From the Doge's Palace, hike six bridges east along the waterfront to the Naval Museum. To see the Arsenale gate, turn left at the museum and follow the canal.*

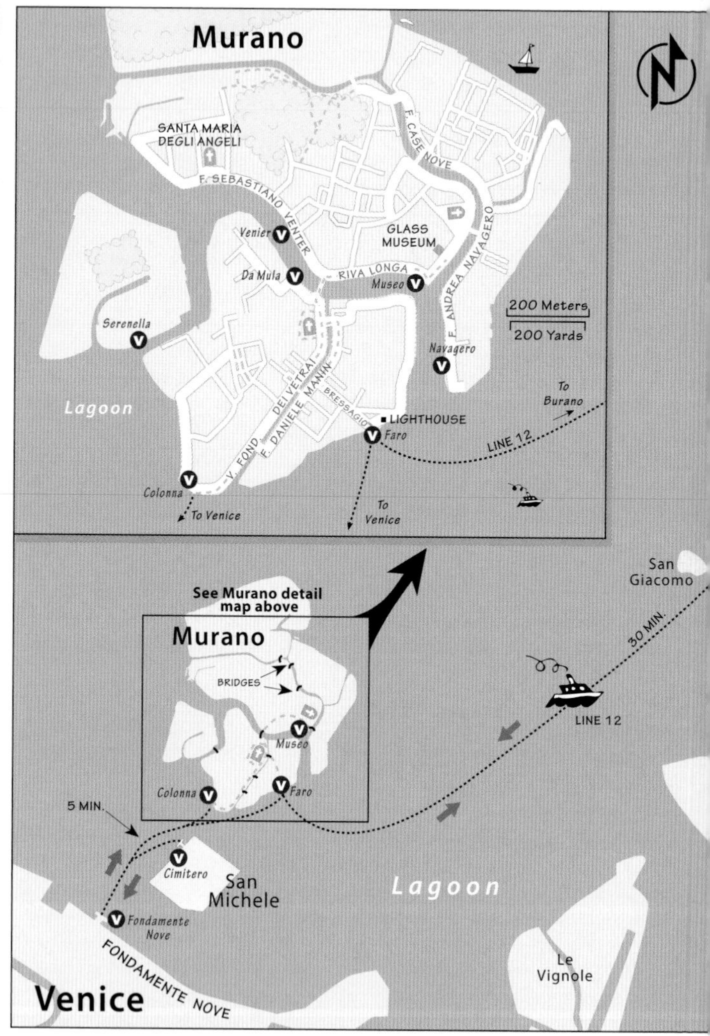
Murano
SANTA MARIA DEGLI ANGELI
F. SEBASTIANO VENIER
F. CASE NOVE
GLASS MUSEUM
F. ANDREA NAVAGERO
Venier
Da Mula
RIVA LONGA
Museo
Serenella
200 Meters
200 Yards
Navagero
Lagoon
V. FOND. DEI VETRAI
F. DANIELE MANIN
BRESSAGIO
LIGHTHOUSE
Faro
To Burano
LINE 12
Colonna
To Venice
To Venice
See Murano detail map above
Murano
BRIDGES
Museo
Colonna
Faro
5 MIN.
Cimitero
San Michele
Fondamente Nove
FONDAMENTE NOVE
Venice
Lagoon
San Giacomo
30 MIN.
LINE 12
Le Vignole

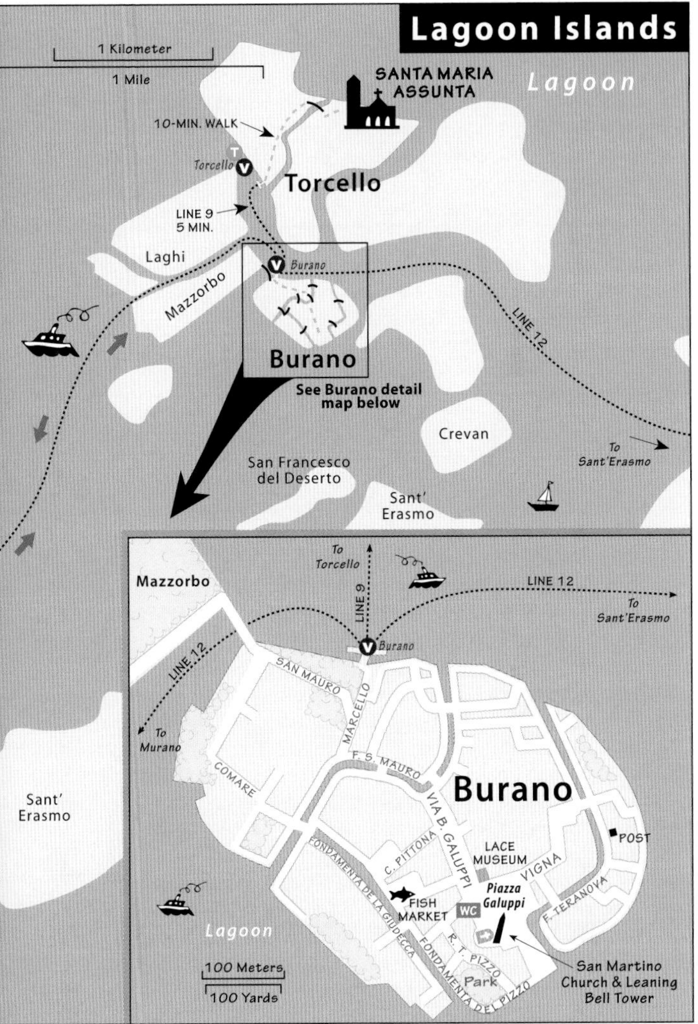
Lagoon Islands
1 Kilometer
1 Mile
Lagoon
SANTA MARIA ASSUNTA
10-MIN. WALK
Torcello
Torcello
LINE 9
5 MIN.
Laghi
Burano
Mazzorbo
LINE 12
Burano
See Burano detail map below
Crevan
To Sant'Erasmo
San Francesco del Deserto
Sant' Erasmo
To Torcello
Mazzorbo
LINE 9
LINE 12
To Sant'Erasmo
Burano
LINE 12
SAN MAURO
MARCELLO
To Murano
F. S. MAURO
COMARE
Burano
VIA B. GALUPPI
Sant' Erasmo
C. PITTONA
LACE MUSEUM
POST
VIGNA
FONDAMENTA DE LA GIUDECCA
FISH MARKET
WC
Piazza Galuppi
F. TERANOVA
Lagoon
FONDAMENTA DEL PIZZO
R. T. PIZZO
Park
San Martino Church & Leaning Bell Tower
100 Meters
100 Yards

La Biennale

Every year (June-Nov), the city hosts a world's fair of art—contemporary visual art in odd years and architecture in even years. Representatives from many nations show off the latest trends, housed in buildings and pavilions scattered throughout Giardini park and the Arsenale.

▶ *Take vaporetto #1 or #2 to Giardini-Biennale. See the events calendar at www.labiennale.org.*

Santa Elena

This 100-year-old suburb at the tip of the fish's tail shows a completely non-touristy, residential side of Venice. You'll find a kid-friendly park, a few lazy restaurants, and beautiful sunsets over San Marco.

▶ *Walk, or catch vaporetto #1 from St. Mark's Square to Santa Elena.*

Venice's Lagoon

North of the city are four islands easily laced together in a pleasant day trip. They sit in Venice's lagoon, a calm section of the Adriatic protected from wind and waves by the natural breakwater of the Lido. The islands offer an escape from the crowds, a chance to get out on a boat, and some enjoyable diversions for fans of glassmaking and lace.

Here they are, from nearest to farthest:

San Michele (at the Cimitero stop on the way to Murano) is the cemetery island, the final resting place of Venetians and a few foreign VIPs, from poet Ezra Pound to composer Igor Stravinsky.

Murano, where glass has been made since the 1200s, has several glass factories giving glass-blowing demonstrations, and the Glass Museum (open daily, tel. 041-739-586, http://museovetro.visitmuve.it). Besides the vaporetto, you can get to Murano from St. Mark's Square by taking a round-trip boat tour (€30, 4 hours) or a free ride that comes with a sales pitch. If you just want a glass-blowing demonstration without leaving St. Mark's Square, ✪ see page 202.

Burano's claim to fame is lacemaking, with shops and a Lace Museum (closed Mon, tel. 041-730-034, http://museomerletto.visitmuve.it). The town itself (pop. 2,700) is a delightful pastel fishing village.

Torcello, population 20, is a marshy wasteland, home to Venice's oldest church (with a Last Judgment mosaic on the back wall), a climbable bell tower, and a modest museum (church open daily, museum closed Mon, tel. 041-730-119).

The island of Burano in the lagoon is a smaller, sleepier version of Venice.

▸ *Of the many transportation options, I suggest this route:*

1. Catch vaporetto #4.1 or #4.2 to Murano-Colonna, departing from San Zaccaria (near St. Mark's, 40 minutes), or the train station (40 minutes), or Fondamente Nova (on the fish's back, 10 minutes).

2. Continue on from Murano-Faro to Burano, on vaporetto #12 (30 minutes).

3. From Burano, take #9 to Torcello (5 minutes).

4. Return home from Burano on the #12 to Fondamente Nova (45 minutes).

Sleeping

For sheer magic, I favor hotels that may be a bit pricier but are close to the action: near St. Mark's, Rialto, and the quaint Accademia/Dorsoduro area. I also list a few hotels near the train station (less charming but handy for train travelers). I like hotels that are clean, central, quiet at night (except for the song of gondoliers), traditional, family-run, and friendly.

Double rooms listed in this book average around €150 (including a private bathroom), ranging from €90 (very simple, with toilet and shower down the hall) to €400 (plush Grand Canal views and maximum plumbing). Many Venetian hotels offer a combination of Old World ambience—wood-beam ceilings, chandeliers, and antique furniture—with modern conveniences. Venice's hotels do their best with the city's substandard plumbing and wiring infrastructure.

Hotel Price Code

$$$ Most rooms are €180 or more.

$$ Most rooms between €130–180.

$ Most rooms €130 or less.

These rates are for a standard double room with bath during high season. Unless otherwise noted, hotels have an elevator, air-conditioning, breakfast included, and Internet access (either free or fee public computer or Wi-Fi). There's an additional hotel tax of €1-4 per person, per night.

A Typical Venice Hotel Room

A €150 double room in Venice is small by American standards and has one double bed or two twins. There's probably a bathroom in the room with a toilet, sink, and bathtub or shower. Rooms generally have a telephone and TV, and may have a safe. Most hotels at this price will have air-conditioning—cheaper places may not. Some rooms have a small fridge stocked with drinks for sale.

Breakfast is generally included. It's usually a self-service buffet of cereal, ham, cheese, yogurt, and juice, while a server takes your coffee order.

The hotel will likely have some form of Internet access, either free or pay-as-you-go. It may be Wi-Fi in your room or a public terminal in the lobby. The staff speaks at least enough English to get by. Night clerks aren't paid enough to care deeply about problems that arise.

In addition to hotels, I also list a few alternatives: bed-and-breakfasts (B&Bs); hostels (for more listings see www.hostelz.com or www.hihostels.com); and church-run places with good prices in an institutional, twin-bed setting. Renting an apartment can be a great value for groups at around €100-200 per day, usually with a week minimum (see www.homeaway.com).

Making Hotel Reservations

Reserve at least a few weeks in advance in peak season (April-June, Sept-Oct, and during Carnevale). Do it by email (the best way), phone, fax, or through the hotel's website. Your hotelier will want to know:

- the type of room you want (e.g., "one double room with bath")
- how many nights ("three nights")
- dates (using European format: "arriving 22/7/13, departing 25/7/13")
- any special requests ("with twin beds, air-conditioning, quiet, view").

If the hotel requires your credit-card number for a deposit (even cash-only places may require it), you can send it by email (I do), but it's safer via phone, fax, or the hotel's secure website. Once your room is booked, print out the confirmation, and reconfirm your reservation with a phone call or email a day or two in advance. If you must cancel your reservation, hotels require advance notice or you'll be billed. Even if there's no penalty, it's polite to give at least three days' notice.

Because finding addresses is tricky in Venice, get clear directions to the hotel from the hotelier or their website. Let them know your arrival point in Venice (e.g., the train station, or the airport) and they can suggest the best mode of transportation and walking directions. Alternatively, at www.venicexplorer.net you can find your hotel on a map, if you know the district and address number (click "Venice Civic Number" to start).

Budget Tips

Some of my listed hotels offer special rates to my readers—it's worth asking when you book your room.

Due to supply outstripping demand, Venetian hotel rates can be surprisingly soft, and you can get deals below the quoted rate. Email several hotels to comparison shop, and check hotel websites for promo deals. You may get a better rate if you offer to pay cash, stay at least three nights, skip breakfast, or simply ask if there are any cheaper rooms. There are fewer bargains during peak season. But rates can drop dramatically (50 percent) off-season—roughly November through March and in July and August. Off-season, don't pay the rates I list.

Big expensive hotels are most apt to mark down rooms. You might snag a €300 double for as low as €120 by booking through their website. Try Hotel Giorgione (www.hotelgiorgione.com), Casa Verardo (www.casaverardo.it), Hotel all'Angelo (www.donapalace.it), or Ca' Dei Conti (www.cadeiconti.com). Or check www.venere.com.

Don't be too cheap when picking a hotel in Venice. Having a nice place to call home is part of the romance of this romantic city.

	Price		
NEAR ST. MARK'S SQUARE—Central as can be, near sights, shops, restaurants, and handy vaporetto stop San Zaccaria			
Hotel Campiello	$$$	East of the square, ideal location, tranquil, lacy and bright, family-run professional refuge, apt. available	
Hotel Fontana	$$$	Nice, old-time, family-run, near school, two bridges east of St. Mark's, terrace rooms extra	
Hotel Flora	$$$	West of St. Mark's Square, amid fashion boutiques on Grand Canal, formal uniformed staff, but homey warm oasis	
Locanda al Leon	$$	Reasonably priced, feels a little like a medieval tower house	
Hotel al Piave	$$	North of St. Mark's Square, fresh modern comfortable rooms above bright and classy lobby, nice neighborhood, cheery welcome	
Locanda Silva	$$	Big basic functional 1960s-era hotel, decent old-school rooms, good location	
Locanda Casa Querini	$$	Bright, high-ceilinged rooms tucked away behind St. Mark's, enjoy sunny breakfast on the quiet square	
Hotel Mercurio	$$	Near La Fenice, warm welcome and 29 peaceful, comfortable rooms, some with canal views	
Albergo Doni	$	Dark and quiet, well-worn once-classy rooms up a creaky stairway, friendly owners, overflow apts. available	
Casa per Ferie Santa Maria della Pietà	$	Church-run institution, dorm-style rooms w/4-8 beds (€40/person), bathroom down hall, public lagoon-view terrace	
Hotel Riva	$	Gleaming marble hallways, antique furnishings, lots of stairs, on romantic gondola-serenade canal, newly renovated	
Corte Campana B&B	$	Enthusiastic owner, three quiet characteristic rooms (one w/ bath down hall) behind St. Mark's, cash only	

Address/Phone/Website/Email
Castello 4647, near San Zaccaria vaporetto, tel. 041-520-5764, fax 041-520-5798, www.hcampiello.it, campiello@hcampiello.it
Castello 4701, on Campo San Provolo, tel. 041-522-0579, fax 041-523-1040, www.hotelfontana.it, info@hotelfontana.it
San Marco 2283a, tel. 041-520-5844, fax 041-522-8217, www.hotelflora.it, info@hotelflora.it
Castello 4270, just off Campo Santi Filippo e Giacomo, tel. 041-277-0393, fax 041-521-0348, www.hotelalleon.com, leon@hotelalleon.com
Castello 4838, on Ruga Giuffa, tel. 041-528-5174, fax 041-523-8512, www.hotelalpiave.com, info@hotelalpiave.com
Castello 4423, on Fondamenta del Remedio, tel. 041-522-7643, fax 041-528-6817, www.locandasilva.it, info@locandasilva.it
Castello 4388, halfway between San Zaccaria vaporetto stop and Campo Santa Maria Formosa on Campo San Zaninovo/Giovanni Novo, tel. 041-241-1294, fax 041-523-6188, www.locandaquerini.com, info@locandaquerini.com
San Marco 1848, on Calle del Fruttariol, tel. 041-522-0947, fax 041-241-1079, www.hotelmercurio.com, info@hotelmercurio.com
Castello 4656, on Fondamenta del Vin, tel. & fax 041-522-4267, www.albergodoni.it, albergodoni@hotmail.it
100 yards from San Zaccaria-Pietà vaporetto dock, down Calle de la Pietà from La Pietà Church, tel. 041-522-2171, www.pietavenezia.org, info.admin@pietavenezia.org
Castello 5310, on Ponte de l'Anzolo, tel. 041-522-7034, www.hotelriva.it, info@hotelriva.it
Castello 4410, on Calle del Remedio, tel. & fax 041-523-3603, mobile 389-272-6500, www.cortecampana.com, info@cortecampana.com

	Price		
RIALTO BRIDGE—Choose the busy east side of the bridge (10-minute walk to St. Mark's) or less-touristy west side, good vaporetto connections			
Hotel al Ponte Antico	$$$	Professional yet romantic, plush rooms, velvety public spaces, pricey Grand Canal views, better value in back	
Pensione Guerrato	$$	West of the bridge, 800-year-old building near colorful market, simple spacious airy rooms, friendly owners, apts. available	
Locanda la Corte	$$	Perfumed with elegance but not snooty, attractive wood-beamed pastel rooms circling quiet courtyard, some suites	
Foresteria della Chiesa Valdese	$	Hostel-like dorm beds (€35/person) and hotel-like doubles, large, ramshackle, run-down yet charming, nice public spaces	
ACCADEMIA/DORSODURO—Quiet ambience, art galleries, convenient vaporetto stops (Accademia or Zattere)			
Pensione Accademia	$$$	Aristocratic old palazzo with comfortable elegant rooms, grand public spaces, and wistful breezy gardens	
Hotel Belle Arti	$$$	Grand entry, formal stern staff, ambience of a big modern American hotel	
Novecento Hotel	$$$	North of Accademia Bridge, boutique hotel, plush rooms, 1920s decor, big elegant public spaces, lots of stairs	
Pensione la Calcina	$$	Formal professional three-star comfort, intimate nautical-feeling rooms are squeaky clean, peaceful canalside setting, view terrace	
Casa Rezzonico	$$	Tranquil getaway far from crowds, seven quiet rooms, grassy private garden terrace	
Hotel Galleria	$$	Narrow velvety rooms, most with views of Grand Canal, no air-con but fans, family-run	
Don Orione Religious Guest House	$$	Big institution, like a modern retreat center, clean, peaceful, comfortable, strictly run, fine value	
Istituto Ciliota	$$	Big well-run sparkling-clean institution, industrial-strength comfort, little character but good value, twin beds only	

Address/Phone/Website/Email
Cannaregio 5768, 100 yards north of bridge, tel. 041-241-1944, fax 041-241-1828, www.alponteantico.com, info@alponteantico.com
On Calle drio la Scimia at San Polo 240a, tel. & fax 041-528-5927, www.pensioneguerrato.it, info@pensioneguerrato.it
Castello 6317, on Calle Bressana, tel. 041-241-1300, fax 041-241-5982, www.locandalacorte.it, info@locandalacorte.it
Castello 5170, near Campo Santa Maria Formosa on Fondamenta Cavagnis, tel. 041-528-6797, fax 041-241-6238, www.foresteriavenezia.it, info@foresteriavenezia.it
Dorsoduro 1058, on Fondamenta Bollani, tel. 041-521-0188, fax 041-523-9152, www.pensioneaccademia.it, info@pensioneaccademia.it
Dorsoduro 912a, 100 yards behind Accademia art museum, tel. 041-522-6230, fax 041-528-0043, www.hotelbellearti.com, info@hotelbellearti.com
San Marco 2683, on Calle del Dose, off Campo San Maurizio, tel. 041-241-3765, fax 041-521-2145, www.novecento.biz, info@novecento.biz
Dorsoduro 780, near Zattere vaporetto stop at south end of Rio de San Vio, tel. 041-520-6466, fax 041-522-7045, www.lacalcina.com, info@lacalcina.com
Dorsoduro 2813, near Ca' Rezzonico vaporetto stop on Fondamenta Gherardini, tel. 041-277-0653, fax 041-277-5435, www.casarezzonico.it, info@casarezzonico.it
Dorsoduro 878a, 30 yards from Accademia art museum, tel. 041-523-2489, fax 041-520-4172, www.hotelgalleria.it, info@hotelgalleria.it
Dorsoduro 909a, on Rio Terà A. Foscarini near Zattere vaporetto, tel. 041-522-4077, fax 041-528-6214, www.donorione-venezia.it, info@donorione-venezia.it
On Calle delle Muneghe just off Campo San Stefano north of Accademia Bridge, tel. 041-520-4888, www.ciliota.it, info@ciliota.it

	Price	
ACCADEMIA/DORSODURO—Quiet ambience, art galleries, convenient vaporetto stops (Accademia or Zattere)		
Foresteria Levi	$$	Foundation-run, 20 quiet comfortable spacious yet institutional rooms, no air-con but fans, prices vary wildly
Casa di Sara	$	Colorfully decorated little B&B, maximum privacy hidden on quiet leafy back street, tiny roof terrace
Venice's youth hostel	$	On Giudecca Island south of Dorsoduro, 260 bunk beds in 8-20-bed rooms (€26/person), full facilities, grand views, great deal for backpackers
NEAR THE TRAIN STATION—It's charmless, but if you must stay here, these places stand out		
Hotel Abbazia	$$$	Big former abbey has history and class, grand living room and garden, fun staff, lots of stairs
Locanda Ca San Marcuola	$$	Peaceful characteristic well-worn oldie-but-goodie, 14 fine rooms, some canal views
Locanda Herion	$	16 beige-tiled homey rooms, decent price, near San Marcuola vaporetto
Hotel Henry	$	Near Jewish Ghetto, tiny and family-owned, 15 simple and flowery rooms, no public spaces, no breakfast

Address/Phone/Website/Email
San Marco 2893, on Calle Giustinian just north of Accademia Bridge, tel. 041-786-711, fax 041-786-766, www.foresterialevi.it, info@foresterialevi.it
Dorsoduro 1330, mobile 342-596-3563, fax 041-241-2296, www.casadisara.com, info@casadisara.com
Fondamenta Zitelle 86, tel. 041-523-8211, fax 041-523-5689, www.ostellovenezia.it, info@ostellovenezia.it
Cannaregio 68, 2 blocks from the station on quiet Calle Priuli dei Cavaletti, tel. 041-717-333, fax 041-717-949, www.abbaziahotel.com, info@abbaziahotel.com
Cannaregio 1763, near San Marcuola vaporetto stop, tel. 041-716-048, www.casanmarcuola.com, info@casanmarcuola
Cannaregio 1697a, on Campiello Augusto Picutti, tel. 041-275-9426, fax 041-275-6647, www.locandaherion.com, info@locandaherion.com
Cannaregio 1506e, on Calle Ormesini at Campiello Briani, tel. 041-523-6675, fax 041-715-680, www.alloggihenry.com, info@alloggihenry.com

MENÚ € 19,50

(1) LASAGNE AL FORNO
ZUPPA DI VERDURA
SPAGHETTI AL POMODORO
SPAGHETTI AGLIO-OLIO-PEPERONCINO
TORTELLINI AL POMODORO

(2) FEGATO "ALLA VENEZIANA"
BRACIOLA DI MAIALE AI FERRI
SCALOPPINE "PIZZAIOLA"
PETTO DI POLLO AI FERRI

(3) PATATE AL FORNO
VERDURA COTTA

COPERTO E' SERVIZIO
COMPRESI

Eating

Venetians enjoy some of the best seafood and greatest dining ambience in the world. Lingering over a multicourse meal with loved ones while you sip wine and watch the play of light on the water...it's one of Venice's great pleasures.

On the other hand, Venetian restaurants are inevitably touristy (no restaurant can survive on locals alone) and pricey (since all produce must be shipped in). But Venice offers dining experiences found nowhere else in Italy.

I list a full range of restaurants and eateries—from budget options for a quick bite to multicourse splurges with maximum ambience. I prefer mom-and-pop, personality-driven places, offering fine value and high quality with a local reputation.

Restaurant Price Rankings

$$$ Most main courses €20 or more.

$$ Most main courses €15-20.

$ Most main courses €15 or less.

Based on the average price of a meat or seafood dish (a *secondo*) on the menu. Pastas, salads, and appetizers are generally a couple of euros cheaper. So a typical meal in a $$ restaurant—including appetizer, main dish, house wine, water, and service—would cost about €35. The circled numbers in the restaurant listings indicate locations on the maps on pages 176-183.

When in Venice, I eat on the Venetian schedule. For breakfast, I eat at the hotel or grab a pastry and cappuccino at the neighborhood bar. Lunch is fast and simple to make time for sightseeing—a sandwich in a bar (as locals do), a slice of pizza, or a self-service cafeteria. Evening time is for drinks and appetizers in a *cicchetti* bar, or for slowing down and savoring a full restaurant meal.

Restaurants

Restaurants serve lunch 12:00-15:00. Dinner is served to Venetians after 21:00 and to tourists at 19:00 (quality restaurants rarely open much earlier). Reservations are not always necessary but can be smart, especially on busy weekends.

Get used to the reality that most restaurants (even my recommendations) are frequented by fellow tourists. Minimize the tourist hordes by eating later, by avoiding triple-language-menu places, or by escaping to the less-touristed Dorsoduro area. Choose between romantic canalside ambience with overpriced food, or hole-in-the-wall places with a local clientele—it's hard to get both.

A full restaurant meal comes in courses: appetizer *(antipasto),* a plate of pasta, meat or seafood course *(secondo),* salad, dessert, coffee, liqueurs, and so on. It can take hours, and the costs can add up quickly, so plan your strategy before sitting down to a restaurant meal.

For light eaters, there's nothing wrong with ordering a single dish as your meal—a plate of pasta, an antipasto, or a salad. Ordering an individual-size pizza and a carafe of wine can buy you a great canalside setting for a reasonable price. Couples could each order a dish (or two) and share. If you want a full meal at a predictable price, consider the *menu turistico*—a fixed-price multicourse meal where you can choose from a list of menu items. It includes the service charge, and is usually a good value for non-gourmets.

In Venice, only rude waiters rush you. For speedier service, be prepared with your next request whenever a waiter happens to grace your table. You'll have to ask for the bill—mime-scribble on your raised palm or ask: *"Il conto?"*

Quick Budget Meals

Venice offers many budget options for hungry travelers.

Italian "bars" are cafés, not taverns. These neighborhood hangouts serve coffee, sandwiches (grilled *panini* or cold *tramezzini*), mini-pizzas, pre-made salads, fresh squeezed orange juice *(spremuta),* and drinks from the cooler.

Various cafeteria-style places dish out fast and cheap cooked meals to eat there or take out. You can buy pizza by the slice at little hole-in-the-wall places, sold by weight (100 grams for a small slice). Ethnic joints serve Turkish *döner kebabs* (meat and veggies wrapped in pita bread). *Cicchetti* bars (✪ see next page) serve small build-a-meal toothpick snacks for the local crowd at lunch and evening.

At any eating establishment (however humble), be aware that the price of your food and drink may be 20-40 percent more if you consume it while sitting at a table instead of standing at the bar. This two-tier price system will always be clearly posted. Don't sit without first checking out the financial consequences. Also, at many bars, the custom is to first pay the cashier for what you want, then hand the receipt to a barista who serves you. Because Venice has so few public places to sit and relax, it can be worth a few extra euros to enjoy your coffee, sandwich, or gelato while seated in an air-conditioned café.

Venice is not a great town for picnics. The city prohibits picnics in most public spaces, so don't sit down and spread out a lavish feast in a highly touristed area. But even locals grab a sandwich or slice of pizza "to go" *(da portar via)* and eat discreetly outside the tourist zone. Buy some fruit, refill your water bottle at a public tap...and dine like a doge. The Rialto

Market (west end of the bridge) is a picnic-buyer's paradise. Hole-in-the-wall grocery stores *(alimentari)* can be hard to find in the tourist zones. There's a produce stand 100 yards behind St. Mark's Basilica, just north of Campo Santi Filippo e Giacomo. A tiny deli lurks along the main drag between St. Mark's and Accademia (at #2512, on the zigzag bridge). When buying produce, it's customary to let the merchant pick it out. If something is a mystery, ask for a small taste—*"Un assaggio, per favore?"*

Cicchetti Pubs

Pubs *(bacari)* are a big part of the Venetian scene. Locals stop in at lunch or early evening for a drink and to snack on various finger foods *(cicchetti)*. The foods range from cheese to olives to deep-fried artichokes to crostini to calamari to anything ugly on a toothpick. It's easy to build a €10 meal out of small €2-3 servings. Or get an assortment *(un piatto di misti)* for around €8. Just belly up to the bar, point to the *cicchetti* you want (it's displayed on trays), and eat, either standing or sitting at a table—for *cicchetti,* the cost is usually the same. Many pubs also serve pastas and meat dishes.

For drinks, you'll find a variety of wines by the glass (*un ombra* for as little as €1). The dominant pre-dinner drink *(aperitivo)* is a white-wine-and-spirits cocktail called a spritz. A *spritz con Compari* (the traditional man's choice) is bitter; a *spritz con Aperol* (which many women prefer) is sweeter. Another Venetian specialty is a sparkling, peach-flavored Bellini.

Bars don't stay open very late, the food selection is best 18:00-20:00, and most places are closed Sunday. To do a pub crawl *(giro d'ombra)*, there's a great area west of the Rialto Bridge (✪ see the "*Cicchetti* Strip" listing, page 170). Come ready to mingle. Boldly order a spritz or a Bellini, and draw approving looks from the natives.

Venetian Cuisine

Along with the basic dishes you'll find all over Italy, Venice has its signature specialties—mainly, a wide variety of catch-of-the-day seafood. Venetian cuisine relies heavily on fish, shellfish, risotto, and polenta.

For appetizers, try a marinated seafood assortment *(antipasto di mare)* or asiago cheese. Risotto (rice simmered in broth) and polenta (grilled cornmeal) are more traditional than pasta. Seafood is the classic main dish. The more exotic it is, the more local: fish (generally smaller varieties like sardines, not salmon or trout), shellfish, octopus, eel, weird crustaceans, and cuttlefish *(seppia).* Seafood is often sold expensively by the gram—confirm the total price before ordering. On a menu, "x2" means the price per person for a large, two-person dish.

No meal in Italy is complete without wine. Even the basic house wine (*vino da tavola* or *vino della casa*) is fine with a meal. The island of Venice produces no wine, but the mainland Veneto region is known for Soave (crisp white, great with seafood), Valpolicella (light fruity red), Amarone (very intense red), and Prosecco (a dry sparkling wine, easy to drink too much).

Italian coffee is some of the world's best. Even the most basic hole-in-the-wall bar serves quality espresso, *macchiatos,* and cappuccinos. Popular liqueurs to finish a meal are *amaro* (various brands) and anise-flavored Sambuca. Venetians love dipping Burano biscotti in *fragolino,* a strawberry dessert wine. Or pick up a cup or cone of gelato at a *gelateria* and stroll the streets with the rest of Venice, enjoying a bit of edible art.

	Price	
RIALTO: North of the Rialto Bridge, near the Strada Nova (see map, pages 176-177)		
❶ Trattoria da Bepi	$$	Bright and alpine-paneled, traditional cuisine, sit inside or out, trust owner's seafood recommendations
❷ La Cantina	$$	Rustic yet sophisticated wine bar serving cold meat, cheese, fish plates, and *cicchetti;* not cheap but great scene
❸ Vini da Gigio	$$	Small place with big enthusiasm for traditional food
RIALTO: East end of the Rialto Bridge (see map, pages 176-177)		
❹ Osteria di Santa Marina	$$$	Highly regarded by locals, dressy dining room or pleasant outside, impressive but borderline stuffy, reservations smart
❺ Rosticceria San Bartolomeo	$	Cheap self-service diner for take out or eat in (but skip their restaurant upstairs), surly staff
❻ Osteria al Portego	$$	Friendly neighborhood eatery, fine meals at tables (reserve) or *cicchetti* at bar
❼ Osteria alle Testiere	$$$	My top dining splurge in Venice for creative seafood, budget €50 and trust your host, reservations mandatory

Operating Hours and Days	Address/Phone
Fri-Wed 12:00-14:30 & 19:00-22:00, closed Thu	Half a block off Campo Santi Apostoli on Salizada Pistor at #4550, tel. 041-528-5031
Closed Sun	Facing Campo San Felice on Strada Nova near Ca' d'Oro, tel. 041-522-8258
Wed-Sun 12:00-14:30 & 19:00-22:30, closed Mon-Tue	Four blocks from Ca' d'Oro vaporetto stop on Fondamenta San Felice at #3628a, tel. 041-528-5140
Mon-Sat 12:30-14:30 & 19:30-22:00, closed Sun	On Campo Marina at #5911, between Rialto Bridge and Campo Santa Maria Formosa, tel. 041-528-5239
Daily 9:00-21:30	Find it by going through the covered passageway near the statue on Campo San Bartolomeo, tel. 041-522-3569
Daily 10:30-15:00 & 18:00-22:00	Near Campo Marina at #6015 on Calle Malvasia (from the Rosticceria San Bartolomeo, continue east to Campo San Lio and turn left), tel. 041-522-9038
Closed Sun-Mon	On Calle del Mondo Novo, just off Campo Santa Maria Formosa, at #5801; tel. 041-522-7220

	Price	
RIALTO: West end of the Rialto Bridge (see map, pages 176-177)		
8 The "Bancogiro Stretch"	$-$$$	Several eateries near lively Rialto Market with seating along Grand Canal; serving lunch, between-meal bar snacks, dinner, or late drinks with a youthful crowd; great for a spritz and *cicchetti*
9 The "*Cicchetti* Strip"	$-$$	Classic bars serving *cicchetti* (and some meals) two blocks inland from Rialto Market—look for Cantina Do Spade, Osteria ai Storti, Bar all'Arco, and Cantina Do Mori
10 Pronto Pesce	$	Hole-in-the-wall, freshest catch amid market action, helpful owners, unbeatable €10 mixed fish plate offered at 13:00
11 Al Mercà	$	Lively nook (no tables) with happy local crowd for light fare, tourists don't faze them
12 Ristorante Vini da Pinto	$	Tourist-friendly forgettable food at decent prices, good service, relaxed outdoor seating
13 Trattoria alla Madonna	$	A hundred noisy tables, old-school formal waiters, tour groups and families, no romance but reliable food
14 Antica Birraria la Corte	$$	Everyday eatery on family-filled square, pizza and salads, beer hall inside or outside
15 Trattoria Pizzeria al Nono Risorto	$	Unpretentious, youthful, garden setting, good pizza, salads, and grilled meat or fish
16 Rialto Bridge Tourist Traps	$$-$$$	Gauntlet of restaurants along the Grand Canal offering lousy overpriced food, aggressive waiters, lots of tourists...and stunning views—to enjoy the ambience on the cheap, order a simple pizza/pasta and drink (confirm minimum charge before you order)

Operating Hours and Days	Address/Phone
Long hours daily	Along Grand Canal near the Rialto Market
Long hours daily	Along Sotoportego dei Do Mori and Calle de le Do Spade
Tue-Sat 10:00-15:00 & 17:30-19:30, closed Sun-Mon	Facing the fish market on Calle de le Becarie o Panataria at #319, tel. 041-822-0298
Mon-Sat 9:30-14:30 & 18:00-21:00, closed Sun	On Campo Cesare Battisti at #213
Long hours daily	Facing the fish market, tel. 041-522-4599
Closed Tue	Tucked away on Calle della Madonna, 2 minutes west of Rialto Bridge, tel. 041-522-3824
Daily 12:00-15:30 & 18:00-22:30	On Campo San Polo at #2168, between Rialto Bridge and Frari Church, tel. 041-275-0570
Thu 19:00-22:30, Fri-Tue 12:00-14:30 & 19:00-22:30, closed Wed	Walk 3 minutes away from Rialto to Sotoportego de Siora Bettina at #2338, tel. 041-524-1169
Long hours daily	Along Grand Canal near the Rialto Bridge

	Price	
NEAR ST. MARK'S SQUARE: In addition to the ultra-atmospheric cafés directly on the square, here are some other options nearby (see map, pages 178-179)		
⑰ Ristorante Antica Sacrestia	$$$	Hands-on owner, creative €33-50 fixed-price meals or a la carte in lovely setting, reasonable pizza for lunch
⑱ "Sandwich Row"	$	Calle de le Rasse, just east of St. Mark's Square, is lined with several bars offering sandwiches, salads, and a place to sit (€1 extra); I like Birreria Forst (#4540) and Bar Verde (#4526)
⑲ Ristorante alla Basilica	$	Institutional-feeling place serves a solid €14 fixed-price lunch (nothing else), air-con
⑳ Rizzo	$	Eat-at-the-counter sandwiches and pizza, tiny grocery assortment
㉑ Picnicking in Giardinetti Reali Park	$	Though you can't picnic on St. Mark's Square, you can in Giardinetti Reali park, west along the waterfront
㉒ Canalside Tourist Traps	$$-$$$	While tourist traps, Ristorante alla Conchiglia and Trattoria da Giorgio ai Greci have romantic tables by gondolier-frequented canals
ACCADEMIA/DORSODURO: Near Accademia Bridge (pretty touristy), Zattere vaporetto (less touristy), and Campo San Barnaba (most charming) (see map, pages 180-181)		
㉓ Ristorante/Pizzeria Accademia Foscarini	$	OK pizzas, interesting toasted *farciti* sandwich, some Grand Canal views, no cover or service charge
㉔ Enoteca Cantine del Vino Già Schiavi	$	Wine shop much-loved for cheap *cicchetti* and sandwiches, bottles to go
㉕ Terrazza del Casin dei Nobili	$$	Enjoy a warm romantic evening along the canal, creative specialties at tolerable prices
㉖ Ae Oche Pizzeria	$	Casual tables on canal or sprawling pizza parlor interior, youthful, fun, good prices
㉗ Ristoteca Oniga	$$	Chic-and-shipshape interior or on the square, accessible, fresh fish and vegetarian options (€12 pastas, €20 *secondi*), €2 cover, reservations smart

Operating Hours and Days	Address/Phone
Tue-Sun 11:30-15:00 & 18:00-23:00, closed Mon	Immediately behind San Zaninovo/Giovanni Novo Church on Calle de la Sacrestia at #4442, tel. 041-523-0749
Most places open daily 7:00-24:00	From the Bridge of Sighs, head down the Riva and take the second lane on the left
Lunch served daily 11:45-15:00	One block behind St. Mark's Basilica on Calle dei Albanesi at #4255, tel. 041-522-0524
Mon-Sat 8:00-20:00, closed Sun	Just north of square on main drag, on Calle dei Fabbri at #933a, tel. 041-522-3388
Long hours daily	Along the waterfront west of St. Mark's
Long hours daily	Several blocks behind St. Mark's, on Fondamenta San Lorenzo near the Ponte dei Greci bridge
May-Oct Wed-Mon 7:00-22:30, Nov-April Wed-Mon 7:00-21:00, closed Tue year-round	Next to Accademia Bridge on Rio Terà A. Foscarini at #878c, tel. 041-522-7281
Mon-Sat 8:00-20:30, closed Sun	Facing Accademia museum, go right and then a forced left at the canal to the second bridge to #992; tel. 041-523-0034
Fri-Wed 12:00-23:00, closed Thu	At Zattare—from Zattere vaporetto stop, turn left to #924; tel. 041-520-6895
Daily 12:00-15:00 & 19:00-23:00	250 yards west of Zattere vaporetto stop, tel. 041-520-6601
Closed Tue	On Campo San Barnaba, tel. 041-522-4410

	Price	
ACCADEMIA/DORSODURO: Near Accademia Bridge (pretty touristy), Zattere vaporetto (less touristy), and Campo San Barnaba (most charming) (see map, pages 180-181)		
28 Osteria Enoteca Ai Artisti	$$	Well-presented, small wine-snob interior or romantic canalside tables, wines by the glass
29 Pizzeria al Profeta	$	Big casual woody interior or leafy garden, pizza and steak, convivial atmosphere
30 Enoteca e Trattoria la Bitta	$$	Tiny "slow food" bistro for serious locavores (but no fish dishes), reservations required, cash only
TRAIN STATION/CANNAREGIO: Residential area northeast of the station, beyond the Jewish Ghetto; explore at sunset, then grab a bite (see map, pages 182-183)		
31 Pizzeria Vesuvio	$	Popular neighborhood favorite, classy indoor seating and pleasant tables outside
32 Enoteca Ciccheteria Do Colonne	$	Local dive with loyal following, okay *cicchetti* and sandwiches, fun scene feels real
33 Brek	$	Near the station, self-service cafeteria chain, efficient and cheap
34 Osteria L'Orto dei Mori	$$$	Chic, nicely presented, creative Venetian cuisine, elegant modern interior or on classic neighborhood square
35 Osteria Ai 40 Ladroni	$	Characteristic old standby, busy ambience inside or canal tables, good seafood antipasto, reserve for dinner
36 Osteria al Bacco	$$	Simple, rustic and traditional, a few canalside tables

Operating Hours and Days	Address/Phone
Closed Sun	Fondamenta della Toletta, tel. 041-523-8944
Closed Tue	From Campo San Barnaba, walk to the end of Calle Lunga San Barnaba; tel. 041-523-7466
Mon-Sat 18:30-23:00, closed Sun	Just off Campo San Barnaba on Calle Lunga San Barnaba, tel. 041-523-0531
Long hours, closed Tue	On Rio Terà Farsetti, up from San Marcuola vaporetto stop, tel. 041-795-688
Daily	Near Pizzeria Vesuvio, on Rio Terà del Cristo, tel. 041-524-0453
Daily 11:30-22:00	Head left as you leave the station, past the bridge, along Rio Terà Lista di Spagna to #124
Closed Tue	On Rio della Sensa at Calle Larga, on Campo dei Mori, tel. 041-524-3677
Closed Mon	Fondamenta della Sensa at Calle del Capitello, tel. 041-715-736
Closed Mon	On Fondamenta Capuzine at Calle Girolamo, tel. 041-721-415

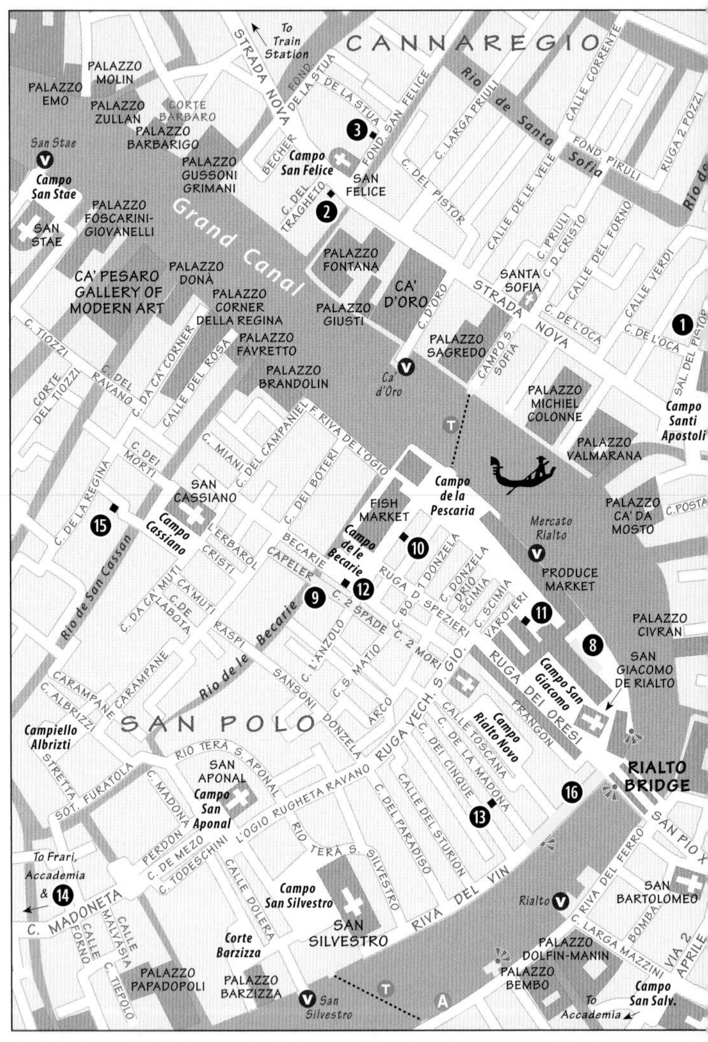
CANNAREGIO
SAN POLO
Grand Canal
To Train Station
STRADA NOVA
PALAZZO MOLIN
PALAZZO EMO
PALAZZO ZULLAN
CORTE BARBARO
PALAZZO BARBARIGO
San Stae
Campo San Stae
SAN STAE
PALAZZO GUSSONI GRIMANI
PALAZZO FOSCARINI-GIOVANELLI
CA' PESARO GALLERY OF MODERN ART
PALAZZO DONÀ
PALAZZO CORNER DELLA REGINA
PALAZZO FAVRETTO
PALAZZO BRANDOLIN
Campo San Felice
SAN FELICE
PALAZZO FONTANA
CA' D'ORO
PALAZZO GIUSTI
Ca' d'Oro
PALAZZO SAGREDO
SANTA SOFIA
PALAZZO MICHIEL COLONNE
PALAZZO VALMARANA
Campo Santi Apostoli
Rio de Santa Sofia
FOND. PIRULI
C. LARGA PRIULI
CALLE CORRENTE
RUGA 2 POZZI
C. DEL PISTOR
CALLE DE LE VELE
C. PRIULI
C. D. CRISTO
CALLE DEL FORNO
CALLE VERDI
C. DE L'OCA
SAL. DEL PISTOR
CAMPO S. SOFIA
FOND. SAN FELICE
DE LA STUA
FOND. DE LA STUA
BECHER
C. DEL TRAGHETO
C. D'ORO
C. TIOZZI
CORTE DEL TIOZZI
C. DEL RAVANO
C. DA CA' CORNER
CALLE DEL ROSA
C. DEI MORTI
C. DE LA REGINA
SAN CASSIANO
Campo Cassiano
Rio de San Cassan
C. MIANI
C. DEL CAMPANIEL
F. RIVA DE L'OGIO
C. DEI BOTERI
L'ERBAROL
CRISTI
BECARIE
CAPELER
FISH MARKET
Campo de la Pescaria
Campo de le Becarie
Mercato Rialto
PRODUCE MARKET
PALAZZO CA' DA MOSTO
C. POSTA
PALAZZO CIVRAN
SAN GIACOMO DE RIALTO
Campo San Giacomo
Campo Rialto Novo
RUGA DEI ORESI
PRANGON
RIALTO BRIDGE
C. DA CA' MUTI
CA' MUTI
C. DE LABOTA
RASPI
Rio de le Becarie
C. 2 SPADE
RUGA D. SPEZIERI
C. DONZELA
DRIO SCIMIA
C. SCIMIA
VAROTERI
C. BO
C. 2 MORI
C. L'ANZOLO
C. S. MATIO
SANSONI
ARCO
DONZELA
RUGA VECH. S. GIO.
CALLE TOSCANA
C. DE LA MADONA
C. DEI CINQUE
CARAMPANE
C. ALBRIZZI
Campiello Albrizti
STRETTA
SOT. FURATOLA
RIO TERA S. APONAL
SAN APONAL
Campo San Aponal
C. MADONA
PERDON
C. DE MEZO
C. TODESCHINI
L'OGIO RUGHETA RAVANO
RIO TERA S. SILVESTRO
C. DEL PARADISO
CALLE DEL STURION
RIVA DEL VIN
CALLE DOLERA
Campo San Silvestro
SAN SILVESTRO
Corte Barzizza
PALAZZO BARZIZZA
PALAZZO PAPADOPOLI
San Silvestro
To Frari, Accademia & 14
C. MADONETA
CALLE FORNO
CALLE MALVASIA
C. TIEPOLO
Rialto
C. RIVA DEL FERRO
SAN PIO X
SAN BARTOLOMEO
C. LARGA MAZZINI
BOMBA
VIA 2 APRILE
PALAZZO DOLFIN-MANIN
PALAZZO BEMBO
To Accademia
Campo San Salv.
1
2
3
8
9
10
11
12
13
15
16

Restaurants near the Rialto Bridge

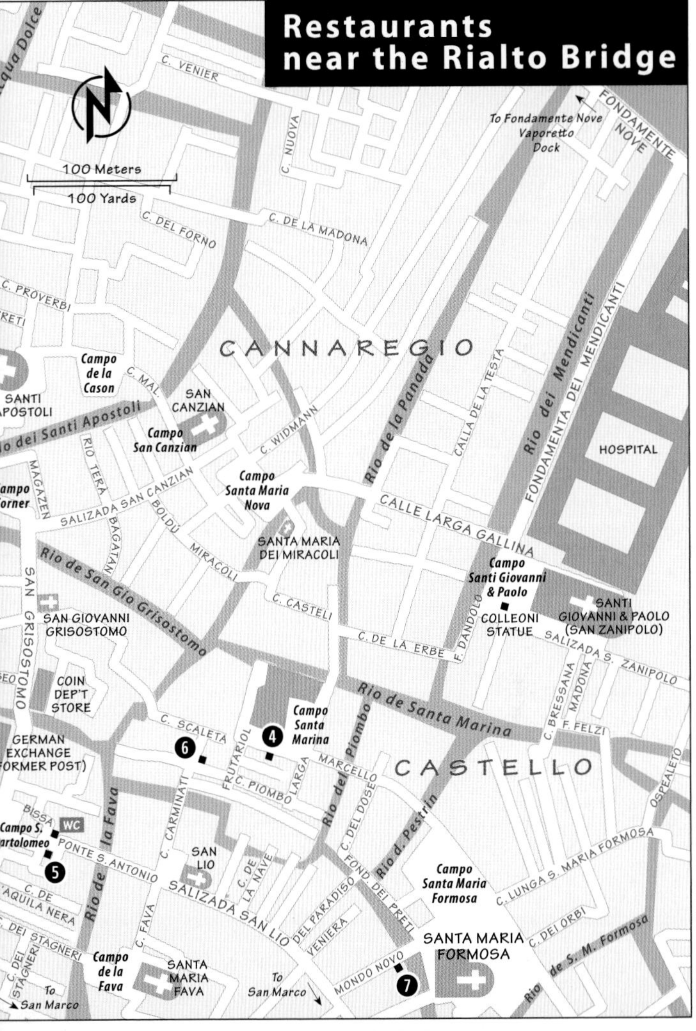

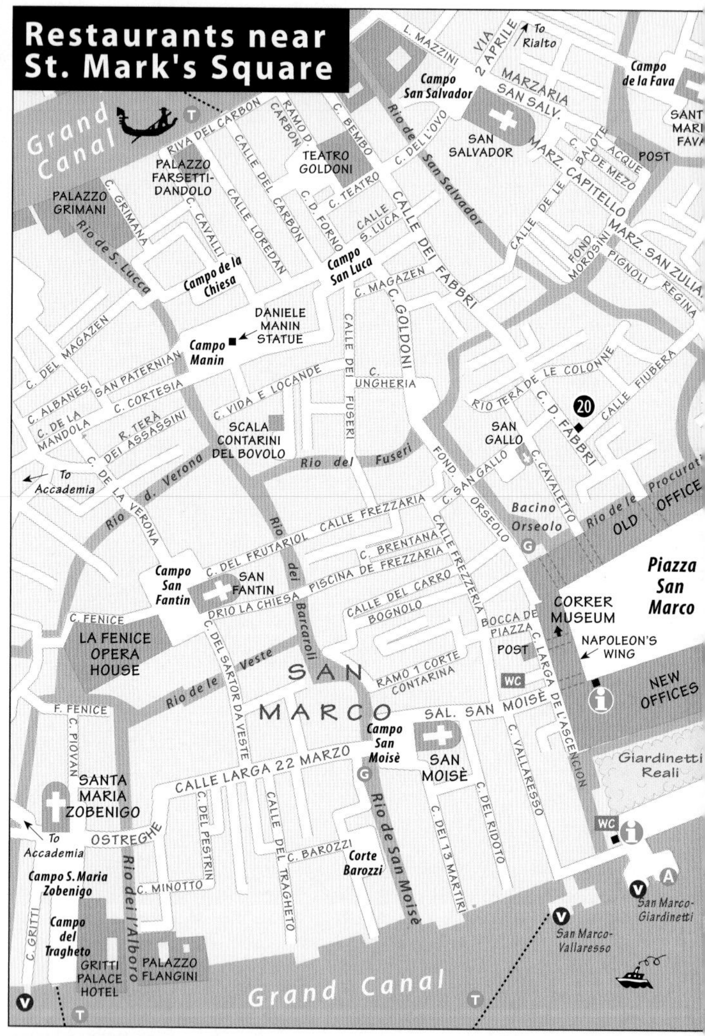
Restaurants near St. Mark's Square
Grand Canal
Campo San Salvador
SAN SALVADOR
Campo de la Fava
TEATRO GOLDONI
PALAZZO FARSETTI-DANDOLO
PALAZZO GRIMANI
Campo de la Chiesa
Campo San Luca
DANIELE MANIN STATUE
Campo Manin
SCALA CONTARINI DEL BOVOLO
To Rialto
To Accademia
20
SAN GALLO
Bacino Orseolo
OLD OFFICE
Piazza San Marco
CORRER MUSEUM
NAPOLEON'S WING
NEW OFFICES
Campo San Fantin
SAN FANTIN
LA FENICE OPERA HOUSE
SAN MARCO
Campo San Moisè
SAN MOISÈ
SANTA MARIA ZOBENIGO
Campo S. Maria Zobenigo
Campo del Tragheto
GRITTI PALACE HOTEL
PALAZZO FLANGINI
Corte Barozzi
Giardinetti Reali
San Marco-Vallaresso
San Marco-Giardinetti
POST
WC

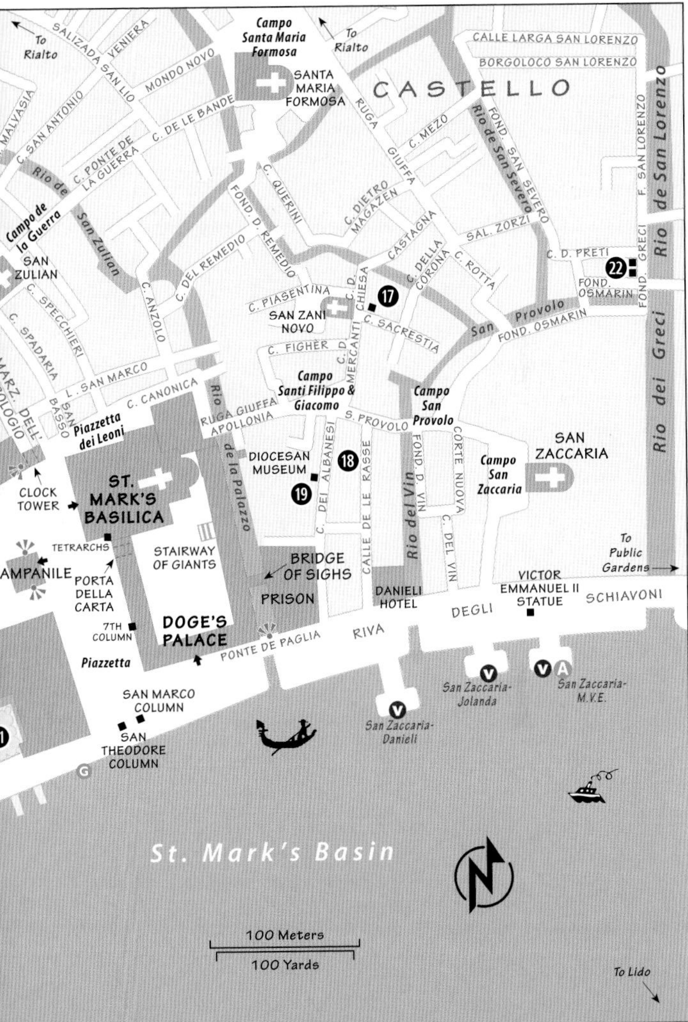
Campo Santa Maria Formosa
SANTA MARIA FORMOSA
CASTELLO
To Rialto
To Rialto
SALIZADA SAN LIO
VENIERA
MONDO NOVO
C. DE LE BANDE
RUGA GIUFFA
C. MEZO
CALLE LARGA SAN LORENZO
BORGOLOCO SAN LORENZO
FOND. SAN SEVERO
Rio de San Severo
Rio de San Lorenzo
F. SAN LORENZO
C. SAN ANTONIO
R. MALVASIA
C. PONTE DE LA GUERRA
Rio de San Zulian
Campo de la Guerra
SAN ZULIAN
C. QUERINI
FOND. D. REMEDIO
C. DIETRO MAGAZEN
SAL. ZORZI
C. D. PRETI
FOND. GRECI
Rio dei Greci
FOND. OSMARIN
Rio di San Provolo
FOND. OSMARIN
C. DEL REMEDIO
CASTAGNA
C. DELLA CORONA
C. ROTTA
C. PIASENTINA
C. D. CHIESA
SAN ZANI NOVO
C. SACRESTIA
C. SPECCHIERI
C. SPADARIA
C. ANZOLO
C. FIGHER
C. D. MERCANTI
L. SAN MARCO
C. CANONICA
Campo Santi Filippo & Giacomo
Campo San Provolo
S. PROVOLO
MARZ. DELL' OROLOGIO
SAN BASSO
Piazzetta dei Leoni
RUGA GIUFFA APOLLONIA
Rio de la Palazzo
DIOCESAN MUSEUM
C. DEI ALBANESI
CALLE DE LE RASSE
Rio del Vin
FOND. D. VIN
CORTE NUOVA
C. DEL VIN
Campo San Zaccaria
SAN ZACCARIA
CLOCK TOWER
ST. MARK'S BASILICA
TETRARCHS
STAIRWAY OF GIANTS
CAMPANILE
PORTA DELLA CARTA
BRIDGE OF SIGHS
PRISON
DANIELI HOTEL
VICTOR EMMANUEL II STATUE
To Public Gardens
RIVA DEGLI SCHIAVONI
7TH COLUMN
DOGE'S PALACE
PONTE DE PAGLIA
Piazzetta
SAN MARCO COLUMN
SAN THEODORE COLUMN
San Zaccaria-Jolanda
San Zaccaria-M.V.E.
San Zaccaria-Danieli
St. Mark's Basin
100 Meters
100 Yards
To Lido
17
18
19
21
22

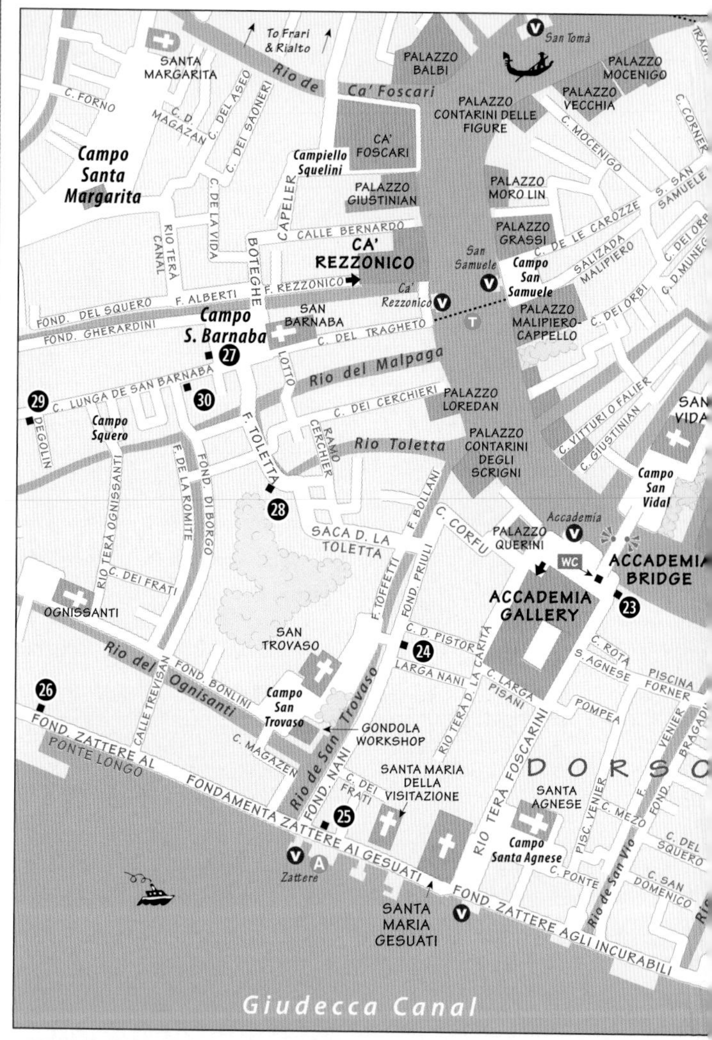
To Frari & Rialto
San Tomà
SANTA MARGARITA
PALAZZO BALBI
PALAZZO MOCENIGO
Rio de Ca' Foscari
C. FORNO
C. D. MAGAZAN
C. DEL ASEO
C. DEI SAONERI
PALAZZO CONTARINI DELLE FIGURE
PALAZZO VECCHIA
C. MOCENIGO
C. CORNER
CA' FOSCARI
Campiello Squelini
Campo Santa Margarita
C. DE LA VIDA
CAPELER
PALAZZO GIUSTINIAN
PALAZZO MORO LIN
S. SAN SAMUELE
PALAZZO GRASSI
C. DE LE CAROZZE
CALLE BERNARDO
RIO TERÀ CANAL
BOTEGHE
CA' REZZONICO
San Samuele
Campo San Samuele
SALIZADA MALIPIERO
C. DEI ORBI
C. D. MUNEGA
F. REZZONICO
Ca' Rezzonico
F. ALBERTI
FOND. DEL SQUERO
FOND. GHERARDINI
Campo S. Barnaba
SAN BARNABA
C. DEL TRAGHETO
PALAZZO MALIPIERO-CAPPELLO
C. DEI ORBI
27
LOTTO
Rio del Malpaga
C. LUNGA DE SAN BARNABA
30
29
DEGOLIN
Campo Squero
C. DEI CERCHIERI
PALAZZO LOREDAN
C. VITTURI O FALIER
C. GIUSTINIAN
SAN VIDAL
RAMO CERCHIER
F. TOLETTA
Rio Toletta
PALAZZO CONTARINI DEGLI SCRIGNI
F. DE LA ROMITE
FOND. DI BORGO
RIO TERÀ OGNISSANTI
28
F. BOLLANI
Campo San Vidal
SACA D. LA TOLETTA
C. CORFU
PALAZZO QUERINI
Accademia
WC
ACCADEMIA BRIDGE
C. DEI FRATI
F. TOFFETTI
FOND. PRIULI
ACCADEMIA GALLERY
23
OGNISSANTI
C. D. PISTOR
24
SAN TROVASO
LARGA NANI
C. LARGA PISANI
C. ROTA
S. AGNESE
PISCINA FORNER
Rio del Ognisanti
FOND. BONLINI
CALLE TREVISAN
Campo San Trovaso
Rio de San Trovaso
RIO TERÀ D. LA CARITÀ
POMPEA
26
GONDOLA WORKSHOP
FOND. ZATTERE AL PONTE LONGO
C. MAGAZEN
FOND. NANI
RIO TERÀ FOSCARINI
DORSO
VENIER
BRAGADIN
SANTA MARIA DELLA VISITAZIONE
SANTA AGNESE
PISC. VENIER
C. MEZO
FOND.
C. DEI FRATI
25
FONDAMENTA ZATTERE AI GESUATI
Campo Santa Agnese
C. DEL SQUERO
Rio de San Vio
Zattere
C. PONTE
C. SAN DOMENICO
SANTA MARIA GESUATI
FOND. ZATTERE AGLI INCURABILI
Giudecca Canal

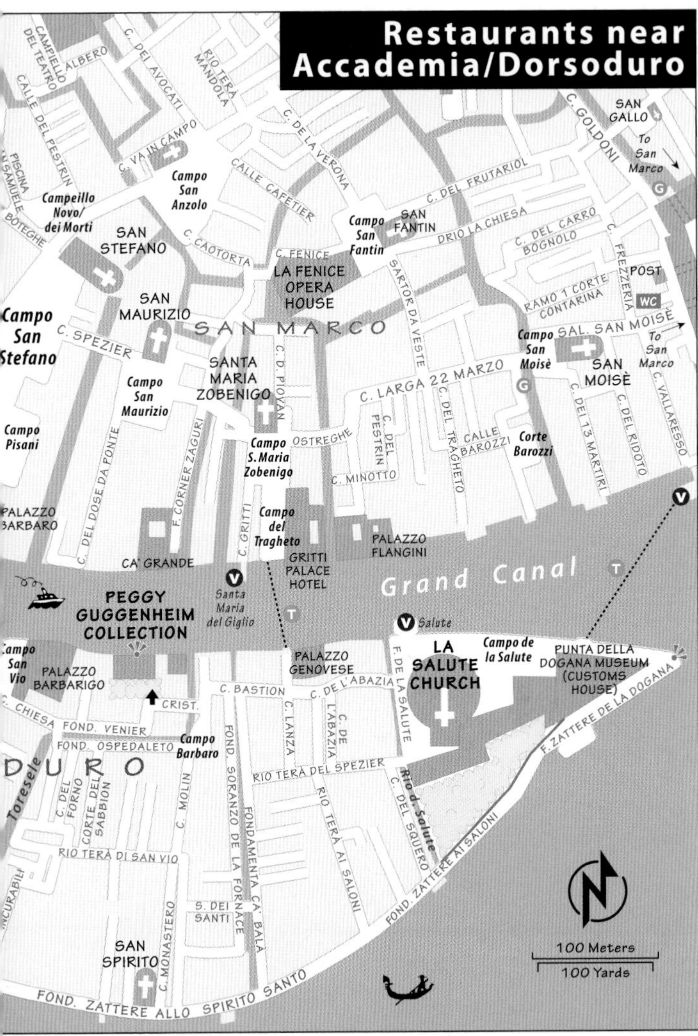
Restaurants near Accademia/Dorsoduro
Campo San Stefano
Campo San Anzolo
Campo San Fantin
LA FENICE OPERA HOUSE
SAN MARCO
Campo San Maurizio
SANTA MARIA ZOBENIGO
Campo S. Maria Zobenigo
Campo San Moisè
SAN MOISÈ
Corte Barozzi
Campo del Tragheto
GRITTI PALACE HOTEL
PALAZZO FLANGINI
Grand Canal
PEGGY GUGGENHEIM COLLECTION
Santa Maria del Giglio
Salute
LA SALUTE CHURCH
Campo de la Salute
PUNTA DELLA DOGANA MUSEUM (CUSTOMS HOUSE)
PALAZZO GENOVESE
PALAZZO BARBARIGO
Campo San Vio
Campo Barbaro
CA' GRANDE
PALAZZO BARBARO
DURO
SAN SPIRITO
FOND. ZATTERE ALLO SPIRITO SANTO
FOND. ZATTERE AI SALONI
F. ZATTERE DE LA DOGANA
To San Marco
100 Meters
100 Yards

Restaurants near the Train Station/Cannaregio
Rio de San Giobbe
SAN GIOBBE
FOND. DE CANNAREGIO
C. SAN GIOVANNI
CHIOVERETE
Canale de Cannaregio
FOND. PESCARIA
FOND. SAVORGNAN
C. DE LA 2 CORTI
CALLE RIELO
100 Meters
100 Yards
CALLE DELLA MISERICORDIA
SAN GEREMIA
RAMO DEI SCALZI
C. PRIULI DEI CAVALETTI
RIO TERÀ LISTA DI SPAGNA
FORNO
33
SANTA LUCIA TRAIN STATION (FERROVIA)
SCALZI
Grand
Ferrovia W
SCALZI BRIDGE
Ferrovia Scalzi
Campo San Simeon Grande
CALLE PISTOR
CORTE PISANI
Rio Marin
FOND. DE SAN SIMEONE PICCOLO
C. LUNGA CHIOVERETTE
C. NOVA DE S. SIMEON
WC
Ferrovia
To Calatrava Bridge
To Piazzale Roma
SAN SIMEONE PICCOLO
SAN SIMEONE GRANDE
LISTA

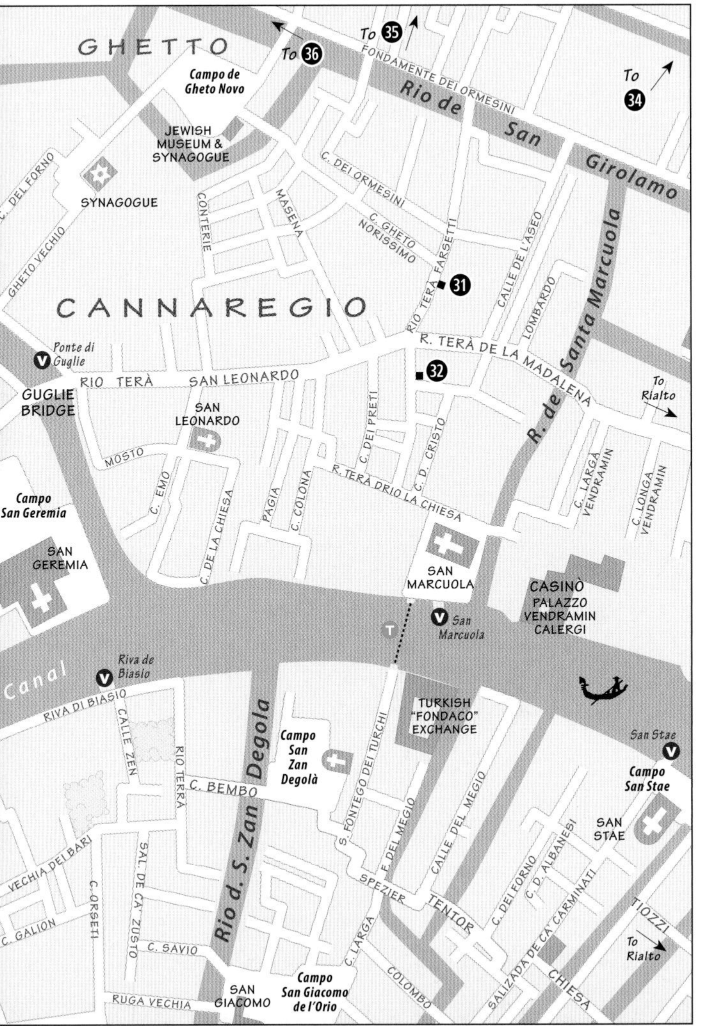
GHETTO
To 36
To 35
To 34
Campo de Gheto Novo
JEWISH MUSEUM & SYNAGOGUE
SYNAGOGUE
FONDAMENTE DEI ORMESINI
Rio de San Girolamo
C. DEI ORMESINI
C. GHETO NORISSIMO
C. DEL FORNO
GHETO VECHIO
CONTERIE
MASENA
RIO TERÀ FARSETTI
CALLE DE L'ASEO
LOMBARDO
R. de Santa Marcuola
31
32
CANNAREGIO
Ponte di Guglie
GUGLIE BRIDGE
RIO TERÀ SAN LEONARDO
R. TERÀ DE LA MADALENA
To Rialto
SAN LEONARDO
MOSTO
C. EMO
C. DE LA CHIESA
PAGIA
C. COLONA
C. DEI PRETI
C. D. CRISTO
R. TERÀ DRIO LA CHIESA
C. LARGA VENDRAMIN
C. LONGA VENDRAMIN
Campo San Geremia
SAN GEREMIA
SAN MARCUOLA
CASINÒ PALAZZO VENDRAMIN CALERGI
San Marcuola
Riva de Biasio
Canal
RIVA DI BIASIO
CALLE ZEN
RIO TERRÀ
C. BEMBO
Rio d. S. Zan Degola
Campo San Zan Degolà
S. FONTEGO DEI TURCHI
TURKISH "FONDACO" EXCHANGE
F. DEL MEGIO
CALLE DEL MEGIO
San Stae
Campo San Stae
SAN STAE
VECHIA DEI BARI
C. GALION
C. ORSETI
SAL. DE CA' ZUSTO
C. SAVIO
RUGA VECHIA
SAN GIACOMO
Campo San Giacomo de l'Orio
C. LARGA
SPEZIER
TENTOR
COLOMBO
C. DEI FORNO
C. D. ALBANESI
SALIZADA DE CA' CARMINATI
TIOZZI
CHIESA
To Rialto

Eating

Actv 99

Practicalities

Planning 186
Money. 186
Arrival in Venice. 187
Helpful Hints 192
Getting Around Venice 194
Communicating. 197
Sightseeing Tips 198
Theft and Emergencies. 200
Activities 201
Resources from Rick Steves 206
Italian Survival Phrases 207

PLANNING

When to Go

Venice's best travel months (also its busiest and most expensive) are May, June, September, and October. These months combine the convenience of peak season with pleasant weather. July and August are more temperate (high 70s and 80s) than in Italy's scorching inland cities. Between November and April, expect mild winter weather (with lows in the 30s and 40s), occasional flooding, shorter sightseeing hours, cheaper hotel rates, and fewer tourists (except during the busy Carnevale festival, generally in February). March and April offer a good balance of low-season prices and comfortable weather.

Before You Go

Make sure your passport is up to date (to renew, see www.travel.state.gov). Call your debit- and credit-card companies about your plans (see below). Book hotel rooms in advance, especially for travel during peak season or holiday weekends. Consider buying travel insurance (see www.ricksteves.com/insurance). If traveling beyond Venice, research transit schedules (trains, buses) and car rentals. If renting a car, you're technically required to have an International Driving Permit (sold at your local AAA office), though I've often rented cars in Italy without one. Consider making reservations for key sights. Get a current list of museum hours at www.turismovenezia.it.

MONEY

Italy uses the euro currency: 1 euro (€) = about $1.30. To convert prices in euros to dollars, add about 30 percent: €20 = about $26, €50 = about $65. (Check www.oanda.com for the latest exchange rates.)

Withdraw money from a cash machine using a debit card, just like at home. Visa and MasterCard are commonly used throughout Europe. Before departing, call your bank and credit-card company: Confirm that your card will work overseas, ask about international transaction fees, and alert them that you'll be making withdrawals in Europe. Many travelers bring a second debit/credit card as a backup.

While American credit cards are accepted almost everywhere in

Helpful Websites

Italian Tourist Information: www.italia.it
Venice Tourist Information: www.turismovenezia.it
Other Helpful Venice Websites: www.hellovenezia.com (vaporetto and event schedules), www.museicivicivenezianі.it (civic museums in Venice), www.venicexplorer.net (interactive maps), www.venicefor visitors.com, and www.aguestinvenice.com
Cheap Flights: www.kayak.com (for international flights), www.sky scanner.com (for flights within Europe)
European Train Schedules: www.bahn.com
General Travel Tips: www.ricksteves.com (trip planning, packing lists, and more—plus updates for this book)

Europe, they will not work in some automated payment machines. Instead, pay with cash, try your PIN code (ask your credit-card company or use a debit card), or find a nearby cashier who should be able to process the transaction.

To keep your valuables safe, wear a money belt. But if you do lose your credit or debit card, report the loss immediately. Call these 24-hour US numbers collect: Visa (tel. 303/967-1096), MasterCard (tel. 636/722-7111), and American Express (tel. 336/393-1111).

ARRIVAL IN VENICE

Marco Polo Airport

Venice's small, modern airport (airport code: VCE) is on the mainland shore of the lagoon, six miles north of the city. There's one sleek terminal, with a TI, ATMs, car-rental agencies, and a few shops and eateries. For flight information, call 041-260-9260, visit www.veniceairport.com, or ask at your hotel.

To get between the airport (on the mainland) and downtown Venice (on an island) can easily take two hours, so allow plenty of time. Here are your options:

Alilaguna Boats—Slow But Easy: These 50-passenger boats

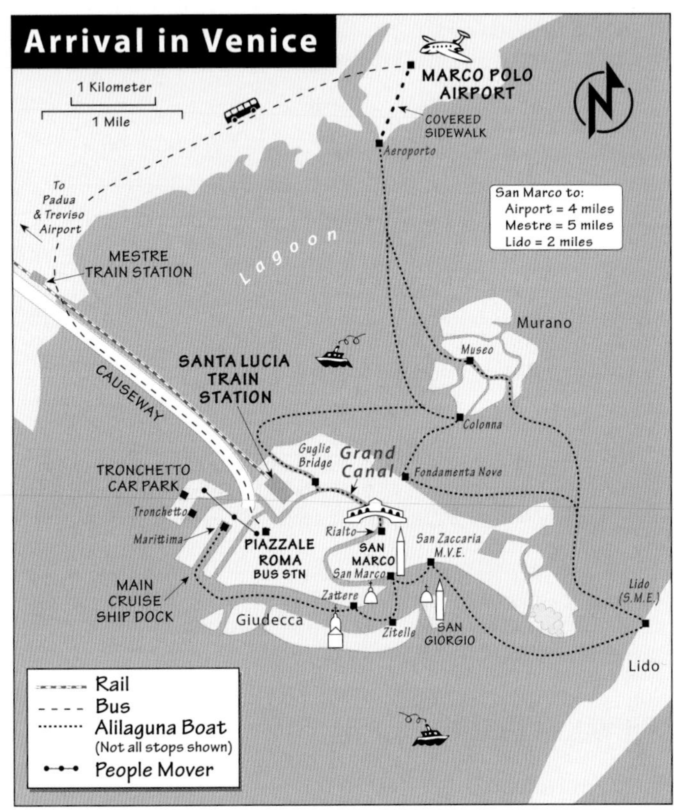

make the hour-plus journey between the airport dock (a short walk from the terminal) and various points in Venice. There are three Alilaguna lines—blue, red, and orange. Some of the main stops include: San Marco, San Zaccaria (near San Marco), Rialto, Guglie (near the train station), Zattere (the Dorsoduro neighborhood), and Fondamente Nove (on the fish's back). You can reach most of this book's recommended hotels very simply by Alilaguna, with no changes. The cost is €15 (€25 round-trip, not covered by city transit passes). Boats depart roughly every 30 minutes. Get a full schedule at the TI or your hotel, call 041-240-1701, or see www.alilaguna.it.

For the trip from the airport into Venice, buy tickets inside the terminal at the TI or the Alilaguna ticket desk, or outside at the dock. To get to the boat dock, exit the arrivals hall and turn left. It's an eight-minute walk away, following signs along a paved, level, covered sidewalk (easy for wheeled bags).

From Venice to the airport, boats start leaving as early as 3:40 in the morning. Alilaguna boats can fill up, so arrive early.

Water Taxis—Fast and Direct, But Pricey: Luxury taxi speedboats zip directly between the airport and the closest dock to your hotel, getting you within steps of your final destination in about 30 minutes. The official price is €110 for up to four people; add €10 for every additional person (10-passenger limit). You may get a higher quote—politely talk it down. A taxi can be a smart investment for small groups and those with an early departure.

From the airport, arrange your ride at the water-taxi desk or with the boat captains lounging at the dock (the same dock as the Alilaguna boats).

From Venice to the airport, book a day ahead, either through your hotel (easiest) or at tel. 041-522-2303 (www.motoscafivenezia.it).

Airport Shuttle Buses—Cheapest, But to Only One Destination: Buses make the 25-minute trip across the bridge from the mainland to the island, dropping you at Piazzale Roma, a major transportation hub at the "mouth of the fish." (✪ See "Piazzale Roma Bus Station," next page.) From there, you can walk farther into Venice or catch a vaporetto down the Grand Canal. Two different, equally good bus companies (ACTV and ATVO) make the trip—just jump on whichever one's leaving next (€5, runs about 5:00-24:00, 2/hour, only 1/hour early and late, check schedules at www.atvo.it or www.actv.it).

From the airport to Venice, both bus companies leave from just outside the arrivals terminal. Buy tickets inside the terminal (at the TI or ticket desk), from ticket machines at curbside, or from the driver. ATVO tickets are not valid on ACTV buses and vice versa. Double-check the destination; you want Piazzale Roma. If taking ACTV, you want bus #5.

From Piazzale Roma to the airport, buy your ticket from the ACTV windows or ATVO office before heading out to the platforms.

Santa Lucia Train Station

Venice's train station (Ferrovia) is located at the head of the Grand Canal, an easy vaporetto ride or fascinating 40-minute walk to St. Mark's Square. (Don't confuse Santa Lucia station—called "Venezia S.L."—with Venezia Mestre on the mainland.)

Minimize your time in the often-crowded station. Baggage check is at track 1 (€11/24 hours, no lockers). WCs (€0.80) are at track 1 and in the back of the big bar/cafeteria. The station's TI is not worth a long wait for a so-so map. If you need train tickets or seat reservations (required for many Venice-Florence-Rome trains, even with a railpass) consider doing it online or at downtown travel agencies: Try Oltrex Change and Travel (one bridge east of the Bridge of Sighs, on Riva degli Schiavoni, tel. 041-524-2828) or Kele & Teo Travel (between St. Mark's and Rialto Bridge, along the main route, tel. 041-520-8722).

The Ferrovia vaporetto stop is right out the station's front door—vaporetto #1 (slow boat down the Grand Canal, with many stops) or vaporetto #2 (express). A water taxi into central Venice is about €60.

Piazzale Roma Bus Station

This open-air parking lot, located at the head of the Grand Canal, serves as a transportation hub for buses, vaporettos, cars, and the People Mover monorail. The square is a jumble of different operators, platforms, and crosswalks over busy lanes of traffic.

Get oriented. The modern Calatrava Bridge leads to the train station, a five-minute walk away. The vaporetto dock is just left of the modern bridge, where vaporetto #1 (slow) or #2 (fast) can take you down the Grand Canal to San Marco. The ACTV bus (including #5 to Marco Polo Airport) has a ticket window by the vaporetto. The ATVO bus ticket office (also to the airport) is in the big, white building. Also on the square are two big parking garages and the People Mover monorail to the cruise port and Tronchetto parking lot. A baggage-storage office is next to the monorail at #497m (€5/24 hours).

Parking Garages

The freeway dead-ends after crossing the causeway to the traffic-free island of Venice. At the end of the road you have two parking choices: garages at Tronchetto or Piazzale Roma. As you approach, signs tell you which lots are full.

Tronchetto garage is a bit farther out, a bit cheaper, and well-connected by vaporetto (€21/24 hours, discounts for longer stays, tel. 041-520-7555, www.veniceparking.it). There's little else at Tronchetto besides the helpful HelloVenezia public transport office, aggressive salesmen, and travel agencies masquerading as TIs.

To get into downtown Venice, the easiest and cheapest way is by vaporetto #2. To find the dock, exit the garage, cross the street, and walk to the right, looking for *"ACTV"* signs. Line 2 has two different routes to San Marco: down the Grand Canal (more scenic, stops at Rialto, 40 minutes to San Marco), or via Giudecca (around the city, faster, no Rialto stop, 30 minutes to San Marco). A water taxi to San Marco (you'll be approached by boatmen) costs around €100. The People Mover monorail—a long walk from the parking garage—can zip you to Piazzale Roma (buy €1 monorail tickets with coins from a machine).

Piazzale Roma's two garages are closer to the center of town and have more transportation options, but they're a bit more expensive and likelier to be full. The big white Autorimessa Communale garage on the right is cheapest (€25/24 hours, tel. 041-272-7211, www.asmvenezia.it). The other is Garage San Marco (€30/24 hours, tel. 041-523-2213, www.garagesanmarco.it). At either garage, you'll have to give up your keys.

Cruise Ports

Most cruise ships visiting Venice dock at Stazione Marittima, located in the jaw of the fish's mouth. There's a good map of Venice's port area at www.port.venice.it/en/terminals.html.

To get to St. Mark's Square, catch the Alilaguna blue line—it takes just 20 minutes. Buy tickets at the kiosk in front of building #103 at the top of the harbor (€8, €3 per big bag). Get more info at www.alilaguna.it. The People Mover monorail to Piazzale Roma is a five-minute walk inland from the port (you'll see its elevated platform). A water taxi to anywhere in town costs around €80.

HELPFUL HINTS

Tourist Information (TI): Venice's crowded and clunky TIs aren't all that helpful, but their shared website is good: www.turismovenezia.it. Click on "Venezia," then the English icon, and you'll find info on current events, the vaporettos ("Getting Around"), current museum hours (click "Art & Culture," then select "Museums"), and more. Or call the TI at 041-529-8711.

If you must visit a TI, you'll find offices at the train station (daily 8:00-18:30), on St. Mark's Square (daily 9:00-15:30, in far-left corner with your back to the basilica), nearby at the San Marco-Vallaresso vaporetto dock (daily 11:00-18:00), and at the airport (daily 9:00-20:00).

Hurdling the Language Barrier: Most people in the tourist industry—and virtually all young people—speak at least a little English. Still, learn the pleasantries like *buon giorno* (good day), *mi scusi* (pardon me), *per favore* (please), *grazie* (thank you), and *arrivederci* (goodbye). For more Italian survival phrases, ✪ see page 207.

Time Zones: Italy's time zone is generally six/nine hours ahead of the East/West Coasts of the US.

Watt's Up? Europe's electrical system is 220 volts, instead of North America's 110 volts. Most newer electronics (including hair dryers, laptops, and battery chargers) convert automatically, so you won't need a voltage converter—but you will need a special adapter plug with two round prongs, sold inexpensively at US and Canadian travel stores.

Numbers and Stumblers: What Americans call the second floor of a building is the first floor in Europe. Europeans write dates as day/month/year, so Christmas is 25/12/13. Commas are decimal points and vice versa—a dollar and a half is 1,50, and there are 5.280 feet in a mile.

Italy uses the metric system: A kilogram is 2.2 pounds; a liter is about a quart; and a kilometer is six-tenths of a mile. Temperature is measured in Celsius. 0°C = 32°F. To convert Celsius to Fahrenheit, double the number and add 30.

Holidays: Many sights and banks close down on national holidays (though Venice stays open more than most Italian cities). Verify dates at www.italiantourism.com or www.turismovenezia.it, or check www.ricksteves.com/festivals.

Business Hours: Most businesses are open Monday through Saturday 10:00-19:00 (a bit longer in tourist areas). Though many stores

Tipping

Tipping in Europe isn't as automatic and generous as it is in the US. At Italian restaurants that have waitstaff, a 10-15 percent "service" charge *(servizio)* is usually included in your bill's grand total. Italians don't tip beyond this, but if the service is exceptional, you can round up the bill by a euro or two. At hotels, it's polite to give porters a euro for each bag (another reason to pack light). If you like to tip maids, leave a euro per night in your room at the end of your stay.

close on Sunday, you'll find more open here than anywhere else in Italy. Hours can vary widely from store to store. Some small businesses close for lunch (roughly 13:00-15:30). Banking hours are generally Monday through Friday 8:30-13:30 and 15:30-16:30.

Bookstores: The small Libreria Studium, a block behind St. Mark's Basilica, has new English books, including my guidebooks (daily 9:00-19:30, at Calle de la Canonica #337, tel. 041-522-2382). The funky Acqua Alta ("high water") used bookstore has prepared for the next flood by shelving its wares in bathtubs and a gondola (daily 9:00-21:00, just beyond Campo Santa Maria Formosa on Calle Lunga Santa Maria Formosa at #5176, tel. 041-296-0841).

Laundry: The coin-operated "Orange" launderette is across the Grand Canal from the train station on Ramo de le Chioverete at Santa Croce 665b (€14/load, daily 7:30-22:30). For a full service laundry (drop off and pick up two hours later), Lavanderia Gabriella is a few streets north of St. Mark's Square on Rio Terà de le Colonne at #985 (€15/load, Mon-Fri 8:00-12:30, tel. 041-522-1758).

***Sestieri* and Addresses:** Venice is divided into six districts *(sestieri)*: San Marco (from St. Mark's Square to the Accademia Bridge), Castello (the area east of St. Mark's Square), Dorsoduro (the belly of the fish, on the far side the Accademia Bridge), Cannaregio (between the train station and the Rialto Bridge), San Polo (west of the Rialto Bridge), and Santa Croce (the "eye" of the fish, across the canal from the train station).

Most addresses (e.g., "Santa Croce 665b") list only the district and house number—not the street. This makes it confusing to find a specific address, so get as much information as you can. For example, the full address for Hotel Guerrato is: Calle Drio La Scimia (the street), 240/a (house number), Rialto (nearest landmark), San Polo (district).

Free Water: Carry a water bottle to refill at public fountains fed by pure, tasty water piped in from the (surprisingly close) Alps.

Services: WCs are scarce. Use them when you can, in any café or museum you patronize. Handy public WCs (€1.50) are near major landmarks. (At St. Mark's Square, it's behind the Correr Museum.)

Pigeon Poop: If your head is bombed by a pigeon, resist the initial response to wipe it off immediately—it'll just smear into your hair. Wait until it dries, and it should flake off cleanly. But if the poop splatters on your clothes, wipe it off immediately to avoid a stain.

Be Prepared to Splurge: Venice is expensive for residents as well as tourists, as everything must be shipped in and hand-trucked to its destination. I find that the best way to enjoy Venice is just to succumb to its charms and blow a little money.

GETTING AROUND VENICE

On Foot

Venice is delightfully car-free, making pedestrians suddenly feel big, important, and liberated.

The city's "streets" are narrow pedestrian walkways connecting its docks, squares, bridges, and courtyards. To navigate, follow yellow signs on street corners pointing you to *(per)* the nearest major landmark: San Marco, Rialto, Accademia, Ferrovia, or Piazzale Roma.

Some helpful street lingo: *Campo* means square, *calle* is a street, *fondamenta* is an embankment along a canal, *rio* is a small canal, *sotoportego* is a covered passageway, and *ponte* is a bridge.

If you're a map reader, invest in a good one (around €5), sold at bookstores and newsstands.

Dare to turn off the posted routes and make your own discoveries. Don't worry about getting lost. Keep reminding yourself, "I'm on an island, and I can't get off." When it comes time to find your way, just follow the signs or simply ask a local, *"Dov'è San Marco?"*

By Vaporetto

These motorized bus-boats run by the public transit system (ACTV) work like city buses except that they never get a flat, the stops are docks, and if you get off between stops, you might drown. For schedules and general information about the vaporettos, see www.hellovenezia.com or www.actv.it.

Tickets and Passes: A single-ride ticket (€7 for most trips) is good for one hour in one direction, with unlimited stops and transfers during that time. Or you can buy a pass: €18/12 hours, €20/24 hours, €25/36 hours, €30/48 hours, €35/72 hours, or €50/7-day pass. A pass can pay for itself in a hurry, so think through your Venice itinerary before you pay for your first vaporetto trip. On the other hand, many tourists just walk and rarely use a boat.

Buy tickets and passes from booths at the docks or from small "HelloVenezia" shops around town. Tickets are electronic, so you can reuse them for your next trip by putting more money on it at the automated kiosks (avoiding lines). If the ticket booth at your dock is closed, buy from the conductor when you board. Riding without a ticket risks a €50 fine.

Riding the Vaporetto: It's very much like catching a bus. Before you board, validate your ticket or pass by holding it up to the small white machine on the dock until you hear a pinging sound. To find your boat, follow signs directing you to the right dock. Each departing boat has a route number (e.g., #1) and also the direction it's headed—for example, "#1 *per* San Marco." Find that dock and wait for your boat to arrive. The system is simple, though some large stops have multiple docks and multiple lines going in various directions.

Grand Canal Lines #1 and #2: For most travelers, only these two vaporetto lines matter. They leave every 10 minutes or so and go up and down the Grand Canal, between the "mouth of the fish" at one end and San Marco at the other. Line #1 is the slow boat, taking 45 minutes and making every stop along the way. Line #2 takes 25 minutes, making only select stops, including the Tronchetto parking lot, Piazzale Roma, Ferrovia (train station), Rialto Bridge, Accademia Bridge, San Marco, and San Zaccaria (east of St. Mark's Square). Avoid rush hour, when boats can be packed: during mornings heading in from Piazzale Roma, and in evenings heading out to Piazzale Roma. Riding at night, you'll enjoy nearly empty boats and views of chandelier-lit palace interiors.

Handy *Vaporetti* from San Zaccaria: About 150 yards east of St. Mark's Square are the four San Zaccaria docks, where several helpful boats depart:

- Line #1 goes up the Grand Canal. In the other direction it goes east to Arsenale, Giardini (the Biennale site), and the Lido.
- Line #2 goes up the Grand Canal. In the other direction, it zips over to San Giorgio Maggiore (✪ see page 132).
- Lines #4.1 and #7 both go to Murano in 45 minutes.
- Lines #5.1 and #5.2 make a circular loop around the island—perfect if you just like riding boats.
- The Alilaguna airport shuttle to and from the airport stops here.

By *Traghetto*

These gondola-like, oar-powered boats shuttle locals and in-the-know tourists across the Grand Canal. (Find the stops on the color map at the front of this book.) Just step in, hand the gondolier €2, and enjoy the short ride—standing or sitting. Note that some *traghetti* are seasonal, some stop running as early as 12:30, and all stop by 18:00.

By Water Taxi

Venetian taxis, like speedboat limos, hang out at busy points along the Grand Canal. Prices are regulated: €15 for pick-up, then €2 per minute (plus other supplements; get details at www.turismovenezia.it). A typical trip from the train station to Rialto would cost about €40. Despite regulation, prices can be soft; negotiate and settle on the price before stepping in. For travelers with lots of luggage, or small groups who can split the cost, taxi boat rides can be a time-saving convenience. For a little more than €100 an hour, you can have a private, unguided taxi-boat tour. It's pricey, but skipping across the lagoon in a classic wooden motorboat is a cool indulgence.

COMMUNICATING

Telephones

Making Calls: To call Italy from the US or Canada: Dial 011-39 and then the local number (011 is our international access code; 39 is Italy's country code).

To call Italy from a European country: Dial 00-39 followed by the local number (00 is Europe's international access code).

To call within Italy, just dial the local number (Italy does not use area codes).

To call from Italy to another country: Dial 00, the country code (for example, 1 for the US or Canada), the area code, and number. If you're calling European countries whose phone numbers begin with 0, you'll usually have to omit that 0 when you dial.

Phoning Inexpensively: Since coin-op pay phones are virtually obsolete, you'll need a phone card. The best option is a €5 international phone card *(carta telefonica internazionale)*, which works with a scratch-to-reveal PIN code. This gives you pennies-per-minute rates on international calls, decent rates for calls within Italy, and can even be used from your hotel phone. Buy them at newsstands and *tabacchi* (tobacco) shops. Tell the vendor where you'll be making the most calls (*"per Stati Uniti"*—to America), and he'll select the most economical brand.

Mobile Phones: A mobile phone—whether your own from home if it'll work in Italy, or a European one you buy when you arrive—is handy but can be pricey. You'll find mobile-phone stores selling cheap models with prepaid minutes and SIM cards at the airport, train station, and throughout Florence.

If traveling with a smartphone, switch off data-roaming until you have free Wi-Fi. Make phone calls for free or cheaply using Skype, Google Talk, or FaceTime.

For more on the fast-changing world of telephones, talk to your service provider or see www.ricksteves.com/phoning.

Internet Access

Almost all hotels have some form of Internet access—either a computer in the lobby or Wi-Fi. Most provide these services for free for a small fee. Otherwise, handy if pricey little Internet places with public computers are

Useful Phone Numbers

English-Speaking Police Help: Tel. 113
Ambulance: Tel. 118
Directory Assistance: Tel. 170 (free, in English) or tel. 12 (€0.50, in Italian)
US Embassy (in Rome): 24-hour emergency line—tel. 06-46741, non-emergency—tel. 06-4674-2406, www.usembassy.it
US Consulate (in Milan): Tel. 02-290-351 (Via Principe Amedeo 2/10, Milan, http://milan.usconsulate.gov)
Canadian Embassy (in Rome): Tel. 06-854-441, www.italy.gc.ca

scattered around town (usually on back streets, marked with an @ sign, and charging €5/hour). Many cafés offer Wi-Fi (usually free for customers).

SIGHTSEEING TIPS

Crowd Control: The city—especially the area from St. Mark's Square to Rialto—is inundated with cruise-ship crowds and day-trippers daily from 10:00 to 17:00, especially on weekends. Sights are most crowded around 11:00-12:00. Visit the St. Mark's Square area early or late, and do your midday sightseeing elsewhere. At St. Mark's Basilica, avoid the line by checking a bag (✪ see page 46), and avoid crowds inside by visiting near opening or closing times. At the Doge's Palace, skip the line by buying your combo-ticket (or a Museum Pass) at the uncrowded Correr Museum (✪ see page 68). At the Campanile and Accademia, visit early or late.

Hours: Most sights keep stable hours, but you can easily confirm the latest at a TI, or tel. 041-529-8711, or www.turismovenezia.it.

Venice Early and Late: Sights that open before 10:00 include the Accademia, Doge's Palace, Campanile, and many churches. Sights that stay open later than 18:00 (at least on some days) include the Accademia, Campanile, Correr Museum, and the Doge's Palace.

Typical Rules: Important sights have metal detectors or conduct bag searches that will slow your entry. Some don't allow large bags. Photos and videos are normally allowed, but flashes or tripods usually are not. Many sights stop admitting people 30-60 minutes before closing time, and guards start shooing people out, so don't save the best for last.

Dress Code at Churches: Basilica San Marco allows no bare shoulders or knees. Other churches encourage modest dress but don't enforce it.

Discounts: Youth and senior discounts are available to Americans and other non-EU citizens (bring ID) at a few museums, including the Doge's Palace, Correr Museum, and Ca' Rezzonico. Other museums generally do not offer discounts, but you can always ask.

Pace Yourself: Venice's endless pavement, crowds, and tight spaces are hard on tourists. Schedule cool breaks to refresh. If you must, pay for a drink in a café for the privilege of sitting.

Rick Steves' Free Audio Tours: I've produced free, self-guided audio tours of the Grand Canal, St. Mark's Square, St. Mark's Basilica, and the Frari Church. Download them for free via the Rick Steves Audio Europe smartphone app, www.ricksteves.com/audioeurope, iTunes, or Google Play.

Sightseeing Passes for Venice

Venice offers an array of passes for sightseeing and transit. None of the options are a must-have, but for most people, the **Museum Pass** (€20) can save some money and time in line. It covers the Doge's Palace/Correr Museum, the Ca' Rezzonico, Palazzo Mocenigo Costume Museum, Ca' Pesaro, and several lesser museums. If you see the Doge's Palace/Correr Museum, and even just one other museum, the pass pays for itself. Buy the Museum Pass at any participating museum. Families get a price break on multiple passes—ask.

Venice's other passes—e.g., the Chorus Pass (covering churches, €10) and the Venice Card (churches plus museums, €40)—are unlikely to pay for themselves. Note that a few major sights are not included in any pass: Accademia, Peggy Guggenheim Collection, Scuola San Rocco, Campanile, and the three museums within St. Mark's Basilica.

THEFT AND EMERGENCIES

Theft

While violent crime is rare in Venice, thieves—mainly well-dressed pickpockets—thrive in crowds. Be alert to the possibility of theft, even when you're absorbed in the wonder and newness of Venice. Be on guard whenever crowds press together, while you're preoccupied at ticket windows, and anywhere around major sights. Be especially alert inside St. Mark's Basilica, along the Mercerie shopping street, and on crowded vaporettos (boarding and leaving, in particular). Assume that any commotion nearby is a distraction by a team of thieves. On the plus side, the dark, late-night streets of Venice are generally safe. I keep my valuables—passport, credit cards, crucial documents, and large amounts of cash—in a money belt that I tuck under my clothes.

Emergency Help: Dial 113 for English-speaking police help. A handy *polizia* station is on the right side of St. Mark's Square (near Caffè Florian). If you feel ripped off by any gondoliers, shop-owners, hotels, or restaurants, submit your complaint in writing to the Venice TI (complaint.apt@turismovenezia.it, fax 041-523-0399).

Lost or Stolen Items: To replace a passport, contact an embassy or consulate (for contact info, ✪ see page 198). File a police report without delay; it's required to submit an insurance claim for lost or stolen railpasses or travel gear, and can help with replacing your passport or credit and debit cards. For more information, see www.ricksteves.com/help.

Medical Help

Dial 113 for English-speaking police/medical emergencies, or 118 for an ambulance. If you get sick, do as the Italians do and go to a pharmacy, where qualified technicians routinely diagnose and prescribe. Or ask at your hotel for help—they'll know the nearest medical and emergency services. Venice's hospital ("Ospedale"), officially called Santi Giovanni e Paolo Hospital, is a 10-minute walk east of Rialto or 10 minutes north of San Marco, on Fondamenta dei Mendicanti.

ACTIVITIES

Shopping

Venice is a great shopping town, known for its sense of style since it first dealt in exotic imports from the East. It offers the full range, from glitzy high-fashion boutiques to street vendors selling wacky T-shirts. Remember, anything not made locally is brought in by boat—and therefore more expensive than elsewhere in Italy. But in this city of aristocrats and luxury goods, shopping has a charm that makes paying too much strangely enjoyable.

Shops are typically open Monday to Saturday 10:00-19:30, and more stores are open on Sunday here than in the rest of the country. If you're buying a substantial amount from nearly any shop, bargain—it's accepted and almost expected. To get the best price, offer to pay cash.

Sizes: European clothing sizes are different from the US. For example, a woman's size 10 dress (US) is a European size 40, and a size 8 shoe (US) is a European size 38-39.

Getting a VAT Refund: If you spend more than €155 on goods at a single store, you may be eligible to get a refund of the 23 percent Value-Added Tax (VAT). You'll need to ask the merchant to fill out the necessary refund document, then process your refund through a service such as Global Blue or Premier Tax Free, with offices at major airports. For more details, see www.ricksteves.com/vat.

Customs for American Shoppers: You are allowed to take home $800 worth of items per person duty-free, once every 30 days. You can also bring in duty-free a liter of alcohol. As for food, you can take home many processed and packaged foods (e.g., vacuum-packed cheeses, chocolate) but no fresh produce or meats. Any liquid-containing foods must be packed (carefully) in checked luggage. To check customs rules and duty rates, visit www.cbp.gov.

Normal Goods: For ordinary clothing and housewares, the best all-purpose department store is the Coin store on the east side of the Rialto Bridge (from the bridge, head north toward Ferrovia).

Cheap Knock-Offs: Along Venice's many shopping streets, fly-by-night street vendors sell fake designer-label handbags at great prices. (Offer even less.) But buyer beware: It's illegal, and if you're caught purchasing fakes, even you could get hit with a fine. Whenever police saunter by, the vendors gather up and scurry away.

Shopping Walk: To get an overview of Venetian shopping, start in St. Mark's Square, with its pricey smorgasbord of Venetian goods. Exit under the Clock Tower onto the Mercerie, lined with fancy window displays. Cross Rialto Bridge (lots of tempting shops) to the west side and walk through a long block of street vendors. Turn left onto the Ruga Vechia San Giovanni, heading into in a neighborhood with plenty of inviting shops, but fewer crowds and better prices.

Souvenir Ideas

Popular souvenirs are Murano glass, Burano lace, Carnevale masks, art reproductions (on posters, postcards, calendars), original art (browse the galleries near the Peggy Guggenheim Collection), traditional stationery (pens and marbled paper), high-fashion clothing (silk ties and scarves), and plenty of goofy knickknacks—Titian mousepads, gondolier T-shirts, or little plastic gondola condom holders.

Venetian Glass: Since medieval times, Venetian glassmakers have created vases, wine glasses, jewelry, sculptures, and more. If you buy, shops will ship it home for you, though the shipping can cost as much as the purchase. Make sure they guarantee to replace any items that arrive broken. For a less-fragile, packable souvenir, consider a glass-bead necklace.

To watch a quick glassblowing demonstration, try Galleria San Marco, on St. Mark's Square at #139 (near the Clock Tower). Every few minutes they do a demo, followed by a soft-sell sales pitch. Though it's designed for tour groups, they let individual travelers flashing this book sneak in. Enter the shop and climb the stairs (daily 9:00-18:00, tel. 041-271-8671, info@galleriasanmarco.it).

If you're serious about glass, visit the island of Murano, with its glass museum and many shops (✪ see page 150). You'll find greater variety on Murano, but prices are about the same as in Venice. Beware glass products made in China—genuine Venetian glass comes with the Murano seal.

Masks: In the 1700s, when Venice was Europe's party town, masks were popular to preserve the anonymity of visiting nobles doing things forbidden back home. The tradition continues today at Carnevale (Mardi Gras). Masks are papier-mâché: you make a mold of clay, drape layers of paper and glue atop the mold, let it dry, remove, and paint it. There are shops all over town. Near the Church of San Zaccaria (just north, on Fondamente de l'Osmarin) try Ca' del Sol and Atelier Marega (and also visit the wood-carving shop next door). Near the Frari Church is Tragicomica (✪ see page 116).

Nightlife

You must experience Venice after dark. The city is quiet at night, as the masses of day-trippers return to their cruise ships and cheap mainland hotels. When the sun goes down, a cool breeze blows in from the lagoon, the lanterns come on, the peeling plaster glows in the moonlight, and Venice resumes its position as Europe's most romantic city.

For me, the best evening entertainment is simply wandering. (Even Venice's dark and distant back lanes are considered safe after nightfall.) Enjoy the orchestras on St. Mark's Square. Pop into small bars for an appetizer and a drink. Lick gelato.

Though Venice comes alive after dark, it does not party into the wee hours. By 22:00, restaurants are winding down; by 23:00, many bars are closing; and by midnight, the city is shut tight.

Get the latest on Venice's busy schedule of events at the TI (www.turismovenezia.it) or the magazine *Un Ospite di Venezia* (free at fancy hotels, or check www.aguestinvenice.com).

St. Mark's Square at Night: For tourists, St. Mark's Square is the highlight, with lantern light and live music echoing from the cafés lining the square. Every night, enthusiastic musicians play the same songs, creating the same irresistible magic. Listen for free from a distance, or spring for a seat and a drink—it can be €12-20 well spent. For more on the cafes and their prices, ✪ see page 36.

Live Chamber Music: Venice is a city of the powdered-wig Baroque era, and composer Antonio Vivaldi is a hometown boy. A number of venues offer Vivaldi's *Four Seasons* and other chamber music, in a candlelit historic ambience, for about €25. You'll see posters all over town, and they rarely sell out. Buy tickets at the door, from your hotel (no service charge), at the handy Vivaldi Store (east end of Rialto Bridge at Fontego dei Tedeschi #5537, tel. 041-522-1343), or from frilly young Vivaldis hawking concert tickets on street corners. San Vidal Church (north end of Accademia Bridge) has concerts almost nightly, featuring what may be the best group in town, the Interpreti Veneziani orchestra (tel. 041-277-0561, www.interpretiveneziani.com). Scuola San Rocco (✪ see page 141) lets you enjoy music beneath Tintoretto's colorful ceiling.

Other Performances: Venice's most famous theaters are La Fenice (grand old opera house, box office tel. 041-2424, ✪ see page 132), Teatro Goldoni (mostly Italian live theater), and Teatro della Fondamenta Nuove (theater, music, and dance). *Musica a Palazzo* is a unique, intimate evening of opera at a Venetian palace on the Grand Canal (mobile 340-971-7272, www.musicapalazzo.com).

Pubs, Clubs, and Late-Night Scenes: Venice's few *discoteche* are overpriced, exclusive, and not tourist-friendly. But there are a few good places people gather to enjoy the late hours. At the west end of Rialto Bridge, there's a cluster of youthful, trendy bars near the Rialto Market (✪ see the "Bancogiro Stretch" on page 170). East of Rialto Bridge is the local-oriented Devil's Forest Pub (San Marco 5185, on Calle Stagneri, www.devilsforestpub.com). The Dorsoduro neighborhood, south of Accademia Bridge, has two late-night zones: Zattere, on the southern bank, and student-friendly Campo Santa Margarita. Near Campo Santa Margarita, the Venice Jazz Club has live music at 21:00 (€20, no music Thu and Sun, Fondamenta del Squero 3102, tel. 041-523-2056, www.venicejazzclub.com).

Gondolas

For centuries, gondolas ferried aristocrats through Venice's watery "streets." Today, they're strictly for tourists. The long, sleek, flat-bottomed boats are perfect for navigating the shallow lagoon, and the oarsman stands up to see. The gondola curves a bit on the oar side so that a thrust sends the gondola in a straight line. Each boat has unique upholstery, trim, and detailing, such as the squiggly shaped, carved-wood oarlock *(forcola)* and metal "hood ornament" *(ferro).* Today, there are about 400 licensed gondoliers. And do the gondoliers sing, as the popular image has it? My mom asked our gondolier that very question, and he replied, "Madame, there are the lovers and there are the singers. I do not sing."

Riding a Gondola: Taking a gondola ride is simple but expensive. For some, it's a cheesy rip-off, while others find it to be one of the great romantic experiences in Europe.

The price starts at €80 per boat—that is, €40 per person for a couple—for a 40-minute ride during the day. Prices jump to about €110 after 19:00, when it's most romantic and relaxing. You can divide the cost—and the romance—among up to six people per boat, but only two get the love seat. Hiring a singer and an accordionist to serenade you on board will cost an additional €120. Prices are standard and listed at www.gondola venezia.it (click on "Using the Gondola," and look under *"charterage"*).

Shop around and choose a gondolier you click with. Striped-shirted gondoliers hang out all over town. Talk to him about the route and how long the ride is. While rates are standard, he may quote a higher price—politely talk him down, or even go lower (prices are soft during the day). Establish the final price, route, duration, and even whether he expects a tip at the end (it's not obligatory). Do all this before you board, and pay only when you're finished. Then relax and enjoy the ride, gliding through Venice with your head on someone's shoulder.

Walking Tours

Many companies offer English-language, 2- to 3-hour small-group tours of Venice's sights, for around €25-75 a person. Some offer a Rick Steves discount—it's worth asking.

Avventure Bellissime offers several different walks, including St. Mark's Square and a boat tour of the Grand Canal (www.tours-italy.com, tel. 041-970-499, info@tours-italy.com). ArtViva's tours include Venice in a Day, Grand Canal, Doge's Palace, and a "learn to be a gondolier" tour (www.italy.artviva.com). Michael Broderick's tours are long and intellectually demanding, for serious students of Venice (www.venicescapes.org, tel. 041-520-6361, info@venicescapes.org). Debonair Alessandro Schezzini takes groups on a fun two-hour pub crawl of back lanes and *cicchetti* bars (www.schezzini.it, alessandro@schezzini.it, mobile 335-530-9024).

You could hire your own private guide for around €140 for a 2-hour tour. Here are a few: "Walks Inside Venice" (www.walksinsidevenice.com, info@walksinsidevenice.com, or call Roberta at mobile 347-253-0560); Elisabetta Morelli (mobile 328-753-5220, www.elisabettamorelli.it, betta morelli@inwind.it); and "Venice with a Guide" (www.venicewithaguide .com).

RESOURCES FROM RICK STEVES

This Pocket guide is one of more than 30 titles in my series of guidebooks on European travel. I also produce a public television series, *Rick Steves' Europe,* and a public radio show, *Travel with Rick Steves.*

My website, www.ricksteves.com, offers a wealth of free travel resources, including my Rick Steves Audio Europe app (featuring audio tours of Europe's greatest sights, museums and neighborhoods), a Travelers Helpline forum, guidebook updates, and my travel blog—plus my travel gear store and information on railpasses and our tours of Europe.

How was your trip? If you'd like to share your tips, concerns, and discoveries after using this book, please fill out the survey at www.ricksteves.com/feedback. It helps us and fellow travelers.

Italian Survival Phrases

English	Italian	Pronunciation
Good day.	**Buon giorno.**	bwohn JOR-noh
Do you speak English?	**Parla inglese?**	PAR-lah een-GLAY-zay
Yes. / No.	**Si. / No.**	see / noh
I (don't) understand.	**(Non) capisco.**	(nohn) kah-PEES-koh
Please.	**Per favore.**	pehr fah-VOH-ray
Thank you.	**Grazie.**	GRAHT-seeay
You're welcome.	**Prego.**	PRAY-go
I'm sorry.	**Mi dispiace.**	mee dee-speeAH-chay
Excuse me.	**Mi scusi.**	mee SKOO-zee
(No) problem.	**(Non) c'è un problema.**	(nohn) cheh oon proh-BLAY-mah
Good.	**Va bene.**	vah BEHN-ay
Goodbye.	**Arrivederci.**	ah-ree-vay-DEHR-chee
one / two	**uno / due**	OO-noh / DOO-ay
three / four	**tre / quattro**	tray / KWAH-troh
five / six	**cinque / sei**	CHEENG-kway / SEHee
seven / eight	**sette / otto**	SEHT-tay / OT-toh
nine / ten	**nove / dieci**	NOV-ay / deeAY-chee
How much is it?	**Quanto costa?**	KWAHN-toh KOS-tah
Write it?	**Me lo scrive?**	may loh SKREE-vay
Is it free?	**È gratis?**	eh GRAH-tees
Is it included?	**È incluso?**	eh een-KLOO-zoh
Where can I buy / find...?	**Dove posso comprare / trovare...?**	DOH-vay POS-soh kohm-PRAH-ray / troh-VAH-ray
I'd like / We'd like...	**Vorrei / Vorremmo...**	vor-REHee / vor-RAY-moh
...a room.	**...una camera.**	OO-nah KAH-meh-rah
...a ticket to ___.	**...un biglietto per ___.**	oon beel-YEHT-toh pehr
Is it possible?	**È possibile?**	eh poh-SEE-bee-lay
Where is...?	**Dov'è...?**	DOH-veh
...the train station	**...la stazione**	lah staht-seeOH-nay
...the bus station	**...la stazione degli autobus**	lah staht-seeOH-nay DAYL-yee OW-toh-boos
...tourist information	**...informazioni per turisti**	een-for-maht-seeOH-nee pehr too-REE-stee
...the toilet	**...la toilette**	lah twah-LEHT-tay
men	**uomini, signori**	WOH-mee-nee, seen-YOH-ree
women	**donne, signore**	DON-nay, seen-YOH-ray
left / right	**sinistra / destra**	see-NEE-strah / DEHS-trah
straight	**sempre diritto**	SEHM-pray dee-REE-toh
When do you open / close?	**A che ora aprite / chiudete?**	ah kay OH-rah ah-PREE-tay / keeoo-DAY-tay
At what time?	**A che ora?**	ah kay OH-rah
Just a moment.	**Un momento.**	oon moh-MAYN-toh
now / soon / later	**adesso / presto / tardi**	ah-DEHS-soh / PREHS-toh / TAR-dee
today / tomorrow	**oggi / domani**	OH-jee / doh-MAH-nee

In the Restaurant

I'd like...	**Vorrei...**	vor-REHee
We'd like...	**Vorremmo...**	vor-RAY-moh
...to reserve...	**...prenotare...**	pray-noh-TAH-ray
...a table for one / two.	**...un tavolo per uno / due.**	oon TAH-voh-loh pehr OO-noh / DOO-ay
Non-smoking.	**Non fumare.**	nohn foo-MAH-ray
Is this seat free?	**È libero questo posto?**	eh LEE-bay-roh KWEHS-toh POH-stoh
The menu (in English), please.	**Il menù (in inglese), per favore.**	eel may-NOO (een een-GLAY-zay) pehr fah-VOH-ray
service (not) included	**servizio (non) incluso**	sehr-VEET-seeoh (nohn) een-KLOO-zoh
cover charge	**pane e coperto**	PAH-nay ay koh-PEHR-toh
to go	**da portar via**	dah POR-tar VEE-ah
with / without	**con / senza**	kohn / SEHN-sah
and / or	**e / o**	ay / oh
menu (of the day)	**menù (del giorno)**	may-NOO (dayl JOR-noh)
specialty of the house	**specialità della casa**	spay-chah-lee-TAH DEHL-lah KAH-zah
first course (pasta, soup)	**primo piatto**	PREE-moh peeAH-toh
main course (meat, fish)	**secondo piatto**	say-KOHN-doh peeAH-toh
side dishes	**contorni**	kohn-TOR-nee
bread	**pane**	PAH-nay
cheese	**formaggio**	for-MAH-joh
sandwich	**panino**	pah-NEE-noh
soup	**minestra, zuppa**	mee-NEHS-trah, TSOO-pah
salad	**insalata**	een-sah-LAH-tah
dessert	**dolci**	DOHL-chee
tap water	**acqua del rubinetto**	AH-kwah dayl roo-bee-NAY-toh
mineral water	**acqua minerale**	AH-kwah mee-nay-RAH-lay
milk	**latte**	LAH-tay
(orange) juice	**succo (d'arancia)**	SOO-koh (dah-RAHN-chah)
coffee / tea	**caffè / tè**	kah-FEH / teh
wine	**vino**	VEE-noh
red / white	**rosso / bianco**	ROH-soh / beeAHN-koh
glass / bottle	**bicchiere / bottiglia**	bee-keeAY-ray / boh-TEEL-yah
beer	**birra**	BEE-rah
Cheers!	**Cin cin!**	cheen cheen
More. / Another.	**Ancora un po.' / Un altro.**	ahn-KOH-rah oon poh / oon AHL-troh
The same.	**Lo stesso.**	loh STEHS-soh
The bill, please.	**Il conto, per favore.**	eel KOHN-toh pehr fah-VOH-ray
tip	**mancia**	MAHN-chah
Delicious!	**Delizioso!**	day-leet-seeOH-zoh

For more user-friendly Italian phrases, check out *Rick Steves' Italian Phrase Book & Dictionary* or *Rick Steves' French, Italian, and German Phrase Book.*

INDEX

A

Accademia (district): 25–26, 135–141
Accademia Bridge: 133, 135
Accademia Gallery: 8, 25, 135–136; map, 134
Accommodations: *See* Sleeping
Acqua alta: 35, 40, 122
Addresses, locating: 7, 193–194
Airport: 187–189
Air travel: 187
Ante-Collegio Hall (Doge's Palace): 75
Armory Museum (Doge's Palace): 78–80
Arrival in Venice: 187–91
Arsenale: 147
Art: La Biennale, 28, 150. *See also* Art museums; Churches and cathedrals; *and specific artists and artworks*
Art museums: passes, 199; Accademia Gallery, 8, 25, 135–136; Ca' Pesaro, 9, 20, 143–144; Ca' Rezzonico, 9, 24, 25, 139–140; Correr Museum, 8, 40, 129–131; Peggy Guggenheim Collection, 8, 25, 136–138; Punta della Dogana, 9, 140; San Marco Museum, 61–65. *See also* Doge's Palace
Assumption of the Virgin (Titian): 87–90
ATMs: 186–187
Audio Tours, Rick Steves': 10–11, 199, 206

B

Basilica di San Marco: *See* Saint Mark's Basilica
Bellini, Giovanni: 91, 121, 131, 135
Bell tower (campanile) of San Marco: 8–9, 39–41, 131
Biennale International: 28, 150
Birth of John the Baptist (Tintoretto): 122
Boat travel: 18, 195–196; to/from airport, 187–189; gondolas, 23, 204–205; *traghetto,* 21, 196; vaporetto, 151, 195–196. *See also* Grand Canal cruise
Bookstores: 193
Bridge of Sighs: 9, 28, 44, 82–83, 129; views of, 119–120, 123–134
Bridges: *See* Accademia Bridge; Bridge of Sighs; Calatrava Bridge; Rialto Bridge
Bronze Horses of St. Mark's: 63–65
Burano: 150; map, 149
Buses: 189, 190
Business hours: 192–193, 198
Byzantium (Byzantine Empire): map, 55; overview, 55

C

Ca' d'Oro: 20–21
Ca' Foscari: 24
Calatrava Bridge: 18, 146
Campanile di San Marco: 8–9, 39–41, 131
Campo Manin: 103–104
Campo San Bartolomeo: 106
Campo San Giacomo: 110–111
Campo San Polo: 115
Canaletto (Giovanni Antonio Canal): 136, 140
Cannaregio Canal: 18–19
Canova, Antonio: 129; Monument, 93–94
Ca' Pesaro: 9, 20, 143–144
Ca' Rezzonico: 9, 24, 25, 139–140
Carnevale: 186
Carnevale masks: 110, 116, 202–203
Carpaccio, Vittorio: 73, 131, 146–147

Cars, parking garages: 190–191
Casino: 19, 107
Cell (mobile) phones: 197
Christ as Pantocrator: 51
Churches and cathedrals: daily reminder, 10; sightseeing tips, 198–199; Church of the Scalzi, 18; La Salute Church, 9, 25, 26, 28, 40, 138–139; San Giorgio Maggiore, 9, 28, 40, 132–134; San Marcuola Church, 19; San Moisè, 100–101; San Polo Church, 115; San Simeon Piccolo, 18; San Stae, 20; San Zaccaria Church, 9, 120–122. *See also* Frari Church; Saint Mark's Basilica
Church of the Scalzi: 18
Cicchetti: 166, 168–174
Climate: 186
Clock Tower, on St. Mark's Square: 28, 38, 108
Collegio Hall (Doge's Palace): 76–77
Concerts: 203–204
Correr Museum: 8, 40, 129–131; map, 130
Credit cards: 186–187, 200
Cuisine: 166–167
Currency and exchange: 186–187
Customs House: 28
Customs regulations: 201

D

Debit cards: 186–187, 200
Discounts: 199
Doge's Apartments (Doge's Palace): 73
Doge's Palace: 28, 67–83, 128; maps, 69, 74, 79, 81; orientation, 8, 68; Seventh Column, 42–44; the tour, 70–83
Donatello: 90
Dorsoduro: 135; eating, 172–175; map, 180–181; sleeping, 158–161
Drinking water: 194

E

Eating: 163–183; listings, 168–175; maps, 176–183; quick budget meals, 165–166
Electricity: 192
Embassies: 198
Emergencies: 198, 200
Entertainment: 203–204
Euro currency: 186–187

F

Feast in the House of Levi (Veronese): 135
Ferrovia: 18, 144, 174–175, 190; sleeping, 160–161
Fish market: 8, 21, 114–115
Foscari, Francesco, tomb of: 90
Frari Church: 85–94, 141; map, 88; orientation, 8, 86; the tour, 86–94

G

Galleria dell'Accademia: 8, 25, 135–136; map, 134
German Exchange: 21–22
Giardinetti Reali: 40, 98
Giudecca Island: 133
Golden Altarpiece (St. Mark's): 59, 61
Golden Staircase (Doge's Palace): 72
Goldoni, Carlo: 106
Gondolas: 23, 204–205
Grand Canal: 6–7, 15; map, 16–17
Grand Canal cruise: 13–28; background, 15; map, 16–17; orientation, 14; the tour, 18–28

Gran Teatro alla Fenice: 101, 103, 132, 203–204
Gritti Palace: 26
Guggenheim Collection: *See* Peggy Guggenheim Collection

H

Hall of the Grand Council (Doge's Palace): 80–82
Harry's American Bar: 98, 100
Helpful hints: 192–194
Holidays: 192
Hospitals: 200
Hotels: 153–161; budget tips, 155; listings, 156–161; reservations, 154–155; typical room, 154

I

International Gallery of Modern Art (Ca' Pesaro): 9, 20, 143–144
Internet access: 197–198
Italian restaurant phrases: 208
Italian survival phrases: 207
Itineraries: 8–11

J

Jewish Ghetto: 18–19, 144–146; map, 145
Jewish Museum: 145–146
John the Baptist (Donatello): 90

L

La Biennale: 28, 150
La Fenice Opera House: 101, 103, 132, 203–204
Language: Italian restaurant phrases, 208; Italian survival phrases, 207
Language barrier: 192
La Quadriga: *See* Bronze Horses
La Salute Church: 9, 25, 26, 28, 40, 138–139
Laundry: 193
Lido: 28
Lodging: *See* Sleeping

M

Madonna and Child with Doge Francesco Dandolo (Veneziano): 90
Madonna and Child with Saints (Bellini): 121
Madonna and Child with Saints and Angels (Bellini): 91
Madonna of Ca' Pesaro (Titian): 94
Manin, Daniele: 103–104, 119
Maps: Burano, 149; Doge's Palace, 69, 74, 79, 81; Frari Church, 88; Grand Canal, 16–17; Murano, 148; Rialto to Frari Church walk, 112–113; St. Mark's Square, 33, 178–179; St. Mark's to Rialto walk, 99; St. Mark's to San Zaccaria walk, 118; Venice, 4–5, 126–127; Venice lagoon, 148–149; Venice's Districts, 7
Marciana National Library: 131
Marco Polo Airport: 187–189
Mark, Saint: 48, 49, 58. *See also* Saint Mark's Basilica
Markets: 8, 21–22; *See also* Rialto market
Marzaria San Zulian: 107–108
Masks: *See* Venetian masks
Medical help: 200
Mercato Rialto: 8, 21–22, 111, 114
Mercerie: 107
Metric system: 192
Mobile phones: 197
Modern art: *See* Peggy Guggenheim Collection

Money: 186–187
Mosaics, of St. Mark's Basilica: 48–57
Mouth of Truth (Doge's Palace): 71
Murano: 150, 202; map, 148
Museo Correr: *See* Correr Museum
Museo di San Marco: 61–65
Museo Storico Navale: 147
Museum of Natural History: 19
Museum of 18th-Century Venice (Ca' Rezzonico): 9, 24, 25, 139–140

N

National Archaeological Museum: 131
Naval Museum: 147
Neighborhoods: 6–7, 193–194
Nightlife: 203–204

O

Open-air markets: *See* Markets; Rialto market
Opera house: *See* La Fenice Opera House

P

Pala d'Oro: 59, 61
Palazzo Balbi: 24
Palazzo Ducale: *See* Doge's Palace
Palazzo Grassi: 24
Palazzo Mocenigo Costume Museum: 144
Paradise (Tintoretto): 80
Parking garages: 190–191
Passports: 186, 200
Peggy Guggenheim Collection: 8, 25, 136–138; map, 137
Piazzale Roma Bus Station: 190
Piazza San Marco: *See* Saint Mark's Square
Piazzetta: 41–42
Piazzetta dei Leoni: 119
Ponte dei Sospiri: *See* Bridge of Sighs
Ponte de la Verona: 103
Ponte della Costituzione: 146
Pubs: 204
Punta della Dogana: 9, 140

R

Resources from Rick Steves: 206
Restaurants: 164–183; listings, 168–175; maps, 176–183
Rialto (district): 22–23, 141–144; eating, 168–171; maps, 99, 112–113, 176–177; sleeping, 158–159; walking tours, 105–106, 109–115
Rialto Bridge: 8, 22, 105–106, 110, 141
Rialto fish market: 8, 21, 114–115
Rialto market: 8, 21–22, 111, 114
Riva: 28, 123, 146
Riva de Biasio: 18–19
Room of the Four Doors (Doge's Palace): 74–75
Ruga: 115

S

Saint Mark's Basilica: 28, 36–37, 45–65, 128; map, 47; orientation, 8, 46; the tour, 48–65
Saint Mark's Campanile: 8–9, 39–41, 131
Saint Mark's Clock Tower: 28, 38, 108
Saint Mark's Square: 28, 31–44, 98, 128; cafés, 36–37; eating near, 172–173; maps, 33, 178–179; at night, 203; orientation, 8, 32; shopping, 202; sleeping near, 156–157; walking tour, 34–44
Sala dei Banchetti (San Marco Museum): 62–63

Index

Sala del Collegio (Doge's Palace): 76–77
Sala del Maggiore Consiglio (Doge's Palace): 80–82
Sala del Senato (Doge's Palace): 77–78
Salviati building: 25–26
San Giorgio Maggiore: 9, 28, 40, 132–134
San Marco (district): 28, 98, 119–120, 128–30; eating, 172–173; map, 99; sleeping, 156–157
San Marco, Piazza: *See* Saint Mark's Square
San Marco Basilica: *See* Saint Mark's Basilica
San Marco Campanile: 8–9, 39–41, 131
San Marco Museum: 61–65
San Marcuola: 19
San Marcuola Church: 19
San Michele: 150
San Moisè Church: 100–101
San Polo (district): 109, 115–116
San Polo Church: 115
San Rocco School: *See* Scuola San Rocco
San Silvestro: 23–24
San Simeon Piccolo: 18
San Stae: 20
Santa Elena: 150
Santa Lucia train station: *See* Ferrovia
Santa Maria del Giglio: 26
Santa Maria della Salute: 9, 25, 26, 28, 40, 138–139
Santa Maria Gloriosa dei Frari: *See* Frari Church
Sant'Angelo: 24
San Toma: 24
San Zaccaria: 9, 29, 120–122
San Zaccaria Church: 9, 120–122
Scala Contarini del Bovolo: 104
Scala dei Giganti (Doge's Palace): 70–71
Scala d'Oro (Doge's Palace): 72
Scuola Dalmata di San Giorgio: 9, 146–147
Scuola San Rocco: 8, 141–143; map, 143
Seasons: 186
Senate Hall (Doge's Palace): 77–78
Shopping: 201–203; souvenir ideas, 202
Sights (sightseeing): 125–151; at a glance, 8–9; daily reminder, 10; general tips, 198–199; itineraries, 8–11; passes, 199. *See also specific sights*
Sleeping: 153–161; budget tips, 155; listings, 156–161; reservations, 154–155; typical room, 154
St. Mark's Basilica: *See* Saint Mark's Basilica
St. Mark's Square: *See* Saint Mark's Square
Stairway of Giants (Doge's Palace): 70–71

T

Tapas: *See Cicchetti*
Taxes: VAT refunds, 201
Teatro Goldoni: 104–105
Telephone numbers, useful: 198
Telephones: 197
Theft: 200
Tiepolo, Giovanni Battista: 115, 136, 139–140; Doge's Palace, 74–75
Time zones: 192
Tintoretto: 100, 122, 133, 136; Doge's Palace, 72, 73–75, 77–78, 80; Scuola San Rocco, 141–143
Tipping: 193
Titian: 136, 139; Doge's Palace, 72, 74; Frari Church, 87–90, 92–93, 94; tomb of, 92–93

Torcello: 150
Torre dell'Orologio: 28, 38
Tour guides: 205
Tourist information: 187, 192
Traghetto: 21, 196
Tragicomica Mask Shop: 110, 116
Train station: *See* Ferrovia
Transportation: around Venice, 194–196; to Venice, 187–91
Treasury: 8, 57, 59
Turkish "Fondaco" Exchange: 19

V

Vaporetto: 151, 195–196
VAT refunds: 201
Venetian glass: 150, 202
Venetian masks: 110, 116, 202–203
Veneziano, Paolo: 92, 122
Venice Biennale: 28, 150
Venice lagoon: 150–151; map, 148–149
Veronese, Paolo: 115, 135; Doge's Palace, 72, 75, 77, 78, 80–81
Vivaldi, Antonio: 203

W

Walking: 194
Walking tours: guided, 205; Rialto to Frari Church, 109–116; St. Mark's Square, 31–44; St. Mark's to Rialto, 97–108; St. Mark's to San Zaccaria, 117–121
Water taxis: 98, 189, 196
Weather: 186

PHOTO CREDITS

Cover

Left photo: Venetian carnival masks on dispay on small stand near Piazza San Marco © Kimberly Coole / Getty Images

Right photo: gondolas docked outside of Piazza San Marcos © Jim Richardson Getty Images / royalty-free

Title Page

© Dominic Bonuccelli

Table of Contents

© Dominic Bonuccelli

Introduction

© Dominic Bonuccelli, Rick Steves

Grand Canal Cruise

© Cameron Hewitt, Rick Steves, Dominic Bonuccelli, Jennifer Hauseman, Gene Openshaw, David C. Hoerlein

St. Mark's Square Tour

© Laura VanDeventer, Dominic Bonuccelli, Anne Jenkins, Rick Steves, Michael Potter

St. Mark's Basilica Tour

Page 49, left © Peter Barritt / Alamy

Other photos © Laura VanDeventer, Ben Cameron, Dominic Bonuccelli, Cameron Hewitt, Gene Openshaw, Rick Steves; additional photos from Wikimedia Commons

Doge's Palace Tour

Page 71, left © Terry Smith Images / Alamy

Other photos © Bruce VanDeventer, Rick Steves, Dominic Bonuccelli, Cameron Hewitt; additional photos from Wikimedia Commons

Frari Church Tour

Page 93, right © Lebrecht Music and Arts Photo Library / Alamy

Other photos © Laura VanDeventer, Michael Potter, Rick Steves; additional photos from Wikimedia Commons

St. Mark's to Rialto Loop Walk

© Laura VanDeventer, Rick Steves, Gene Openshaw, Cameron Hewitt, Dominic Bonuccelli

Rialto to Frari Church Walk

© Laura VanDeventer, Rick Steves, Jennifer Hauseman; additional photos from Wikimedia Commons

St. Mark's to San Zaccaria Walk

Page 121, © Richard Bradley / Alamy

Other photos © Gene Openshaw, Cameron Hewitt, Laura VanDeventer, Rick Steves

Sights

© Dominic Bonuccelli, Cameron Hewitt, Robyn Stencil, Laura VanDeventer, David C. Hoerlein, Rick Steves; additional photos from Wikimedia Commons

Sleeping

© Rick Steves, Dominic Bonuccelli

Eating

© Dominic Bonuccelli

Practicalities

© Cameron Hewitt, Dominic Bonuccelli

Avalon Travel
a member of the Perseus Books Group
1700 Fourth Street
Berkeley, CA 94710, USA

Printed in China by RR Donnelley
Second printing November 2013

ISBN 978-1-59880-383-9
ISSN 2325-985X

For the latest on Rick's lectures, books, tours, public-radio show, and public-television series, contact Europe Through the Back Door, Box 2009, Edmonds, WA 98020, tel. 425/771-8303, fax 425/771-0833, www.ricksteves.com, rick@ricksteves.com.

Europe Through the Back Door
Managing Editor: Risa Laib
Editors: Jennifer Madison Davis, Glenn Eriksen, Tom Griffin, Cameron Hewitt, Suzanne Kotz, Cathy Lu, Gretchen Strauch
Editorial Intern: Michael Maloy
Researcher: Sarah Murdoch
Graphic Content Director: Laura VanDeventer
Maps & Graphics: David C. Hoerlein, Twozdai Hulse, Lauren Mills

Avalon Travel
Senior Editor and Series Manager: Madhu Prasher
Editor: Jamie Andrade
Assistant Editor: Nikki Ioakimedes
Copy Editor: Denise Silva
Proofreader: Janet Walden
Indexer: Stephen Callahan
Production & Typesetting: McGuire Barber Design
Cover Design: Kimberly Glyder Design
Maps & Graphics: Kat Bennett, Mike Morgenfeld

ABOUT THE AUTHORS

Rick Steves

Since 1973, Rick Steves has spent 100 days every year exploring Europe. Along with writing and researching a best-selling series of guidebooks, Rick produces a public television series *(Rick Steves' Europe)*, a public radio show *(Travel with Rick Steves)*, and an app and podcast (*Rick Steves Audio Europe)*; writes a nationally syndicated newspaper column; organizes guided tours that take over 10,000 travelers to Europe annually; and offers an information-packed website (www.ricksteves.com). With the help of his hardworking staff of 80 at Europe Through the Back Door—in Edmonds, Washington, just north of Seattle—Rick's mission is to make European travel fun, affordable, and culturally enlightening for Americans.

Connect with Rick:

facebook.com/RickSteves  twitter: @RickSteves

Gene Openshaw

Gene is a writer, composer, tour guide, and lecturer on art and history. Specializing in writing walking tours of Europe's cultural sights, Gene is the co-author of 10 Rick Steves' books and contributes to Rick's public television series. He lives near Seattle with his daughter and roots for the Mariners in good times and bad.

FOLDOUT COLOR MAP

The foldout map on the opposite page includes:

- **Maps of Venice on one side**
- **Maps of Venice and Italy on the other side**